postcolonial
Dublin

ANDREW KINCAID

postcolonial
Dublin

IMPERIAL LEGACIES AND THE BUILT ENVIRONMENT

University of Minnesota Press
Minneapolis
London

Published by the University of Minnesota Press
111 Third Avenue South, Suite 290
Minneapolis, MN 55401-2520
http://www.upress.umn.edu

Library of Congress Cataloging-in-Publication Data

Kincaid, Andrew, 1968–
   Postcolonial Dublin : imperial legacies and the built environment / Andrew Kincaid.
     p.   cm.
   Includes bibliographical references and index.
   ISBN-13: 978-0-8166-4345-5 (hc : alk. paper)
   ISBN-10: 0-8166-4345-8 (hc : alk. paper)
   ISBN-13: 978-0-8166-4346-2 (pb : alk. paper)
   ISBN-10: 0-8166-4346-6 (pb : alk. paper)
   1. City planning—Ireland—Dublin—History. 2. Urbanization—Ireland—Dublin—History. 3. Urban renewal—Ireland—Dublin—History. 4. Nationalism and architecture—Ireland—Dublin.
5. Urban policy—Ireland—History. 6. Postcolonialism—Ireland.
I. Title.
   HT169.I772D835   2006
   307.1'21609418'35—dc22   2006003031

Contents

Acknowledgments

I am eternally grateful for the endless patience, intelligence, and support of my wife, Lauren Fox. John Archer provided early and ongoing encouragement and support. The faculty of the cultural studies and comparative literature department at the University of Minnesota offered valuable critique and discussion over several years. I would like to thank, in particular, Qadri Ismail and Timothy Brennan. My colleagues in the English department at the University of Wisconsin, Milwaukee, especially Marcus Bullock and Jose Lanters, have given me much intellectual and professional guidance, for which I am grateful. The research for this book was generously supported by the Graham Foundation in Chicago and the Center for Twenty-first Century Studies and the Graduate School at the University of Wisconsin, Milwaukee. I would like to thank, as well, Mary Clark and Andrew O'Brien at Dublin City Archives and Simon Lincoln at the Irish Architectural Archives for their generous assistance. For their friendship and endlessly stimulating conversations, I thank Conor McCarthy, Peter McAuley, Steve Macek, Paul Caprani, and Micheal O'Siochru.

Introduction

Colonialism leaves a physical imprint long after its official departure. From the beginning, colonialism worked through a policy of urbanization. An urban center was the heart of a colonized country, pulling in wealth from the rural fringe and exporting goods internationally, as well as training indigenous populations to be new consumers and citizens.[1] In the New World (Philadelphia, 1682; Savannah, 1732; Charleston, 1672), in Australia (Adelaide, 1830s), in New Zealand (Wellington, 1840; Canterbury, 1852), and in Sierra Leone (Freetown, 1792), the British government laid out new towns, designed to be centers for commerce, defense, and civic life.[2] Referred to as the "Grand Model" of colonial settlement, these towns were plotted in advance (their individual parcels of land marketable to prospective settlers back home), were organized along geometric lines (the gridiron), and were centered on a large public square (symbolizing a range of functions from healthy ventilation to demonstrative democracy).

As expanding trade and industrialization transformed adventurist colonialism into capitalist imperialism, vast port cities—Bombay, Madras, Calcutta, Singapore, Hong Kong, and Gibraltar—developed in those areas under British control, with large migrant populations employed in processing the raw materials and commercial products of an increasingly integrated empire.[3] These mercantile cities expanded rapidly as displaced rural workers flocked to them in search of work. Their exponential growth resulted in many problems that have persisted down to the present day: slums, disease, and the intensification of tensions not only between the colonized and the colonizer, but also between competing ethnic and religious groups. Colonial administrators and planners responded to the growth of these cities by attempting to shape the built environment in ways they thought might lessen the threat of plagues, overcrowding, and violence to Europeans. To varying degrees, officials in Bombay, Madras, and Calcutta relocated the native population to areas outside the city. Singapore segregated the races by establishing homogeneous residential ethnic enclaves, the *campongs*. The creation of New Delhi was an even more radical concept, involving the building of an entire new city in order to concentrate the imperial administration in one place and to remove the government from the potential antagonism of the governed. The supreme example of racial segregation was, of course, South Africa, where the apartheid city separated peoples by both race and class. The origins of the full-fledged apartheid city (Johannesburg and Soweto) can be traced to colonial reactions to slave emancipation (1834) and British reactions to the outbreak of plague at the turn of the twentieth century.

At the beginning of the twentieth century, when many colonies, including Ireland, rose up in violence against colonial oppression, colonialists turned to the new discipline of town planning to try to persuade the natives that their interests (health, jobs, and housing) would be best served by staying within the empire and embracing its ability to provide modern cities. New capitals—Pretoria, Canberra, and New Delhi—were planned for South Africa, Australia, and India. These cities were symbols of a new beginning, with monumental architecture, grand new boulevards, vast public parks, public transport systems, and efficient industrial zones. They promised more in the way of modernization and progress, their proponents hoped, than independence ever could.

A cultural reading of colonialism's urban geographies—its urban planning and architecture—illustrates how imperial ideologies were built in stone. Studying the urban landscape also provides new insights into how nationalists attempted to resist colonialism and sought to establish their own hierarchies and prejudices: Who should live where? What sort of city is best? How should industrialization develop?

For hundreds of years, Ireland had been a laboratory for colonizing techniques. In 1831, for example, the British established a national school system in Ireland, decades before a similar system was implemented in Britain. In 1836 the colonial government formed the Royal Irish Constabulary, the world's first centralized police force (Townsend 1983, 69). Between 1824 and 1841, the Ordnance Survey charted the island in intricate cartographic detail (O'Brien 1993, 345). As policing, education, and mapping were imperial techniques and strategies, so too the urban landscape in Ireland had long been a site for colonial experimentation and practice. The underwriters and settlers of the Munster (1585–86) and Ulster (1610–40) plantations established a series of market towns in each of the vanquished counties. During the second half of the eighteenth century, when Dublin was redeveloped as a colonial capital, the new landed aristocracy sought to carve out state power from the medieval core of the indigenous city. The Commissioners for Making Wide and Convenient Ways, Streets, and Passages (an entity created in 1757) redesigned the city's congested streets and undertook all manner of developments to provide evidence of the essentially liberal nature of colonial occupation: the building of bridges, the connecting of strategic sites with broad avenues, and the standardizing of façades. All of this took place many decades before Haussmann's "creative destruction" of Second Empire Paris, and fifty years before Nash's redesign of Regent and Oxford Streets in London. When modern town planning made its appearance at the beginning of the twentieth century, it was but the latest in a long line of urban tactics implicated in the colonial project of social management.

From its inception, colonialism has worked through the built environment. The tradition of regulating and organizing populations through the production of space did not stop with the departure of the British from Ireland in 1922 and the formation of the Free State. The popular image of the postindependence decades (the 1920s and 1930s) is of a rural, Catholic country in which an agrarian way of life not only predominated but precluded all other possibilities. In fact, during these years, great attention was paid to urban matters, as it had been when the British occupied the country. The quest for garden suburbs—with their fresh air, sunlight, and, consequently, healthy citizens—continued to occupy the agendas of several members of the new Irish administration who were eager to provide the kind of environment in which an indigenous and prosperous middle class could flourish. During the 1920s Dublin Corporation laid out several suburban schemes, including the Marino estate (1923–27) and Fairbrothers Fields (1921–27). By the 1930s Eamon de Valera's government, which is famously depicted as beholden to essentialist visions of an arcadian Gaelic past, was also actively engaged in the mass provision of suburban housing at Cabra and Crumlin. On the one hand, garden suburbs were neocolonial, in that the postcolonial administrations were pursuing policies laid down by the British government and its architects and planners. On the other hand, suburbs were an attempt to bridge the modernizing, even urbanizing agenda of nationalism with its own nineteenth-century language of idyllic pastoralism. Also during the 1930s Dublin Corporation embarked on a major slum clearance and inner-city renewal program. Herbert Simms, the City Housing Department's leading architect, oversaw the construction of more than seventeen thousand new units during these years. Many of the apartment blocks incorporated design features associated with the latest architectural modernisms: expressionism, art nouveau, and international style. These urban renewal schemes were part of a complex ideological project by the state's largest and most populist party to maintain the support of a large class bloc composed of farmers and rural laborers, the Catholic bourgeoisie, and Dublin's working class.

An examination of postindependence Ireland, therefore, from the perspective of architecture and planning, reveals that the urban environment was not ignored by state officials; rather, Dublin and its population lay at the center of energetic debates about power, history, memory, and the shape of independence.

If the 1920s and 1930s represented the change from a colonial to a postcolonial city, with all the accompanying hopes and fears associated with any major cultural and economic transition, the 1960s in Ireland witnessed an ideological transformation of similar proportions. A new generation of planners and economists sought to move the country away from what they saw as its outdated ethos of cultural and economic isolationism. Led by the modernizing Sean Lemass, the ruling Fianna Fáil party lowered corporate taxation and provided subsidies for foreign companies in an effort to internationalize the economy. Alongside these political and economic shifts, Dublin's physical infrastructure was again transformed as the traditionally low-lying historic architecture began to be replaced with modernist office buildings and tower blocks in corporate international style. These physical metamorphoses were the spatial equivalent of the moves within the economic, indeed historiographic, spheres toward functionalism, objectivity, fact, and universalism (and, hence, away from historic prejudices, entrenched myths, and old conflicts).

The present book details the ways in which Irish architecture and urban planning during the twentieth century engaged the legacy of colonialism and the politics of nationalism. In essence, I argue that nationalism in Ireland both before and after independence has been a site of struggle through which competing social forces, individuals, classes, and parties have sought to gain control over geography and people, specifically via the built environment. Ideology always spatializes itself. Theoretical and historical questions, such as "What does it mean to be modern?" "Ought there to be a national architectural style?" and "How does nationalism remember its own past?" manifest themselves in the production of urban space. The competing forces within nationalism have fought over the meaning of inherently abstract words and phrases—"the people," "the land," "the nation," and even "Ireland"—as well as over the more pragmatic concepts of urbanization, modernization, and development. A central theme of the book is nationalism's rewriting of the past for the purposes of the present. History must be made to seem as if it were all the time working, often in a subterranean way, to produce the kind of society that we now inhabit. In each of the chapters in the book I take up this concern about the writing of history. The text I read is the city—the shape, structure, and architecture of which, I argue, narrate the past and attempt to give it meaning as much as any work of literature or history. In the final chapter, for example, I am concerned with how the contemporary forces of global capital are restructuring older urban neighborhoods. Urban renewal is creating a whole series of gentrified apartments and "historic" districts renovated in order to attract well-off young urban professionals and tourists, respectively. Tourism in turn often peddles history, marketing essentialized notions of history and identity. Ireland is currently in a period of massive economic restructuring, having opened itself fully during the 1990s to a wave of American multinational capital, most notably in the form of pharmaceutical and computer companies. Neoliberalism, I argue, appropriates the signs and images of Irish history in order to lend itself an air of permanency. Globalization aims to anchor itself in tradition. As Dublin markets itself as an up-and-coming Euro city, the state has engaged, as never before, in acts of architectural preservation and historical restoration. Such actions inevitably raise questions about what is being preserved, what histories are being restored.

Postcolonial Dublin not only seeks to locate Ireland within the broader field of planning and architectural history, it also engages what I see as the limited scope of Irish studies and postcolonial theory. The field of Irish studies has long been dominated by a literary paradigm. Critical interpretations of Irish writing, most notably studies of the great modernists—Yeats, Joyce, Beckett, and Synge—still make up the majority of books published every year in the field. Even the current generation of leading Irish critics, such as Declan Kiberd, Terry Eagleton, and Seamus Deane, with their awareness of contemporary postcolonial theory and cultural studies, have continued to focus almost exclusively on literature, poetry, and drama. Kiberd's book *Irish Classics,* while a fascinating cultural study of Irish writers, still concentrates on a canonical set of figures. Eagleton's important *Heathcliff and the Great Hunger* engages heavily with Shaw and Wilde. There is, of course, nothing wrong with more analysis of Irish literature. Certainly, every great work needs to be reinterpreted by each generation. The problem with the dominant literary approach to Irish studies lies in what it excludes. *Postcolonial Dublin* emerges out of a desire to do something different in Irish studies, a sense of the need to expand the range of what has traditionally been considered important, and a wish to show that there are other histories, other approaches, and other ways of understanding Irish culture. In writing about Dublin, I wanted to try to branch out from literary representations of the city. Dublin is a material city; it is made up of physical buildings, inhabited streets, and neighborhoods. One of the pitfalls that literary approaches of Dublin has led us into is that the textual city has come to take on a greater degree of reality and importance than the physical city. Millions of readers know that Bloom had a pint at Davy Byrne's pub on the afternoon of June 16, 1904, but few know about the political and ideological factors that shaped the squares and streets through which he made his way. The notion of a modernist city, a city that can only be understood in bits, is, in part, a product of Joycean scholarship. But a city is more than language, more than the pages of a book. My work seeks to bring the material city back into focus.

Within studies of Irish nationalism—its origins, prejudices, and goals—the state itself is often ignored. In my work I have tried to define the state, to examine the ways in which it functions and how it and its leaders maintain power. In architecture and urban planning, we can see how state officials and architects went about building offices for the government and constructing housing for citizens. When approached in this way, the state appears as an institution that is always adapting, always seeking to assimilate potentially resistant populations unto itself, while handily promoting dominant economic policy. In each of my chapters, therefore, I pay attention to the priorities of the government at the period of time in question. By discussing major public projects that have been built in or planned for Dublin over the last century, I have attempted to illustrate how ideologies—indeed how nationalism—actually got built in stone.

Seamus Deane recently suggested that during the nineteenth century, the west of Ireland, the wild landscape of the Atlantic seaboard and the traditional lives that it supported, became, in the minds of the emerging Irish middle class, "the place of authenticity, the place that was not yet subject to the effects of administrative, governmental rules and laws" (1992, 52). Deane is repeating a common notion that Irishness was traditionally defined negatively, constructed in terms of what was not English. If England was industrial and urban, Ireland ought to be agricultural and rural. This essentialist vision of culture continued, the majority of today's critics hold, into the post-independence period, when a new, insecure state demanded allegiance to a simplistic and stable understanding of national life. This equation of rural Ireland with real Ireland has resulted in Dublin gaining little attention in studies of Irish nationalism and state formation. Dublin in the nineteenth and early twentieth centuries has received scant consideration, especially compared with the interest shown in Georgian or contemporary Dublin, which are both regarded as

"European" cities. *Postcolonial Dublin* focuses on Dublin from 1900 until today. The first three chapters examine the city during decades (1900–1960) that many other scholars have written off as being years of urban neglect and stasis that mirrored general cultural stagnancy. My motivation, therefore, has been to bring Dublin back into debates about the formation and consolidation of the modern Irish state.

Of the several important books that treat Irish planning and urban development, none places the physical environment and architecture into a broader context of ideological, political, and cultural debates. The thought and research that went into *Postcolonial Dublin*—a concern with the material rooted in questions about identity and nationalism—required me to pay attention to how the local and global interact and manifest themselves in the physical infrastructure of Dublin. A central concern of this book is how international trends, be they political, intellectual, or architectural, have shaped Ireland. In each of my chapters I examine how spatial changes in Dublin are the product of indigenous, local histories, as well as of the international debates of their day. In chapter 1, for example, I detail the role that British planners played in Ireland, before they went to other parts of the empire to design and build cities. In chapter 3, I illustrate how the arrival of the international style of architecture in Ireland in the 1960s was connected both to attempts to overcome what its proponents saw as a debilitating reliance on postcolonial mythology, and to post–World War II urban trends in Europe. This expansive approach is also an effort to counter a trend in Irish studies. Many scholars of Ireland have fallen prey to its romantic image and bought into the notion of Irish exceptionalism. The Irish themselves have often congratulated themselves on being like no other nation on earth. The evidence suggests otherwise. *Postcolonial Dublin* remains mindful throughout that Irish experience is representative of human experience.

Michael Bannon's book *Planning: The Irish Experience, 1920–1988,* rarely engages the politics and demands of nationalism and never relates the production of space to the production of other cultural trends. This is understandable, given that his work is largely designed for planning professionals. Nevertheless, Bannon's book remains one of the few that puts forth a comprehensive, though legalistic, history of Irish planning. Frank McDonald's two canonical works on the city, *The Destruction of Dublin* and *The Construction of Dublin,* while brilliantly detailed and laden with anecdotes about Irish planning figures, businessmen, and con artists, remain largely journalistic in their scope and execution. Murray Fraser's *John Bull's Other Homes* stands out among histories of Dublin for openly accepting a colonial model of history. British housing policy, for Fraser, was a way of furthering a larger political agenda. His work, however, stops with the foundation of the Irish state in 1922. Fraser also steers clear of reflection on the role that urbanization and Dublin played in the rise and consolidation of Irish nationalism. Ruth McManus's *Shaping the Suburbs* marks a departure from earlier, positivist historical approaches to the city. She shows a willingness to employ cultural studies and gestures toward internationalism with an appendix on Ebenezer Howard's *City of Tomorrow.* For McManus, though, theoretical reflections are never fully elaborated: the broader meaning, history, and function of nationalism and its relationship to the urban remain unaddressed, and many of her own key terms—the state, the suburbs—are not sufficiently analyzed. Furthermore, McManus shows a reluctance, common among a generation of Irish historians, to connect culture and colonialism. My book adds to these and hopes to contribute to the literature a notion of interdisciplinarity and a theoretical analysis centered on the relationship between space and society.

The question of postcolonialism largely revolves around the theme of nationalism. In my thinking about these ideas, I am indebted to a range of renowned postcolonial scholars, including Franz Fanon, Ranajit Guha, Partha Chatterjee, and Gayatri Spivak. For these thinkers, as for many of their European counterparts, spatial metaphors exist at the heart of their theories. Spivak's famous concept of the subaltern requires us to think about the construction of a center and a margin, a site of representation and a place of invisibility and exclusion. For Chatterjee, the possibilities of a genuinely different model of nationalism for the postcolonial world force him to reflect on the history and trajectory of the normative European state, along with its tactics of centralization. What has always interested me about theory are the ways in which abstract ideas such as the nation, modernization, and ideology trickle down and influence the material conditions of our lives. Ideas spatialize themselves. This same key concern stimulated my reading of the major theorists of modernity. From Freud through Benjamin to Habermas, important European thinkers have conceptualized their work around physical metaphors. For Foucault, it was the panopticon as the symbol for modern state power. For Habermas, it was the public sphere, the site of potential communicative rationality. Postcolonial theorists have as one of their major goals the critique of many of the core principles of the European Enlightenment tradition. Freedom, liberty, and representative democracy never traveled well to the colony. My interest in architecture and urban planning led me to question whether these physical disciplines might be added to the canon of postcolonial theory, which often focuses on literature. It is my hope that this book will add to the studies of postcolonial theory, modernism, urbanism, and Irish studies. Perhaps out of this constellation might arise a new way of understanding Dublin and its powerful links to an Ireland still emerging from the legacy of colonialism.

Precedents for Urbanization

Postcolonial Dublin focuses on Dublin in the late nineteenth and early twentieth centuries. But the city did not miraculously appear, fully formed, at the start of the modern era. Nor did the terms I grapple with—hegemony, modernization, nationalism, and the state—arrive on the scene with the dawn of the twentieth century. Both the spatial city and its theoretical counterpart have a long history. The legacy of urbanization foregrounds my analysis of postcolonial Ireland.

Plantation and Market Towns

From the beginnings of modern colonialism in Ireland, the building of towns and cities served as a bridge between the defensive and forcible nature of earlier conquest and the less violent, more persuasive methods of later imperialism. England's colonial strategy at the beginning of the modern period was still one of defensible space and military occupation, but its rhetoric and propaganda were beginning to be inflected with the suggestive tones of paternalism, improvement, and the civilizing notions of a population interested in supporting its continued presence in an unwelcoming landscape. Sir George Carew, president of the Munster Plantation (1585–86), believed that more could be achieved through persuasion than might: "We must change their course of government, clothing, customs, manner of holding land, language, and habit of life, it will otherwise be impossible to set up in them obedience" (Foster 1989, 282). Urbanism would come to play a key role in bringing what the British considered the arts of government, commerce, and culture to a backward Ireland. Sir Edmund Spenser, who had received vast tracts of land in Munster in 1586, wrote, for example, that "nothing doth sooner cause civility in any country than many market towns, by reason that people repairing often thither for their needs will daily see and learn civil manners."[4]

At the center of the Munster and Ulster plantations was a policy of laying out and building new towns. During the plantation of Ulster, representatives of the London Companies, which underwrote the settlement project, set about the construction of twenty-three fortified towns, including Londonderry, Coleraine, Newtownards, and Strabane (McSheffrey 2000, 32). Overseen by the Irish Society, the plantation's regulating authority, these new settlements employed all manner of urban features—wide streets, a grid pattern, a central market square, and commodified parcels of land for sale—that would help draw the line between modernity and tradition, that distinctive yet illusory boundary between the civilizing patterns of the settler and what were perceived as the backward behaviors of the native.

Londonderry's Market House, designed by Thomas Phillips in 1622 (Curl 1986, 22), was one of the first buildings in Ireland to reference what would soon become the dominant vocabulary of classical architecture. Occupying the central position of the new town plan, the market house stood on the space that in earlier times would have been reserved for a church or cathedral. Its Renaissance columns, and its symmetry and openness (on each of the four sides runs an agoric, pillared arcade), might serve as a political statement: citizens are equal under a rational, secular, and economic order. But atop the colonnaded building stood a square, fortified structure, reminiscent of a Norman tower. Surrounded by cannon, Londonderry's central feature expressed simultaneously the confidence, wealth, and insecurity of the colony. In early designs of Londonderry, spacious sites were reserved for church and school, two cultural institutions that would play a crucial role in subsequent generations. Likewise, the architecture of English towns in Ireland differentiated between native Irish and new arrivals. Settlers constructed their two-story houses with cut stone, brick, and slate. These homes stood in contrast to traditional Irish cabins made of mud, thatch, or rough stone. On maps of the period, English homes, behind the fortified walls of the town, perch in tidy rows along straight streets, while Irish houses are clustered haphazardly in the surrounding countryside. Settlers with property inside the town also received a plot of cultivated land outside the city walls, replicating the aristocratic pattern of town and country home ownership. This property arrangement merged middle-class aspirations with aristocratic pretensions, establishing what would become a defining characteristic of colonialism: the transplantation of a nascent middle class to a virgin country, and its subsequent elevation to a ruling elite.

The Move toward Urban Hegemony and the Creation of the Wide Streets Commission

Londonderry was one of the last fortified towns to be built in Western Europe. From the importing of guilds to the building of schools and churches, each element of the philosophically motivated and rationally planned city was underscored by its physical defense. The plantations were never exactly peaceful affairs. Violent resistance against them took two main forms: guerrilla resistance from evicted Irish tenants and more organized, last-ditch rebellions led by former Irish chieftains. In Ulster, for example, Hugh O'Neill led the most concerted attack. In 1601 his army killed several thousand settlers, but his defeat came at the Battle of Kinsale in the same year.

Every political system is a balance between the explicit use of force and the more nuanced tactics of persuasion and development. Despite the early rhetoric about improving the "clothing, customs...language, and habit of life" of the Irish, the plantations in Ireland were held through the use of force: soldiers were given the outermost land in Ulster to facilitate defense; grantees of larger estates were required to construct fortified enclosures; and a Crown official, the director-general of fortifications in Ireland, was appointed to oversee all buildings. Of the twin (and constantly alternating) strategies of control that the British have used in Ireland—coercion and consensus building—the plantations relied heavily on the power of the sword, while never giving up on claims to civilize the local population. In the construction of new towns, for example, we see the beginnings of an attempt, though a colonial one, to construct some semblance of a public sphere in Ireland—that is, a space in which the authorities come to rely less on violence (on which the state claims a monopoly) and more on the possibilities of winning acceptance from the colonized to enter into a mutually beneficial relationship. This relationship must always remain asymptotic, however, for should the vanquished ever prove to be as competent and efficient at running their own affairs as their occupiers, then that would remove the prime putative reason for the presence of the colonizer in the first place: to be a model of order, development, and culture.

The term *hegemony,* according to Antonio Gramsci, refers to the intellectual and moral leadership exercised in society by a class or its intellectuals.[5] More recently, the term has gained a new lease on life in postcolonial studies, with regard to the examination of the nineteenth century, an era commonly referred to as the "age of improvement."[6] Writing about the concept of improvement in the Indian context, at the beginning of this process of intervention and amelioration, Ranajit Guha suggests that the idea found strength during the administration of Lord Cornwallis: "The verb 'improve'... occurred frequently in his correspondence and official pronouncements—something like nineteen times in his two famous minutes of 18 September 1789...in defense of his plan for an immediate Permanent Setlement" (1997, 32). In Ireland, forty years later, the same paternalistic spirit can be seen in the 1828 founding of a Society for the Improvement of Ireland whose mission was to "procur[e] employment and relief for the people of Ireland as appeared to be best suited to preserve domestic tranquility, ensure national happiness, increase the strength and consolidate the resources of the empire at large."[7] Perhaps the apex of these policies, designed to "remedy the Irish problem" (Foster 1989, 222), was reached during Gladstone's tenure. In his three terms as prime minister (1868–74, 1880–85, 1892–94), he committed his energy to the project of bettering colonial societies. In an 1887 speech on the "Irish Question," he argued that Britain's purpose was to "affect the happiness, contentment, social order, and peace of all classes in Ireland" (Hutton and Cohen 1902, 238). His Land Act of 1870, which compensated Irish peasants for "improvements" made to their land, illustrates his thinking. Such concrete reforms, he said, can only "endear" the natives to "the greatness of Empire," and will ultimately enhance its "solidity" and "cohesion" (250). As the nineteenth century progressed, the balance between force and hegemony tilted noticeably toward the policies of consent making.

Any change in ideology sees its reflection in alterations to the built environment. As the nuances of discussion about hegemony shifted, so too did the architectural institutions that were the material means through which attempts at persuasion were implemented. One of the first major urban reconstructions that signaled a decisive change in the strategy of colonial government was the work of the Wide Streets commissioners of the late eighteenth and early nineteenth centuries. The commissioners, appointed by King George II, were part of the Protestant ascendancy. This Anglo-Irish caste was the landed, politically powerful group directly descended from those settlers, soldiers, merchants, and aristocrats who had arrived in Ireland during and after the plantations of the sixteenth and seventeenth centuries. This group ultimately achieved military victories, allowing them a significant degree of economic and cultural control over the island and laying the foundation for Protestant power. The commissioners operated in Dublin between 1750 and 1841. During the eighteenth century, the consolidation of Anglo-Irish power is most clearly visible in architecture across the whole of the country, not just in Dublin. Many landlords, magistrates, and other figures of the ascendancy built large neo-Palladian and Georgian estates throughout rural Ireland.[8]

Many of the owners of these mansions, in addition to being Commissioners for Making Wide and Convenient Ways, Streets, and Passages, were also members of the Protestant Parliament in Dublin. Some of their names now mark Dublin's main thoroughfares: Gardiner, Beresford, Foster, D'Olier. One of the first modern urban renewal authorities, the commissioners created broad new corridors; regulated the height and materials of new buildings; constructed a line of new quays along the Liffey river; erected new bridges; opened up vistas and sites for grand civic structures (Custom House and Four Courts); connected the commercial, administrative military centers

(Dublin Castle, Courts of Justice) to each other with new roads; and integrated the city's canals, riverways, and arterial roads into a comprehensive commercial transport network. Empowered to "carry on improvements by making . . . wide streets . . . through many parts that were before narrow, dangerous and inconvenient," these landowners collected taxes, acquired eminent domain, assessed property valuations, compensated those displaced by clearance, and enforced a series of regulations with regard to the width of pavements and the cleanliness of roads.[9] Such massive urban restructuring could not have occurred outside the context of an authoritarian regime that was allowed to impose its grand vision on the landscape, relatively free of democratic accountability.

Wide streets are one of colonial urbanism's most lasting legacies. From Dublin in 1757, through ceremonial parade routes in Africa and India, to postcolonial efforts to build modern national urban centers (Brasília, Chandigarh, Abuja), the wide street has served a host of ideological functions: efficiency and mobility, improved ventilation and cleanliness, slum destruction, prevention of revolution, urban beautification, display of state power, representation of democracy, gentrification, and land speculation. The commonly told story of urban modernism tends to focus on Paris, with its flaneurs, arcades, boulevards, and poets; or on Vienna, with the Ringstrasse and the coming of age of an ambitious bourgeoisie; or on London, with its Victorian extremes, imperial grandeur, and poverty. Each of these cities has its own story of how the urban environment embodied the dramatic changes that we now think of as the defining characteristics of modernity: capitalism, alienation, leisure, and constant change. The wide streets of Dublin, however, illustrate that many of the developments we associate with European modernity got their start in the colonies, returning home after having been proven a useful tool of population management.

The commissioners' justification for intervening in the spatial layout of Dublin comes through in the language they used. Not just *improvement,* but the words *convenient, trade, healthfulness, ornament,* and *safety* appear time and time again in their tracts and in the minutes of their meetings.[10] The commissioners' initial goal was to create a "Wide and Convenient Way . . . from Essex-Bridge to the Castle of Dublin . . . Whereas the ways, streets, avenues, and passages, leading from Essex-Bridge to the . . . Castle of Dublin . . . are at present narrow, close, and crooked, and the making a wide and convenient way, street, and passage . . . will contribute to the ease and safety of passengers, the adorning those parts of the city, and will be of use and benefit to the publick."[11] The chief secretary, in pushing for funds from London for a new center of commerce, wrote that "[a]s an Exchange for the merchants to assemble for transacting their business has long been wished for, his excellency is of the opinion that the most proper situation for such a building would be in that part of the new street in which it would be a termination of the view from Capel Street, Essex bridge and Parliament Street."[12] The improvements enacted by the commissioners were intended to facilitate the "accommodation of trade."[13] They were also, in the words of Lord Lieutenant Carlisle, aimed at "beautifying the city" and having a "tendency to national improvement."[14]

Having completed the widening of Essex Bridge and the creation of Parliament Street, the commissioners turned their attention to the reordering of Dame Street. Widening this street allowed for smoother travel between places of government (Parliament House), a military location (Dublin Castle), and an Anglican center of learning (Trinity College). This reorganizing also demonstrated that the semiotics of architecture and urban planning were integrating Ireland into a European Enlightenment narrative, one that structured urban space in a new, less obviously defensive way. Henceforth, city spaces would not just be fortresses, they would reflect "great plans of public utility" and demonstrate "great and munificent improvements" that were seen as adding considerably to the "ornament and convenience of the metropolis."[15]

The commissioners integrated large-scale architectural plans, such as the enlargement of the Parliament House in 1782 and the building of the Four Courts in 1786, into their schemes. Gandon's Custom House was the most celebrated neoclassical building in Ireland, and the commissioners oriented roads and views around it. A large statue of Commerce crowns the dome of the Custom House, and on its pediment stand the four figures of Neptune, Mercury, Plenty, and Industry. Edward Smyth, Gandon's sculptor, also designed the keystones that represent the Atlantic Ocean and the thirteen principal rivers of Ireland (Malton 1978, 57–58). At either end of the building, the pavilions display carvings of the Arms of Ireland, a woman and a harp, being enveloped by the lion and the unicorn of Great Britain, which, wrote Malton, "represent the friendly union of Britannica and Hibernia, with the good consequences relating to Ireland" (57).

The iconography and function of the other large architectural projects that were affiliated with Georgian Dublin and the work of the commissioners also presented a favorable view of the English conquest of Ireland and the benefits that accrued from it. John McGregor describes in his travelogue of the period, *A New Picture of Dublin,* the sculptures embedded in the walls of the Four Courts: "[T]he panels over the entrances...represent William the Conqueror establishing Courts of Justice...King John signing Magna Carta, Henry II receiving the Irish Chieftains, and James I abolishing the [Celtic] Brehon laws" (1821, 179). Enlightened English law is both evolutionary and based on the submission of an older, more tribal, Gaelic order. Of the Wide Streets commissioners' work overall, McGregor states, "[I]t must be admitted that no city in Europe can boast of greater improvements in the short space of half a century" (175).

By 1851 the center of Dublin had a rational and highly symbolic infrastructure. The developments mentioned here are but a few of the commissioners' projects. The Wide Streets commissioners clearly had a comprehensive vision of the city; they imagined urban space as a planned and controllable unit, but also one that could be manipulated and made to serve several ideologies at once. The commissioners integrated Dublin's quays into two long continuous arteries, zones of circulation that did away with disjointed work units. But the quays also aided the military, furthering communication between "his Majesty's Castle and the Vice-Regal Lodge in the Park, the Barrack, the Royal Hospital, and Access to the Courts of Justice."[16] Their designs created a ceremonial, almost circular, route that displayed the institutions of modern state and colonial power. Dublin Castle was at the center of much of their early work, as were the new civic institutions. The Wide Streets commissioners also created new zones in the city, new quarters of prestige and expense, and they opened the shops and streets for a sort of early flaneur. Alongside the widened streets, new Georgian residential squares were being laid out, and the commissioners, in a move not unlike contemporary gentrification, laid down design standards and regulated taxes, thereby having a large say in who got to live where. They also took over the job of hygiene managers, insisting on how and when streets should be cleaned and levying fines on those who disobeyed. They controlled street lighting, while also thinking about traffic flow and density. They concerned themselves with aesthetics and with how to ornament and beautify the city. Their work intensified a process that had begun during the plantations with the role of the surveyor: the increasing scope of the expert and professional, namely, the architect and the engineer, new specialists in urban space administration. The commissioners also introduced new styles of classical architecture that were clearly distinguished from older, more indigenous forms and materials. Most important, they provided the streets themselves that encouraged greater mobility, transparency, safety, and order, all euphemisms for modern life.

The Wide Streets commissioners, under the auspices of the ascendancy, sought to build a modern urban capital, but the wide streets and grand architecture of Dublin were never able to hide imperialism's basic contradiction: that improvement was largely a cloak for dominance. The commissioners made themselves almost too visible, for the scale of their plans and their big houses highlighted the contrast between privilege and poverty. Power was put on display in dramatic fashion; a public sphere was constructed, but no real attempt was made to integrate the native language, religion, or customs into the new arrangement. The commissioners never naturalized their rule.

The Colonial State and the Logic of Centrality

By the beginning of the nineteenth century, London had come to regard Ireland's Protestant elite as largely an inefficient governing class: the ascendancy had brought neither peace to the country nor culture to the people. Following the Act of Union in 1800, Ireland had its colonial Parliament removed and was administered by a new generation of unelected rulers appointed by Westminster—a series of viceroys, chief secretaries, and other assorted officials. With the departure of the ascendancy, a new geography of centering paralleled the temporality of development and improvement that was increasingly colonialism's defining ethos. Parliament in London facilitated the creation of the representative buildings and institutions of modernity: museums, libraries, universities, railway stations, and state bureaucracies in the center of Dublin.[17] The native subject became the target of a new tactic aimed at convincing him of the merits of order, obedience, culture, progress, and, ultimately, inclusion in a larger project of creating the greater good.

From the mid-nineteenth century on, the modern imperial state spatialized its role as curator of national culture. The National Gallery at Merrion Square was opened in 1859. The Royal Dublin Society Library was taken over by the state and renamed the National Library of Ireland. A parliamentary committee concluded that "the library ought to be considered as intended not solely for the advantage of the comparatively few individuals who belong to the Dublin society, but as a National Library, accessible under proper regulations to respectable persons of all classes who may be desirous to avail themselves of it for the purposes of literary research."[18] In 1890 the National Museum of Ireland opened its doors. The attempt by state administrators to define everything worth knowing—history, literature, and culture—was reinforced by their ability to claim a monopoly not just on violence but on rationality itself. Colonial government centralized the power of decision, of the decision-making process, in its officials who looked to the metropolitan center, where the new bureaucracies were situated, as the source of regularities and laws. Dublin Castle, after 1800, housed the various offices, boards, and departments that were established to administer the country, including the Department of Agriculture, the Board of Education, Inspector of Factories, the Ordnance Survey, the Land Commission, and the Congested Districts Board.

Economics and transport were also centralized in Dublin as part of the emerging geography. All the great railway stations in Ireland were built in the mid-nineteenth century, generally in the hierarchical Italian Renaissance style.[19] The thirty companies that ran the imperial railways completed a comprehensive and intricate rail network as part of their modernizing infrastructure. Construction of over two thousand miles of track altered the Irish landscape in significant ways: forests were depleted for wooden sleepers; remote areas were opened up to tourism; emigration became easier; local industry had to compete with cheaper, imported goods; and a new architectural and engineering industry created an impressive new system of bridges, tunnels, and stations (Aalen, Whelan, and Stout 1997, 213–14). Another centralized authority emerged in Ireland during the nineteenth century: the Royal Irish Constabulary, an armed national police force. The new force replaced the former system of local magistrates and county constabularies, and, without precedent, was commanded from Dublin by a single figure, the inspector-general. Over the course of the nineteenth century, fourteen hundred new barracks were constructed, while the individual policeman was handed a vast new array of duties. In the 1840s policemen were given the task of compiling a Registry of Households, and by the 1860s their regular duties "included the collection of agricultural statistics, census work, the serving of poor-law election notices, customs duty, weight and measures inspection, factory inspection and the enforcement of extensive new laws governing fishing, to liquor sales to prostitution" (Townsend 1983, 70). The colonial state's fixation on statistics and the centralization of data was built into the penetrating gaze of the police officer and his headquarters in Dublin. Prisons, too, were increasingly centralized and nationalized, as state power steadily advanced through modern institutions that were stages ahead of those in Britain.

The Trust

Toward the end of the nineteenth century, before the arrival of modern town planning, the imperial government promoted the idea of trusteeship in Ireland, India, and elsewhere. The concept derives from Burke, who felt that only an aristocratic minority had the capability of governing: they possessed sufficient leisure time for discussion and gathering of information, and the necessary wealth that placed them above menial dependence and, thus, self-interest. This privileged group, Burke believed, could best represent the general public, whose reason was "weak" and "passions ungoverned" (McDowell 1991, 621). In 1834 Parliament passed a motion calling for the protection of the rights of natives across the colonial world. William Light, for example, who laid out the Australian city of Adelaide, also held the title of "Protector of Aborigines" (Home 1997, 48). By the end of the century, trusts had evolved into municipal authorities consisting of members of the local British elite, who were given a mandate by London to administer the affairs of a city. As challenges to the empire arose, trusts acted as a buffer zone between a distrusted central authority and an increasingly restless local population. Dublin's Guinness Trust was formed in 1890, the Calcutta Improvement Trust in 1897, and the Lucknow Improvement Trust in 1925.[20] By this time, trusts were primarily motivated by the Victorian project of improving urban hygiene and public morality. In 1890, on the back of the Dublin Improvement Act of 1889, a group of Protestant and Unionist businessmen and politicians formed the Guinness, later the Iveagh, Trust. At first, six hundred dwellings were constructed in the center of Dublin. Within a few years, Dublin's Iveagh Trust had turned its attention to reforming public behavior through the eradication of the "grime and smell of the poor" (Aalen 1990, 42). In 1905 it commenced work on a recreation hall and public baths to encourage exercise and essential hygiene. In Ireland, preventing the spread of tuberculosis was the great cause for sanitarians and philanthropists, not least out of the fear that the disease might spread to the suburbs. (In India the discourse of the plague—its cause, prevention, and cure—was the driving factor behind the urban reform movement, including the relief of congestion, the sterilization of land, and the creation of ventilated parks and suburbs.) Dublin's Iveagh Trust remained Protestant dominated and became increasingly marginal in a growing nationalist city. Edward Cecil Guinness's initial statement upon founding the Guinness Trust indicated his aims: "the amelioration of the condition of the poorer of the working classes" (Aalen 1990, 14). Beneath that altruistic statement lay the broader agenda of attempting to suppress socialism and quiet the rising independence movement.

From the founding of Londonderry in the seventeenth century, through the urban reconstruction spearheaded by the Wide Streets commissioners in the eighteenth, to the creation of civic institutions and colonial trusts during the nineteenth, colonial landowners, merchants, government officials, and philanthropists sought to mold the urban environment. When colonialism reached its crisis in the twentieth century, the focal point of nationalist insurgency became the buildings and institutions that were the concrete legacy of those British attempts to win hegemony. During the 1916 Rising, an eclectic mix of ideologues chose the General Post Office (GPO) as their head-quarters. A weeklong bombardment by a British gunboat left it a burned-out shell. Following the Rising, during the War of Independence the city became an arena for modern urban guerrilla warfare. Urban space provided a maze of alleys and side streets, the glens and mountain passes of the city, suitable for Michael Collins's intricate network of spies, assassins, and informers. And the IRA set ablaze Gandon's Custom House. Following the formation of the Irish Free State, the forces that opposed the new regime took over the Four Courts and initiated the Civil War. What the seizure of the GPO, the Four Courts, and the Custom House, and their dramatic conflagration, so vividly displayed was not only the obvious failure of colonialism's institutions to win hegemony, but also the nationalists' recognition that these urban sites were crucial to their own project. *Postcolonial Dublin* takes up the story during these years.

1 | *Dublin of the Future* and the Emergence of Town Planning in Ireland

Dublin is burning. In "The Last Hour of the Night," the frontispiece to Patrick Abercrombie's 1914 town plan, *Dublin of the Future* (Abercrombie 1922), shooting flames soar out of three of the city's imperial buildings, while its citizens, who might naturally be terrified, instead go about their everyday lives (Figure 1). Two policemen watch children play soccer. Weary figures pass by. Their home, a tenement propped up with wooden beams, stands, cracked, on the verge of collapse, in imminent danger of being engulfed. Hovering between the two landscapes—one, colonialism's powerful architecture; the other, its urban underbelly—floats a morbid figure. Stooped and sickly, he is, without doubt, the devil: horns, cloven feet, a cloak of flames. A carrier of the repressed material of the city, this morbid symptom is marked by the forces that gave birth to him. Like the tenement poor, crammed into the decaying buildings of the long-gone Anglo-Irish ascendancy, his body is decrepit, diseased, and threatening. His eyes stare straight at the liberal viewer. Imperialism is dying, but nowhere can the new be seen. A certain space has been shattered, and the fight is on to see what will replace it.

To any Dubliner, the three burning buildings are recognizable at a glance. The General Post Office (built 1814–18) symbolizes the worldwide network of information that colonialism helped produce

1

Figure 1. *The Last Hour of the Night,* frontispiece of Patrick Abercrombie's *Dublin of the Future* (1922).

and regulate. It renders the colony communicative with the wider world, intelligible within a colonial imagination. The Custom House (built 1781–91), constructed downstream from the heart of the old city on reclaimed land to benefit ascendancy speculators, locked Dublin into the laissez-faire world of global trade. Its ambitious architecture and maritime iconography reinforced the mercantilist connection between nation and taxation, state and statistic. The Four Courts (built 1786–1802), rising powerfully above all the other buildings on the Liffey Quays, was constructed during that false dawn between Grattan's Parliament of 1782 and the 1798 rebellion, when it appeared that Protestants and Catholics in Ireland might find some common cause in the struggles for free trade,[1] legislative independence,[2] and even republicanism.[3]

These buildings, celebrated for their grandeur, were the physical representation of a hegemonic colonial attempt to carve out a space of civil society, to put the modern state and its institutions on display. Their Georgian neoclassicism—imposing, uniform façades of granite, Roman columns and arches, a scale at odds with the history of the city—proclaimed permanency and conquest, as if to say, "We have vanquished; we are here to stay!" They stood at the beginning of that long nineteenth-century project to transform what had been acquired haphazardly by the sword into a carefully regulated empire.

These structures represented the areas of greatest state intervention, namely, the means of communication, the economy, and the law. As the mercantilist and predatory colonialism of the sixteenth and seventeenth centuries turned into the systematic imperialism of the eighteenth and nineteenth centuries, the British, having gained some degree of control of the land and economy, sought to reinforce their means of ideological control, disseminating state logic over an ever wider area.

These earlier centuries saw violent attempts by the British to manage a sometimes rebellious, mostly contentious Irish population. The settling of plantations, with its attendant mass importation of alien Protestant settlers; the seizing and redistribution of land from its Catholic and Gaelic landowners to loyal soldiers; and suppression of rebellions, most brutally Cromwell's victory in 1649 over Catholics and Royalists who had fought against the confiscation of their land and status: all attest to the overwhelming violence of a sustained colonial policy in Ireland at the beginning of the modern era. Protestant victories at Boyne and Aughrim in 1690 and 1691 marked the consolidation of Protestant power over the island.

Following these military victories and their associated land redistributions, a new political class came to govern the country. Known as the Protestant ascendancy, they were a select and secure group of landlords, merchants, and lawyers. Partly an aristocratic class, partly a religious affiliation, and partly a social order dedicated to a leisured and cultured way of life, the ascendancy strove to follow the principles of the European Enlightenment: an enthusiasm for reason, science, and learning; a commitment to practical politics and social improvement; and an interest in the high arts, such as classical music, architecture, and literature.[4] The names associated with the eighteenth century in Ireland—Jonathan Swift, Edmund Burke, Bishop Berkeley, Laurence Sterne, Oliver Goldsmith, and Richard Sheridan—testify to the ambitions of this elite. Their concrete legacy lies in the Palladian architecture spread across rural Ireland, as well as in the wide boulevards, baroque planning, and neoclassical buildings associated with Dublin's Wide Streets commissioners (1757–1802). As in colonial America, the aspirations and independence of the ascendancy grew as their wealth and confidence increased. Toward the end of the century, the leaders of the ascendancy had begun to question their relationship with their imperial supervisors in London. Based as they were in trade and the export of agricultural produce, they saw no reason why Westminster should regulate their commercial and administrative affairs. By 1800, particularly on account of the 1798 United Irishmen's rebellion, British officials in London came to believe that Ireland's Protestant ruling class could not be trusted, that they had neither the willingness nor the ability to keep the colony subservient to its dominant partner. From 1801, following the Act of Union, the country was officially incorporated into the United Kingdom and ruled directly from London.

When Ireland became part of Britain, the British Parliament, which had a large block of Irish MPs, aimed to build the infrastructure of a modern, albeit colonial, state. While force was always an option, and one often used, policymakers began to consider the Irish a population to be won over, to be convinced of the benefits of unity within the empire. William Gladstone epitomized this policy. In 1886, during the introduction of the first Home Rule Bill, Gladstone, who had been elected prime minister on a platform of pacifying Ireland, stated that "[o]ur ineffectual and spurious coercion is morally worn out." He continued, "Something must be done . . . to restore to Ireland the first conditions of civil life—the free course of law, the liberty of every individual . . . the confidence of the people in the law . . . apart from which no country can be called . . . civilised" (Hutton and Cohen 1902, 9).

In the introduction of national schools, the building of colleges and universities, the construction of prisons and hospitals; in the modernization of the means of transport, the standardization of building and hygiene codes, the centralization of bureaucracy; in the creation of a national police force, and in many other efforts to further the smooth functioning of society, the rhetoric of development masked the required obedience to the law.[5] The substantial number of troops and police in Ireland reflected the weak hold of civil government on the social order.[6] The regular deployment of the army in day-to-day matters, such as elections and evictions, merely highlighted the failure of hegemony to take root among the Irish whom the British sought to govern. For any state, suggests Terry Eagleton, the greatest test of its hegemonic powers comes from its colonial subjects (1995, 28). Between 1916 and 1922, the suspect ideas of consent, legitimation, and free trade, along with many of the buildings that housed them, were in flames.

Each of the buildings portrayed in "The Last Hour of the Night" became in its turn, a century after it was built, the focal point of revolution. The GPO, center of colonial communications, was captured by rebel forces and subsequently shelled by the British during the Easter Rising (1916). The Custom House was set ablaze by the Dublin Brigade of the IRA on 25 May 1921, as part of an effort to undermine the British-run administration during the War of Independence (1919–21). Pro-Treaty troops bombarded the Four Courts in 1922 with artillery borrowed from Winston Churchill to oust anti-treaty soldiers who had seized the building during the Civil War. During these years, the city became a battleground, a space of revolution against imperialism and its structures in Ireland: Dublin became a major focus of insurrection and its prevention.

In the following pages, I argue that modern town planning in Ireland arose out of an *emergency,* a crisis of imperial proportions, which the new discipline both underscored and sought to solve. For the British, town planning was a key element of the new social imperialism, a paternal effort to impress on colonial subjects that their best interests (jobs, health, housing) lay with the empire and its ability to provide modern cities. In truth, town planning was, for the English, a means of defense, a way of keeping their hold on increasingly contested territories. In 1913, for example, Patrick Geddes, a founding member of the British town planning movement, stressed the urgent need for social and spatial reform in the Irish capital. In evidence given to the Dublin Housing Inquiry, he made his claim by means of a military metaphor: "When people are preparing for war they bring up their resources on every side. You, too, could be drawing up your plans" (Local Government Board [LGB] 1914a, 211).

Town planning offered nationalists, in contrast, a tangible way to anticipate state power and a creative opportunity to build their own ideologies in stone. Following the 1916 Rising, *Studies,* a moderate Catholic journal, published an article by R. M. Butler, Ireland's leading architectural critic, who suggested that the destruction of the city's core raised both an "opportunity" and "a question of national importance": namely, how to best "reconstruct" the city's thoroughfares so that the nation "might be well proud" (Butler 1916, 570). In 1923, following independence, Ernest Blythe, first minister for local government, spoke of how "the character of the capital will have a very important influence upon the progress and development of the state" (Campbell 1994, 43). Town planning, in its potential to deliver healthy cities, to provide municipal government, and to create modern citizenship, appealed to the leaders of the fledgling state—to both their pride and their insecurity.

Dublin and Nationalist Historiography

But these are urban issues, and they arise at the beginning of the twentieth century. Anticolonial resistance in Ireland through the nineteenth century had been predominantly a rural affair, driven by the contradiction between landlord and tenant. This tension manifested itself over the century in many forms, including eviction, famine, and emigration, all of which contributed to the removal of the most unstable class elements from the Irish countryside. In turn, this rural depopulation helped consolidate bourgeois control over the emerging nationalist movement itself by furthering the Anglicization of Irish culture, the enlargement of farm size, and the deindustrialization of southern areas.[7]

In narratives of resistance, urban issues rarely find their way into the story of nineteenth-century Irish nationalism. From the United

Irishmen's peasant uprising in 1798, through the efforts of the Young Ireland movement to reconcile native tenant and foreign landlord via a common Gaelic culture, to the militant Land War of the 1870s, nationalist historians and historians of nationalism make little reference to Dublin's population playing a significant part in the anticolonial struggle. George Boyce writes that "Ireland in the nineteenth century was an overwhelmingly rural country...rural values and ways of life shaped the thinking of the vast bulk of its people" (1990, 5). Joseph Lee, a leading economic historian, foregrounds the lack of industrial development and, hence, the relative historical unimportance of nineteenth-century Dublin. "Why did Ireland, outside the Lagan Valley," he asks, "fail to create her own Bostons and Birminghams? Why did the population of Belfast increase from 100,000 to 400,000 between 1815 and 1914, while that of Dublin only managed to creep up from 250,000 to 300,000?" (1983, 9).

What, then, is significant about the role of the Irish city in the long interplay between colonizers and colonized? If the struggle against colonialism was a rural endeavor, why examine the city, specifically Dublin, with the aim of understanding nation-building? In the decade before the formation of the autonomous Irish Free State in 1922, Dublin represented not only an emergency for the imperial authorities, but also a potential site of crisis and opportunity for the aspiring nationalist movement. Colonialists saw that Dublin's decrepit slums and tenements housed a collective force of inhabitants whose poverty and living conditions might later prove to be an impetus to violence. In Dublin, the transition from what some still refer to as the "glorious days" of the Georgian era into the long period of stagnation associated with the aftermath of the Act of Union was most noticeable in the deterioration of the city's domestic architecture. Rows of Georgian terraces, once inhabited by aristocratic owners, were bought up and subdivided into smaller and smaller units by speculators, who rented to an ever increasing, downwardly mobile class. By the end of the nineteenth century, Dublin's once grand Georgian homes had deteriorated into tenements.

In 1913, the year of the Dublin Lockout, the *Irish Times,* the city's most pro-British newspaper, noted that the notorious condition of housing in the city "is responsible not only for disease and crime but for much of our industrial unrest."[8] An official government inquiry into "the housing conditions of the working classes" followed the strike and called for a massive investment in state-built housing in the city. The large amount of financing that would be required would be many times recuperated, the report suggested, "by raising the moral tone of the people and the almost certain consequent reduction in crime and sickness" (LGB 1914b, 25). Following the 1916 Rising, a new chief secretary, H. E. Duke, was appointed to Ireland. At his first public function, he warned that Dublin's slums were a problem of "tremendous magnitude" and that their improvement was at the heart of the "well-being of the community of this island and the Empire."[9] Despite the laissez-faire reputation of classic colonialism, Ireland was the site of ever increasing state intervention. State housing policy was an attempt to purchase an insurance policy against revolution.

For many nationalists, cultural nationalists in particular, Dublin was simultaneously the urban anomaly in a movement "authenticated" by rural, Gaelic tradition and the symbolic center of any future modern nation-state. Today's revisionist historians portray Patrick Pearse, leader of the Easter 1916 Rising, as someone who advocated a rigid interpretation of Irish culture as rural, Gaelic, and Catholic. His critics highlight his dedication to reinvigorating the Irish language, his commitment to Catholicism, and his descriptions of an idyllic, pastoral nation as evidence of his desire to create a culturally monolithic, rural postcolonial state. But Pearse's ideology was complex. Like all nationalisms, his philosophy was not a reaction against modernity, but a product of it. Pearse believed that any new Irish state would have to be at home in the modern world, and that urbanism would be at the center of the new nation. "A free Ireland," he wrote "would not...have squalor in her cities....A free Ireland would...nationalise the railways...would foster industries, would promote commerce...would beautify the cities, would educate the workers" (Lee 1983, 147). For other, more radical nationalist leaders, such as James Connolly and James Larkin, anticolonial resistance was unthinkable outside of urban socialism. Connolly, founder of the Irish Labor Party and the Irish Citizen's Army, continually railed against the dreadful housing conditions in Dublin. In his paper *The Worker* he urged Dubliners not to be "dazzled into forgetfullness" by the horrors of World War I: "All the fleets and armies of the 'alien enemy' are not as hurtful to our lives, as poisonous to our moral development, as destructive to our social being as any one street of tenement houses in the slums of Dublin" (Ó'Cathasaigh 1997, 154). Urban politics also afforded the greatest possibilities for getting working-class representatives elected, and the housing issue was the first item on the Labour Party's 1914 manifesto: "Vote for Labour and Sweep Away the Slums."[10] Landlord profit was one of Connolly's favorite recurring examples for demonstrating how capitalism in Ireland was a British imposition on an older, collective way of life. Irish society, Connolly propounded, had once "rested upon the communal ... ownership of land." With the breakup of the Gaelic order, however, many of its descendants had become part of the establishment and "[had] a thousand strings binding them to English capitalism." The landlord, he argued, "is now an Irishman," and "we must organize as a class" to confront those who call themselves patriots but who would evict us "same as before" (Connolly 1987, 1: 25).

This fracturing of nationalism along class lines posed a problem for Ireland's more moderate nationalist factions. For the Catholic Church, the established Irish Party at Westminster, and conservative cultural nationalists, Dublin's inner-city population needed to be harnessed to the specific ends of these groups—that is, the attainment of statehood, not a radical economic overhaul. Arthur Griffith, founder of Sinn Féin, which was fiscally conservative in its early incarnation, denounced radicalism as a distraction: "I deny that socialism is a remedy for the existent evils. . . . I deny that capital and Labour are in their nature antagonistic" (Yeates 2000, 355). For the Irish Party at Westminster, the Dublin Lockout of 1913 was a socialist detour away from the evolution toward home rule; Thomas Kettle, the first professor of economics at the nationalist University College, Dublin, attempted to mediate between the two sides in the strike and keenly noted the connection between housing and unrest. In calling for urban reform, he argued that new housing schemes would have to be created, and that they might negotiate "the frenzy of Socialism and the obtuseness of Capitalism." "Not only Dublin but civilisation as we know it" depended on such a compromise.[11] The Catholic Church was the other great hegemonic nationalist institution. And for the Church, radical nationalism, such as Larkin and Connolly's trade unionism, was not only anticlerical but, in its eyes, a product of an alien, British, Protestant system as well. In 1913, Sinn Féin's newspaper published a speech by a prominent priest. "For the first time," wrote Father Phelan, "Ireland has a concrete example of how the two civilisations, Gaelicism and Socialism, mutually repel and antagonise each other.... To any man who wished to see the very antithesis of the dream of Gaeldom, Dublin during the strike has presented it" (Yeates 2000, 356).

But Dublin was not only a problem site for middle-of-the-road nationalists. It also had the potential to be the proud and noble capital of a future state. New ideas about town planning were coming from Britain, from Ebenezer Howard and Raymond Unwin, and from America, from John Nolen in particular. These ideas were beginning to enter Ireland and would come to play an important role in the debates over what the social and physical shape of any new state should be, particularly with regard to suburbanization, industrialization, and how to best reconstruct the city after a decade of turmoil. In 1911 Dublin Corporation, becoming an increasingly nationalist body, sent two of its councilors, Thomas O'Beirne and Charles Travers, to Birmingham to examine that city's approach to working-class housing. Upon their return, O'Beirne and Travers recommended the creation of more parks and civic amenities. Given the approach of home rule (the liberals under Asquith had been reelected in 1910), they also argued that "should Dublin soon become the seat of a National Parliament, the development of the city and all Irish towns on modern town planning lines should begin immediately."[12] When Patrick Abercrombie published his 1914 city plan, he spoke clearly to aspiring nationalists, to whom his language would appeal: "The re-establishment of a National Parliament should give the necessary impetus to set a great Town Plan in motion, and the access of material prosperity which will ensure the means to carry it out" (1922, 3). Likewise, when Raymond Unwin, the theorist and architect behind the creation of Letchworth Garden City (1904) in England, visited Dublin in 1914, he used his lectures to place Dublin in an international context, in which the city would "once again become a pride unto itself and a pride of nations."[13]

When Patrick Geddes, Britain's leading promoter of town planning, traveled to Dublin in 1914, he, too, sought to hitch his ideals about urban reform to the cause of moderate nationalism. In his promotion of slum clearance and garden suburbs, he met with labor representatives as well as members of the Roman Catholic hierarchy. Geddes convinced labor activist Larkin of the need for a "garden village" for the "practically homeless" workers (Kitchen 1975, 248–49). Geddes went so far as to convince Dublin Corporation to offer the land. This would be a minor victory for the advocates of town planning, offering an alternative to the dominant labor trend of creating more inner-city living space. Geddes also sought to convince members of the Catholic hierarchy that modern town planning could address some of their frustrations, including the lack of a Catholic cathedral in a city dominated by two Protestant ones. A new town plan, Geddes argued, could provide a "new Cathedral . . . so making a via sacra . . . [that would be] the best monument for Home Rule . . . and the Irish Race" (Defries 1928, 180). The archbishop was so impressed by the idea that he purchased the site for the building from the corporation.

In the heady days of the early twentieth century, when both town planning and modern nationalism were, not coincidentally, developing with renewed energy, nationalists of various stripes envisioned their own control over Dublin's spaces as central to their political vision. As British authority came under assault in Ireland in the years before and after 1916, British officials also turned to the new discipline of town planning and to its young practitioners, such as Unwin, Geddes, and Abercrombie, in order to pacify the city and ameliorate the causes of unrest. Nationalists, as the speed of planning activity grew, entered into the debates over the location and style of new housing, the future shape of the city, and the changing relationship between town and country.

Dublin and the International Planning Movement

Many major players in the early days of the town planning movement passed through Dublin in the decade before independence. In 1911 Patrick Geddes arrived in Ireland to open an exhibition on "Cities and Town Planning," at the invitation of Lady Aberdeen, wife of the viceroy to Ireland and long a philanthropic champion of urban reform in Ireland. Geddes, an eccentric Scottish promoter of regional planning, civic surveying, and small-scale urban renewal, gave testimony at the 1913 inquiry into "housing conditions of the working class" in Dublin. There—oddly enough, given his ideas about organic town planning and historic preservation (what he called "conservative surgery")[14]—he conjured up links between Dublin's "glorious" baroque past and its potential future: the great university city, he believed, was "destined to become what it was in the 18th century, one of the most important secondary cities in the world" (LGB 1914a, 210). But this could only be realized if an "improved Town Planning Act" were passed, as it had been in England in 1909. In Britain, town planning was tied as much to reforming morals as to improving material conditions. England's 1909 town planning bill aimed to "provide a domestic condition for the people in which their physical health, their morals, their character...can be improved" (Hall 1996, 53). In Ireland the urgency for urban reform was more immediate than in England. When, in the aftermath of the Dublin Lockout, the authorities did not invest in improving the city's housing stock, Geddes lamented that "[a] hundred thousand pounds well spent in carrying out the beginnings of all this—aye—even the half of it—there would have been no Sinn Fein revolution in 1916. I do not merely suggest this: I know it. And from both sides, from all concerned" (Defries 1928, 181).

Geddes was in and out of Dublin in the years surrounding the Rising. In 1914 he helped organize a civic exhibition, which included the display of all manner of interdisciplinary urban data: aerial maps, demographic statistics, urban history, and botany. At this event, he launched a competition for a new and substantial town plan for the city. In 1916 he returned from France to preside over the award. From Ireland, he traveled to India and from there to Palestine and other colonies where he initiated a tradition of sanitary urban reform and garden suburbs, for which Dublin had been an early testing ground.

By the time he arrived in Dublin in 1914, Raymond Unwin was the foremost architect in and promoter of England's garden city movement. In April 1914 he gave a lecture at Trinity College, Dublin, entitled "How Town Planning May Solve the Housing Problem."[15] Following this presentation, Dublin Corporation employed him as a housing consultant, during which time he designed with Geddes a new suburb at Marino, on the northern fringe of the city.[16] This project, according to one biographer, was significant for Unwin, as he "experimented with double and even quadruple blocks," which pointed toward his post–World War I work, defined by the mission of providing pragmatic, functional housing on a large scale (Miller 1992, 131). In the aftermath of World War I, Unwin held the key role in the Tudor Walters Committee, established to assess Britain's postwar housing needs. The result of these efforts would be a million or so homes built in England between the wars, but almost all were in suburban areas, with few conforming to the principles of true garden cities. Unwin's main work in Ireland was overseeing the legislation behind the reconstruction of Dublin's main thoroughfare, Sackville Street, after it was destroyed during the 1916 Rising. The bill sought to negotiate the commercial concerns of business owners, the aesthetic interests of civic leaders, and the separatist feelings of nationalists over the interference in local matters by British planners and architects. His mediations among the various factions in Dublin and between state and local authorities were a good dress rehearsal for the political role he was to play in England as chief housing officer in the 1920s and 1930s. Again, Dublin proved to be a fruitful site of experimentation for a leading English planner.

Patrick Abercrombie had a long affiliation with Dublin. As with Geddes and Unwin, his connection with the city began in 1914, when his submission, *Dublin of the Future,* won Dublin's town planning competition. Following the foundation of the Irish Free State in 1922, Abercrombie's design formed a physical template in debates over suburbanization versus the building of inner-city apartments. His plan firmly advocated garden city principles and commitment to a monumental urban core. In 1937 he was again employed to map out Dublin's future by the increasingly industrially minded postcolonial state. After the first of his Dublin stints, he returned to England, where he drew up plans for the mining communities of Doncaster (1921) and Sheffield (1924) in the Midlands. Abercrombie is best known for his Greater London Plan, which decentralized over a million people and their jobs to suburban rings and satellite towns, and implemented the control of land values (Cherry 1981, 116). But Abercrombie regarded *Dublin of the Future* as his "best piece of constructive regional planning," and as a leading planning critic remarks, with Dublin behind him, "his professional reputation was assured" (Cherry 1981, 108).

Few books on Irish history mention that these foremost players in the founding of town planning as a professional activity were enthusiastically engaged in the politics and landscape of Dublin. In the wider world of planning history, too, Dublin gets barely a nod. Peter Hall, in *Cities of Tomorrow* (1996), mentions Abercrombie's Dublin plan in passing. A typical collection of essays in the field, such as *Urban Planning in a Changing World: The Twentieth Century Experience,* doesn't mention Ireland at all. Cherry's *Pioneers in British Planning* (1981) lays out the chronology of all the major figures in the early urban reform movement, including, very briefly, their Dublin engagements, but never adequately addresses the questions of why, when, and how Dublin came to occupy the important position it did. Gerald Dix writes that Patrick Abercrombie's "success in the Dublin Town Planning Competition in 1914 marked his entry into the leading ranks of the young planning profession" (Cherry 1981, 105). But Dix never considers the ways in which Abercrombie's *Dublin of the Future* plan engaged the politics of colonialism in Ireland: how, for example, its imposing beaux arts design of ceremonial axes and sweeping vistas simultaneously reinforced imperial power and appealed to the middle-class nationalists, who desired a space in which political power could be centralized. Mervyn Miller's essay on Raymond Unwin in the same collection does not reference Dublin. Helen Meller's study of Patrick Geddes comes closest to theorizing the symbiotic relationship between town planning and the context of colonialism: "The city of Dublin," she writes, "provided a favorable setting for a Geddesian social experiment since, as a colonial city, the free play of social and political factors was stifled" (1990, 58). Yet this, too, reveals a reductive reading of Irish culture. Ireland at the beginning of the twentieth century was a ferment of political and cultural activity on the eve of a revolution—a revolution that existed in a world context, and one whose tragedy, Lenin wrote, was that it broke "prematurely" (Pyle 1968, 195). Meller's idea of a repressed political climate does an injustice to the social discontent and rebellious energies that necessitated the need for town planning in the first place. Far from social factors being stifled, everyday life in the colony was intensely political, and the 1913 Lockout, the thirty-year-old campaign for home rule, the Gaelic renaissance, and the Easter Rising itself, all attest to this.

Turning to studies specifically on Irish planning by Irish writers, one might expect to find a more politically engaged analysis of the ideological interests behind urban reform. Colonialism, after all, works to gain control over physical space, and in Ireland land has always been the most contested category of all. Historically, there has always been a correspondence between changes in how the country was governed and how the land was controlled and used. The settlers in the Ulster plantation, for example, created a series of market towns in order to promote commerce and private property. At the end of the eighteenth century, when power across the island was more securely held by the ascendancy, the Wide Streets commissioners extensively replanned the congested streets of Dublin and undertook all manner of redevelopments to demonstrate what they considered to be the essentially liberal nature of colonial rule. At the end of the nineteenth century doctors and sanitation experts set about controlling public health by eradicating the slums. With such a fraught history of land management, it is surprising that the few historians of Irish planning are not more attuned to the spatial, particularly urban, practices of empire. Irish scholars might mention that Dublin played a role in the early town planning movement, but they are reluctant to consider, and even insecure about suggesting, that Dublin might hold a significant and unique position as the capital of the only Western European nation colonized by another in the history of planning. They tend to see Irish cities as marginal to the processes of modernity and colonialism, both of which justified themselves, in part, by transforming the urban landscape.

Scholars of modernity have most often turned to definitive moments in the history of large European cities to chart the ways in which modern ideologies of state and class power found physical expression. The shaping of Paris under Haussmann, for example, becomes the Ur-site for explaining modernity's penchant for "creative destruction." Fin de siècle Vienna, with the construction of the monumental Ringstrasse, is often held up as a central venue to illustrate the power and narcissism of a new European middle class. The grime and overcrowding of Victorian London in the nineteenth century are represented as the quintessential example of unregulated industrial capitalism. Urban historians of Ireland, however, are slow to connect Dublin to this broader story.

When we look more closely, we see that Ireland not only has a long history of urban development, but that this history continually interacts with the forces of urbanism and modernism. The urban Irish landscape reveals the ways in which the colonial environment in particular was a site for many of the signatures of urban modernity, but out of their context, misplaced. Modernity is a clash, a shock, the product of a tension between two competing cultures. In countries where colonialism is not a factor, this tension may arise somewhat organically and may work itself out through the ritualized institutions of society, such as parliamentary democracy. In Ireland, however, as in other colonies, colonization causes more of a rupture, and this rupture is literally visible in the city. Looking at town planning in colonial Dublin—its importation and appropriation—draws attention to the self-justifying language and the privileged and militaristic ideology that disguises itself in the cloak of liberalism, improvement, order, and efficiency. Ireland, after all, holds the central position in "British" modernist literary production (Yeats, Joyce, Wilde). The country also played an important role in the formation of British economic policy. The laissez-faire policies that contributed to the famine at the start of the nineteenth century had, by that century's end, turned into the politics of state intervention, as subsidies for Irish land reform and public housing, along with a host of other welfare initiatives, remained more advanced in Ireland than they were in England. Modern town planners, like the purveyors of other cultural discourses during the nineteenth and twentieth centuries, used Ireland as a site of experimentation, inspiration, and domination. Planning helped consolidate the process of modernization in the colonies. It was inevitable that, as nationalism began to take root in Ireland, its practitioners would appropriate this language to further their own ends: the creation of an independent state.

Town planning discourse always boasts of its own modernity. The first issue of *Town Planning Review,* one of the discipline's earliest journals, claims that after the extremes of the Victorian city, "the modern city is awakening to a new dawn of civic design" (Adshead 1908, 10). In *Dublin of the Future* Abercrombie promises "to create the capital of a modern country" (1922, 3). A few years later, Horace O'Rourke, Dublin Corporation architect, argues that "modern times" require a new survey of the city. Debates about the term *modernity* are endless. My goal is not to arrive at a definition of the concept on which everyone can agree. By examining town planning, I hope to gain insight into the ways in which the terms *modernity* and *the modern* have been used by their self-proclaimed practitioners in the colonial urban context. My emphasis, therefore, is on the ways in which the urban environment became the focus of various attempts to define and control modern life: its values, its scale, its economy, and its history. These theoretical questions are missing from most of the literature by Irish urban historians.

In *The Emergence of Irish Planning,* Michael Bannon, a leading Irish planning critic, writes that "before and after independence . . . Ireland has been an essential stopping-off point for many planning advocates" (1985, 14). This analysis of the relationship between Dublin and the international planning movement typifies the attempt at objectivity, the aim to be apolitical, that characterizes much social science writing. Town planning, Bannon writes, was a tool used to resolve "the dominant problem of the time . . . urban housing" (15). Overlooked is the fact that housing and "the associated problems of environmental decay" (15) were symptomatic of deeper political problems that hinged on the position of Ireland within the British empire — underdevelopment, absentee landlordism, and lack of self-determination. In other words, Bannon evaluates Irish town planning and, at the same time, refuses to place Ireland within the context of colonialism. Indicative of this approach is his idea that "planning . . . was not to form any significant part of the emerging nationalist policies" (18). On the contrary, while not always immediately striking, nationalist notions about what an ideal city ought to look like were foundational during these years. As today's Dublin undergoes the rapid changes associated with globalization, a new interest in the history of the city has arisen. Ruth McManus's *Dublin, 1910–1940: Shaping the City and Suburbs* (2002) addresses, in a more interdisciplinary manner, the evolution of Irish planning. But she fails to theorize the terms she employs. What is "the state" and how did town planning help to create it? What distinguished the Irish Free State from its colonial predecessor? Likewise, she overlooks the pluralism of the term *nationalism,* which, like town planning itself, is not a singular entity, but a site of struggle.

I seek to highlight here the theoretical as well as empirical strands that connect planning in Ireland to wider developments of international urban reform, which themselves cannot be thought of outside of the colonial context. It is this story of the relationship among colonialism, modernity, and urbanism that I seek to tell.

Modernity and Urbanism

Outside the Irish framework, modernity and urbanism have had a long and fruitful relationship. Situating European modernity in its urban context allows us to better read the ways in which Irish modernity will ultimately interact with it, coming in and out of its story and adding to it. For many of the major theorists, the causes and the effects of modernization—the institutional changes associated with modern life—whether positive or negative, can best be observed through an examination of the changes that took place in Western cities from the eighteenth century onward. For Jürgen Habermas, the defining feature of post-Enlightenment society was the rise of what he called "the public sphere," a "realm of our social life in which something approaching public opinion can be formed" (1990, 49). The public sphere is both real and figurative. It identifies a series of physical, material institutions—theaters, salons, museums, for example—where an independent bourgeoisie "assembled to form a public body" and "confer in matters...of general interest" (49). Habermas represents his theory in spatial terms to best convey the physical alterations that were taking place in European cities alongside, and on account of, changes in the political sphere. He charts the transformation of Europe from a feudal to a modern, bourgeois society. Beginning in the eighteenth century, the framework of the public sphere allows one to theorize a whole host of urban changes, such as parks, markets, urban squares, civic architecture, and space. For Habermas, the political changes associated with modernity take place in and through physical space.

For Michel Foucault, the modern city is associated with the state, as they both relied on the forces of surveillance. One of Foucault's key concepts, the panopticon, is both an architectural structure and a metaphoric means to understand the rise of the individual and his attendant incarceration by the channels of discourse. Geography is central to Foucault's schema for understanding the mechanics of modern state power. From cartography through the beginnings of street lighting and policing to the creation of modern schools and hospitals, society has reproduced its citizens through an intensely focused attention on the physical arrangements of all aspects of urban living.

An earlier generation of thinkers also placed the city at the center of their theories of modern life. An ideal city, for Max Weber, is what we might now call a cosmopolitan one, but one he considered as a place that hosts "a set of social structures that can produce a multitude of concretely different styles of life . . . that encourage social individuality and innovation, and is thus the instrument of social change" (Sennett 1969, 6). By contrast, the modern city is a retrograde urban environment, a product of the "impersonal" forces that underlie capitalism. The result, Weber concludes, is a city of faceless bureaucracies and rational market processes. Weber was nostalgic for the city of the late Middle Ages, the Renaissance city, that cultivated rich and diverse urban styles of life and promoted personal reciprocal acquaintances (ibid., 23–47).

Another influential scholar of the city, Georg Simmel, arrives at a similar conclusion to Weber's: that the modern city breeds anonymity. For Simmel, the alienating effects of contemporary urbanism are sociopsychological. Speed, traffic, advertising, noise, and crowds, the distinguishing characteristics of the new metropolis, continually bombard the senses. This assault forces the individual, in a move of self-preservation, to live in a nonemotional and controlled manner, and to keep all aspects of his life—family, work, friends—separate from each other. To protect the emotions against continual shock, urban dwellers develop a "blasé attitude," a "matter-of-fact" demeanor, which appears "cold," "heartless," "indifferent," and "apathetic."[17]

For Walter Benjamin, the flaneur, "the man of the crowd," is the central figure in an attempt to understand the poetry of Baudelaire, whom Benjamin regards as the quintessential modern urban poet. Set on the streets and in cafés of nineteenth-century Paris, Baudelaire's poems reflect on the meaning of memory and experience in a rapidly changing city. The flaneur, a more confident version of Simmel's "blasé" citizen, walks among the urban crowds but remains aloof from them, in a kind of existential security. The flaneur finds it possible, as Baudelaire put it, "to be away from home and yet to feel everywhere at home; to see the world and be the center of the world, and yet to remain hidden from the world" (Frisby 1985, 18–19). For Benjamin, the flaneur is an important symbol of modern urban experience, of something that is fading and disappearing in an increasingly rationalized and expanding city: a figure who resists the developing forces of capitalism and refuses the blandness of the urban landscape.

Sigmund Freud, too, depended on the city. There all manner of fears arose in the middle class, who then required the treatment of psychoanalysis to rid them of the neuroses of everyday life.

For all these thinkers, the city is the site of modernity, where the planned practices of modernization run into resistance from alternative economies, languages, and cultures. Because urbanization is one of the greatest legacies of colonialism, Ireland stands inextricably connected to this lengthy story of change and progress. The arrival of town planning in Ireland, complete with new legislation and a renewed commitment to public improvement, was, for its modernizing advocates, the latest in a long line of professional discourses employed in the colonial project of urban social management.

Nationalism and Modernization

Dublin in the nineteenth and early twentieth centuries was considered by many observers to be a hybrid city: "the capital and center of British rule for centuries, the entrepôt for British trade and commercial influence and the main gateway for the diffusion of British culture in Ireland" (Daly 1984, 1). The city, in many Irish modernist texts, is inhabited by the functionaries, merchants, and administrators of colonial government. These characters "fumble in a greasy till / And add the halfpence to the pence" in the words of Yeats's "September 1913." In Joyce's *Dubliners,* the city becomes the scene of decay and the center of paralysis. The idea that Dublin, crass and materialistic, is more of an English than an Irish city arises from a structuralist reading of culture: that every power develops its opposite in order to bring itself into being. Structuralist critics have pursued the theory that during the nineteenth century in Ireland (the years that gave us the "birth of Irish nationalism") and during the Victorian period in England, literature and popular entertainment in both countries projected emotions and instincts onto their cultural counterparts as foils for their own identities and evolutions. In English writing, from Brontë's primordial Heathcliff through Engels's unhygienic peasants in Manchester to Conrad's mix of Russian and Fenian terrorist stereotypes in *The Secret Agent,* the implications are that Paddy the Irishman is lazy, dangerous, and impulsive, whereas the Englishman John Bull is mature, rational, and hardworking.[18] The same structure is at work in many Irish texts of the same period. From the antiquarianism and Celticism of Thomas Moore's *Irish Melodies* through James Clarence Mangan's translations of Irish poetry to the Celtic revival led by Yeats and Synge, the typical subject of the Irish nation tended to be an inverted image of the English imperial character: spirited, rooted, and traditional. These differences highlighted the separate rural "nature" of the Irish character, so contrary to industrial and urban England.

Binaries are always ripe for deconstruction. The values of modernity (enlightenment, pluralism, democracy, and progress) are as much in evidence in nineteenth-century Irish nationalism as the traits of traditionalism (religion, inherited privilege, and cultural nativism) are visible in Victorian and imperial Britain. For nationalism to work, its advocates must connect with the daily lives and "structures of feeling" of those whose support they seek to win. The strategies through which Irish nationalist leaders and movements won legitimacy were highly innovative. Nationalism is not inherently an antimodern movement, despite the inward-looking and past-centered portrayal many contemporary critics and historians give it.[19] Nationalism, for Benedict Anderson, emerges out of the growth of print capitalism, the rise of national languages, the development of state apparatus, and the unleashing of the secular ideologies of enlightenment and emancipation. For Ernest Gellner, nationalism is a response to industrialization; it provides cultural coherence in an increasingly mobile and fragmented society. Industrialism's "membership is fluid, has a great turnover, and does not generally engage or commit the loyalty and identity of members.... The *nation* is now supremely important, thanks both to the erosion of sub-groupings and the vastly increased importance of a shared, literary-dependent culture"

(1983, 63). National feeling and community, in other words, helps to ease the pain of modernization.

Nationalism is a product of modernity. Those who live with it also live with its paradoxes, pushing forward while remaining troubled about their legacy to the past. Modernity's contradiction consists of two antagonistic elements. On the one hand, modernity promotes the narrative of progress and development, the idea that society can improve itself through the use of technology, reason, and enlightened ideas. On the other hand, it creates dislocations, victims: morals and values that no longer hold up in the face of encroaching consumerism and bureaucratic anonymity, communities that are overtaken by economic forces beyond their control. The result of this contradiction is that to live in modernity is to be troubled by the past and enticed by the future. A modern citizen simultaneously rejects and remains beholden to tradition. Nationalism is a variant of these contradictions. The ideology offers promises of a better future. But to appeal to its constituents, to afford them continuity and community in the face of unavoidable change, nationalist leaders are forced to dress their rhetoric in the garb of the past.

Modernity and nationalism, then, have always supplied each other with the material circumstances in which the other can thrive. In the 1820s, for example, Daniel O'Connell's Catholic Association mobilized tens of thousands of supporters under the leadership of a group of Catholic lawyers, provincial merchants, and journalists to campaign against the denial of Catholic civil rights. Between 1830 and 1845, an essentially "alternative parliament" met in O'Connell's headquarters at the Corn Exchange Building on Dublin's Burgh Quay. O'Connell and his disciplined lieutenants established a series of national bodies and associations—the Catholic Association, the Repeal Association, and the Anti-Tory Association—that served as electoral clearinghouses, ladders for political talent, and media relations centers for his parliamentary organization. O'Connell's campaigns are notable for their modern elements: the use of the crowd, of "monster meetings" (mass political rallies), to stir up public emotion and opinion; the formation of a disciplined parliamentary party to win concessions from Westminster; and the use of newspapers and pamphlets to inform and propagandize. This is, in other words, the creation of an indigenous populist public sphere. No political leader, writes Joseph Lee, "has subscribed more passionately than O'Connell to the idea of progress" (1984, 72). He campaigned for the repeal of the Act of Union so that the Irish economy could experience free trade and less taxation, the keys to stimulating industrial development, the only long-term solution to the country's poverty. He spoke Irish, but realized the "superior utility of the English tongue as the medium of all modern communication" (Curtis 1995, 26). He campaigned to win power for the Catholic middle class by gaining Ireland a respectable position in the empire: "The people of Ireland...are ready to become a kind of West Britons if made so in benefits and in justice; but if not, we are Irishmen again" (32). Yet despite his commitment to modernization, O'Connell's vocabulary "remained incongruously rooted in historical imagery...[and] no romantic nationalist relied more heavily on the rhetoric of reincarnation" (Lee 1984, 72). In O'Connell and his movement, then, one finds all the contradictions and characteristics that arise from the union of modernity and nationalism: the collision between the contemporary and customary; the blending of internationalism and parochialism; the competition between secularism and religion; and the performance of politics and populism.

Again, in the 1870s and 1880s, in the aftermath of the Land War, Charles Stuart Parnell forged an even larger and more disciplined party to demand the devolution of Irish affairs to a "Home Rule Parliament" in Dublin. The legacy of his campaign includes some of the first sustained uses of parliamentary obstruction—making speeches that lasted through the night (to be effective at Westminster, the Irish had to be troublesome), as well as cooperation with militant nationalists who wearied of constitutionalism. At the same time, he formed alliances with the Catholic Church, a move that connected his progressive ideology with one of the most traditionalist elements of Irish society.

Contrary to the idea that rural land redistribution lay at the heart of the "Irish Question," nationalist leaders remained determined to find ways to industrialize the country. A century-long economic depression close on the heels of the Act of Union gave rise to a powerful economic narrative: that the loss of an Irish parliament and subsequent direct control from London precipitated the country's industrial underdevelopment. Throughout the nineteenth century,

Irish nationalists propounded the message that the country had the raw materials and manpower to be able to "sustain a strong industrial nation" (Daly 1992, 4). A number of economists at the time, such as Hely Hutchinson, W. E. H. Lecky, and George O'Brien, confirmed Ireland's modern potential and pinned its sluggishness on British legislation (ibid., 5). Along with these thinkers, more pragmatic politicians sought to solve this problem by implementing policies geared toward development. Thomas Davis suggested that, with European-style tariff protection in tandem with an independent parliament, "Ireland could support a population of up to 35 million people" (ibid.). Parnell and O'Connell advocated industrial revival. The thread of progress continued through to the beginning of the twentieth century. Arthur Griffith, founder of Sinn Féin, while no radical, campaigned for Irish independence on the basis that Britain had deliberately stifled Irish industry and commerce. D. P. Moran, editor of the nationalist newspaper, *The Leader*, spoke for the Catholic middle class, which he saw as being denied any advancement by a residual Protestant ruling class. Often cited as a prototypical cultural nationalist, Moran "aspired to the creation of an industrialized and urbanized Ireland coexisting with a modern agricultural sector" (ibid., 8). Contrary to how it has been portrayed, Irish nationalists, bred in the shadow of colonialism and its strategies of improvement, were strong supporters of industrialization and modernization.

The history of nationalism in the nineteenth century, then, both in its constitutionalist and separatist varieties, is the story of how Irish resistance learned to confront imperial ideology in terms comprehensible to the colonial state itself: nationalist movements became increasingly centralized, well regulated, and infused with the principles of modernization. The notion of economic progress became so embedded in the minds of Irish leaders, from O'Connell to Griffith, that the prime argument against the union with Britain was that it actually hindered Irish development. The British state, after all, only reluctantly accommodated an emerging Irish middle class. Westminster enacted trade laws that made it difficult for Irish businesses to compete. And the system of landlordism repatriated Irish capital to England. Modernization, according to these leaders, would be better accomplished if the Irish were left to run the place on their own. If development were the original intent behind colonialism, then that goal would be best served by a British departure.

And yet nationalists, in asserting the right of Ireland to develop and to be independent, had to find commonality with other nations: the path of modernization leads to the convergence and increasing similarity of societies (McCarthy 2000, 15). Yet the idea of the nation implies a community, a unique and common cultural identity. Each nation, therefore, must have its own style within the pattern of sameness. So, for example, at the same time that Arthur Griffith argued for a pro-development, independent Irish parliament, his paper, the *United Irishman,* reinforced the need to protect Irish customs and pastimes in a manner of which the most romantic nationalist would be proud. The *United Irishman* published Irish ballads, detailed the etymology of Irish place names, and even extolled the virtues of Irish limestone over inferior English concrete (Maume 1999, 48). Griffith was opposed not to modernization but to Anglicization, so he denounced what he saw as the prim and proper culture of "West Britons." By contrast, he espoused Gaelic sports, Irish dances, and Catholic religious excursions. Along with Griffith, at the beginning of the twentieth century D. P. Moran, champion of the Catholic middle class, argued that the educated Catholic community should exert itself economically and culturally until Britain accepted its denizens as managers of an autonomous Ireland. At the same time that he campaigned for Irish industry—its products needed to be as good and as cheap as English ones—Moran asserted the superiority of Gaelic culture, its language, rituals, and religion.

The forces at work at the end of the nineteenth and the beginning of the twentieth centuries—industrialization, nationalism, and colonialism—were all caught up in the same contradiction. How might city leaders best provide developed yet historically resonant, industrial yet healthy, efficient yet leisurely, thriving yet organized modern urban spaces? How to progress and develop economically yet not betray the principles of the past? As it developed in England and in the colonies through its early practitioners (Patrick Geddes, Raymond Unwin, H. V. Lanchester, Patrick Abercrombie), the answer would be found in the new discipline of town planning. These planners sought to convince colonial and nationalist leaders that investment in their ideas would guarantee political success. At the heart of town planning's promise were certain core principles: low-density garden suburbs; efficient, zoned, and compartmentalized commercial, residential, and industrial sectors; rational and speedy modes of communication; monumental civic institutions such as museums, art galleries, and government buildings; and open, family-centered recreational spaces. Town planning, in other words, promised, according to its followers, regulated, communal, and profitable modernization.

Colonialism, Nationalism, and Town Planning

Emerging out of a critique of European industrialization and the major changes that modernization wrought, town planning has been most commonly represented as a response by Western states to the excesses of nineteenth-century laissez-faire capitalism: horrendous slums, dreadful public health, and violent social unrest. Highlighting the limits of philanthropy and promoting the necessity of state intervention in the regulation of capitalism, town planning in the West is a way of coordinating the increased complexity of metropolitan life. Accumulating and distributing food, moving and resting the labor force, generating and distributing power: all demonstrate the need to integrate aspects of modern city life into a singular "planning mentality" (Boyer 1983, 60–83).

As an academic discipline, town planning established its own body of experts (planners as social scientists above the fray of politics), created its own method (the civic survey), maintained its own reservoir of knowledge (statistical data on all aspects of urban life, including geography, geology, and history), and constructed its own object of study (the city in evolution).[20] As a modern art of governmentality, it brought together architects, engineers, and sociologists to produce an urban fabric in which housing, circulation, work, hygiene, and aesthetics all functioned in unison to regulate industrial society.

The planning of towns is as old as the history of cities. But the idea of urban design as a science appeared at the beginning of the twentieth century out of a series of interrelated events. Garden city principles dominated the early years of the town planning movement. (The term *town planning* is credited to John Sulman, an Australian architect, who first used it in 1890 [Home 1997, 3].) Ebenezer Howard's 1898 book, *Garden Cities of Tomorrow*, was the culmination of a century-long socialist-cum-anarchist critique of the modern industrial city. The ideas contained within this seminal book led directly to the formation of the Garden City Association, which set about gaining the finances, land, and industries required to realize Howard's vision: a city that would wed the principles of town and country, capitalism and socialism, individualism and communalism. The Garden City Association further formalized the concept of town planning with the launch of its journal, *Garden City*, in 1904. Its early volumes are full of sociological rationales for the reform of cities: "The commercial era...has been insidiously preparing the way for our ruin....It has been undermining the health of the people....The task [we set ourselves] is the decentralizing of industries, the adequate designing and the ordered development of towns."[21] Along with the pioneering work of notable figures, such as Howard or Geddes, planning was garnering institutional support. In 1910 the "First International Conference of 'Town Planning'" was held in London. Hosted by the Royal Institute of British Architects, the conference gave more than one thousand architects the opportunity to gain more influence, even commissions, in an age when a growing liberal consensus held that reforming cities was the key to social stability, moral and physical health, and even economic efficiency. In 1909 the University of Liverpool formed the first Department of Town Planning, funded, in part, by William Lever, the soap manufacturer. Patrick Abercrombie, the first chairman of the new program, edited another new journal, *Town Planning Review*, beginning in 1910. Also in 1909 Westminster passed the first Town Planning Act, which encouraged local authorities in England to devise town planning schemes, zone land for particular uses, clear slums, and stipulate housing designs and densities. By 1910, then, the idea of legislative planning and the academic and literary institutionalization of the new discipline were well entrenched.

The formal establishment of the discipline was rooted in the ideals of reforming the Western, industrial city. These foundations were intricately connected to the understanding that the imperial project also required transformation to remain viable. In its first issue, *Garden City* argued, in an article titled "The Basis of British Efficiency," that without urban reform "our civilization is going the way of all others which have preceded it ... and either the civilization of the West is doomed, or our race is no longer competent to play the role of pioneer.... The advanced position that our society has thrust upon us, nevertheless demands that we shall do this or perish."[22] The accumulation of wealth from trade, extraction, and production depended on the exploitation of colonial resources, peoples, and cultures. "It is due to Manchester," wrote Gandhi, "that Indian handicraft has all but disappeared" (Chatterjee 1986, 86). Not only were Western cities adorned with statues, arches, and parks commemorating imperial figures and soldiers, their museums full of orientalist treasures, but their very expansion was predicated on the creation of markets in areas halfway across the globe. From the beginning, town planning was implicated in the colonial project. Influential figures, such as Geddes and the architects-cum-planners H. V. Lanchester and Edward Lutyens, carried with them (though in different ways) Western assumptions about how order, health, industry, housing, family structure, and public space ought to appear in the urban environment. Lutyens, Lanchester, and Abercrombie sought to transpose the regularity and scale of baroque planning into India, South Africa, and Ireland. Their designs adopted a universalizing gaze and proposed similar solutions for radically different geographies and cultures. Salubrious garden suburbs would appease and provide for modern workers, rationalized communication networks would create greater speed and mobility, and demonstrative spaces of public democracy would encourage active citizenship.

Geddes, however, was contemptuous of what he saw as "death-dealing Haussmannizing," and he struggled to introduce alternative ideas about historic preservation, organic development, and intimate scale to native governors and colonial officials. His antimodernism was just as rooted, though, in European and romantic ideas about what cultures in the colonies ought to be: traditional, decentralized, and nonhierarchical. Geddes was also convinced that his methods might play a role in keeping the empire together. He wrote to his son in 1915: "I increasingly feel the value of our own exhibitions in India and that of my conservative yet constructive attitude and influence in cities and towns to be of direct political as well as social value ... of an unexpectedly direct bearing on order and stability—even of the Empire—not only by economy etc. but by tending to check the revolutionary spirit by the Eutopian one" (Meller 1990, 235). These pioneers of town planning, then, invested their cause with two urgent imperatives: rescuing the empire and saving modern industrial culture from its own excesses. Early town planning journals blended reports on town planning in Calcutta, Alexandria, Rangoon, and Palestine[23] with articles calling for the reform of industrial and agricultural practices in England, America, and Germany.[24] Internationalist in outlook, style, and personnel, town planning was a symbol of modernism's cosmopolitanism at the turn of the century.

From town planning's inception, its language revealed deep ambiguities about the relationship of planning to the nation and to internationalism. The rhetoricians of planning positioned the discipline against the nation, which they viewed as an isolated, even a dying, entity. "The idea of the city as a unit of life and culture," said Raymond Unwin at the 1914 Dublin School of Civics, "is emerging after a period during which the civic unit has been obscured by the nation and national policies.... Town Planning is the outcome of a new recognition of the importance of the city unit" (Miller 1992, 265). An early article in *Town Planning Review* suggests that "as time goes on it will become ever more and more clear that nationality is purely a political phenomenon.... National temperament grows weaker every day... and uniform methods of industry and commerce and travel are destined to do much to establish one single civilization across the globe" (Edwards 1914, 16). In a similar fashion, Geddes saw himself as a world citizen promoting the ideal that revitalized cities, as centers of economic and social dynamism, "could replace the nation-state as the basic political unit" (Sutcliffe 1981, 164). Regional and world government, he said during his time in Dublin, might be "secured by a federation of cities" (ibid.). One push behind the British origins of town planning, therefore, was a desire to counter the rising demands of nationalists: cultural distinction and political separatism.

But planners could not ignore nationalism, either; it was too strong a force. To say that planning arose to meet the needs of empire is merely to say that planning fit into the dialectic of imperialism and nationalism. During the nineteenth century imperialism increasingly made allowances for the expression of national identity within the overall system of empire. The Act of Union that integrated Ireland into the United Kingdom was premised on the concept of national difference. Without distinction, after all, there can be nothing to unify. (It was Ireland's dangerous alterity that necessitated the Union in the first place.) By becoming part of the United Kingdom, Ireland was recognized as a formal partner: it was given parliamentary seats in London, and it shared free trade, postal services, and an exchequer with Britain (Eagleton 1995, 131). Despite the semblance of equality, however, Ireland's colonial status continued to be reinforced by a 12,000-strong paramilitary police force, a large number of permanently garrisoned troops (25,000 in 1881), the maintenance of a viceroy and chief secretary, and the preservation of a separate civil service in Dublin Castle (Matthew 2000, 145). This ambivalence about Ireland's status—whether it was metropolitan enough to be part of the center or marginal enough to remain a colony—reinforced the notion that Ireland possessed its own national identity. The history of Anglo-Irish relations in the nineteenth century is largely the story of various attempts to define the national differences between England and Ireland and to see how they could find adequate political expression. Imperialists, for the most part, continued to try to accommodate Irish nationalism within the United Kingdom. At the heyday of empire, for example, Gladstone recognized, even encouraged, Irish nationality, seeing it as something that would bring greater strength to both parties: "Distinct nationality... does not mean disunion from England. It is the recognition of the distinctive qualities and the separate parts of great countries and empires which constitutes the true basis of union, and to attempt to centralize them by destroying those local particularities is the shallowest philosophy and the worst of all practical blunders" (Hutton and Cohen 1902, 226). The same ideology that recognizes the separate national character of Ireland motivates Matthew Arnold's reflections in *On the Study of Celtic Literature.* In Arnold's opinion, a better, more integrated British subject results from the combination of the Gaelic qualities of "wit" and "perceptive instinct" (which cuts the Irishman off from the "world of fact") and the Anglo-Saxon ability to move "steadily along close to the ground," patiently waiting for the opportunity to "deal with the fact" (Arnold 1900, 111). As nationalism became more organized and coherent, the language of imperialism recognized it and, by somewhat unsubtly embracing some of its spirit, tried to appease it.

When planning arrived on the scene, it was hardly surprising that its practitioners, often working under an imperial rubric, were at the same time able to evoke the desires of nationalists. In 1914, while working as a planning consultant with Geddes in Dublin, Unwin conjured up grand patriotic images of what the Irish capital could become: "Dublin...possesses some of the most beautiful buildings around which it should not be impossible to group a city which may yet again stand foremost among the metropolitan cities of the world."[25] In a 1911 lecture titled "Dublin and City Development," Geddes placed the Irish capital firmly within the history of the European Enlightenment, describing "the cultural resources of Dublin, its vast scientific equipment, its magnificent universities, all of which expressed the increased possibilities of development, not only for this metropolis, but for the greater part of Ireland, thus affording a promise that this country should once more recover its world-wide influence throughout European civilization."[26] In the early days of planning, before the Easter Rising that (re)radicalized nationalists with a separatist republican ideology, imperialist reformers and moderate patriots used "metropolitanism" as a synonym for a kind of nationalism of universal ideals: a nationalism defined by liberal democracy, a thriving intellectual culture, and cosmopolitanism.

Other advocates of planning appealed not to a modernizing nationalism within the broad vision of European classicism, but to a romantic Celticism that combined mythic characteristics with a pragmatic industrializing vision. Lady Aberdeen mixed folkish essentialisms with hard-headed rhetoric in a 1911 brochure for Ireland's first town planning conference: this "magic isle's...natural gift for music and song...[and] her power to enter deeply into the joys and sorrow of life" now combine with "the happy tales of increasing wealth and industry...to prove her native wit and talent" (Ui Breasail 1911, 2). Upon the inauguration of the Housing and Town Planning Association of Ireland (HTPAI) in 1911, J. V. Brady, a founding member, wrote of the "increasing spirit of national pride among all creeds and classes throughout the country, and great hopes for prosperity." The ability of planning, he continued, to "provide a comprehensive, orderly and healthy system of development cannot fail to appeal to the too long-neglected imaginative and artistic qualities of the practical-minded Celt."[27] Exaggerated proclamations of Irishness were commonplace at the beginning of the twentieth century. Anglo-Irish writers, such as Yeats and Lady Gregory, asserted their attachment to native culture right at the moment that their class and cultural presence were fading in historical importance. The interest shown in town planning by Irish Protestants, therefore, might have been a way by which this class sought to gain some relevancy in, even a degree of control over, the growing, but still ideologically eclectic, nationalist movement. The blend of sentimental and realist rhetoric highlights planning's early ambiguity—its simultaneous appeal both to cultural distinction and to humane modernization modeled on Western industrial reform.

Middle-class Catholic nationalists, the backbone of the home rule movement and of the Irish Parliamentary Party at Westminster, generally had a less romantic view of nationalism. In the editorials of their newspapers, town planning was seen as a practical means of achieving greater material advancement. Upon the founding of the HTPAI, the *Irish Industrial Journal* wrote, "If we cannot promote the health of our workers, we cannot secure the efficiency of our nation in trade and manufactures. We must study . . . our own cities . . . in the light of their growth and conditions. . . . Here in Ireland, where nature strews her charms with lavish hand, there is no excuse for the monstrosity of modern town building" (HTPAI 1911, 6). The *Tuam Herald* urged its readers to think of planning as "a very needed reform. There is no one with a spark of patriotism but must wish to see our ill-planned, ill-kept towns arranged on a better plan, divested of their repulsive suburbs and unhealthy quarters, and made generally more civilized and comfortable" (ibid.). The hope, for moderate nationalists, was that town planning could harmonize practical development with nature, beauty, and healthful living.

By 1913 the Irish Parliamentary Party (IPP), the party of home rule, increasingly turned its attention toward urban matters, in order to appease the growing discontent of workers and to halt their possible mass support for an independent Irish Labor Party (formed by Connolly and Larkin in 1913). Urban anger had increased in Dublin, most notably during the 1913 Lockout, and the condition of the slums became the focus of greater scrutiny. The 1914 government report, *Inquiry into Housing Conditions,* documented all manner of urban horrors in the city's 5,322 tenement houses. As early as 1907 the IPP's spokesman on housing, J. J. Clancy, recognized the need for an urban housing bill, similar to the Laborers' Acts that had created so many homes for the nation's rural poor in the 1880s and 1890s as part of Gladstone's mission to pacify Ireland. Clancy declared, "I regard it as a crime against God and man that those who are responsible for the government of this country should have allowed this state of things [the housing of the working classes] to continue so long. . . . If we cannot carry it [better housing] . . . then one more irresistible argument will be furnished against foreign rule in this island" (Fraser 1996, 87).

A division had opened up in nationalist urban politics over what exactly constituted the best vision for the city. Some moderates saw town planning—defined by the drive for garden suburbs and civic beautification—as an impractical alternative to inner-city housing, which would be closer to where workers actually lived. Furthermore, the construction costs of new, centrally located housing had recently become subsidized by the Imperial Exchequer under a new housing act.[28] (The premise of reformist, rather than separatist, nationalism was to extract as much money as possible from London.) Promoting city center housing rather than suburbanization, Clancy told Chief Secretary Birrell in 1913 that it was not town planning "or such ornamental development" that was required in Dublin, "but something that will house the people afresh in those localities in which now the conditions of life are abominable and intolerable" (Fraser 1996, 136). Other moderate nationalist members of Dublin Corporation were also opposed to planning. Edmund Eyre, treasurer of Dublin Corporation, argued that "garden suburbs do not lighten the lot or brighten the lives of the great number of poor people. . . . [We] cannot expedite the transfer of these poor people."[29] Some Sinn Féin members were also against planners' efforts to reduce urban density. In corporation proceedings, councillors Kelly and Cosgrave repeatedly put forth motions to eliminate all references to garden cities.[30] In part an effort to reduce reliance on Britain, and in part an attempt to harness working-class energies to its own agenda, Sinn Féin championed inner-city housing schemes. For constitutionalists such as Charles Murray, chairman of the Housing Committee of

Dublin Corporation, radical nationalists, in opposing home rule, were operating out of pettiness, dooming their own constituents to poverty and substandard housing. While James Larkin "damned" the empire, moderates such as Murray attacked him for "obstructing liberal and humanitarian measures for the housing of workers."[31]

During the years 1910–25, when the political conditions in Ireland were in constant turmoil, nationalists of various stripes, British colonial officials, and the decaying Anglo-Irish class all sought to make their mark on the regulation of the urban environment. If some defined urban reform in terms of inner-city housing, there were also those who advocated for fully fledged town planning principles. Town planning as a discourse was setting down the spatial and ideological roots that would find full expression in the autonomous Irish Free State after 1922. While most histories of planning in Ireland consign town planning aims to the idealistic, or even aristocratic, longings of a minority group fighting a small and losing battle, town planning played a large part in drawing the contours of the new independent capital. Suburbanization and the debates surrounding it were already helping to define the new nation. Town planning did take root in Ireland.

The Origins of Town Planning in Ireland

City space in the colony had long been the most material manifestation of centralized power, both the hero and structure of modernity's story. It displayed the symbols of administration, progress, and surveillance. The imperial government encouraged the rhetoric of urban improvement and state munificence to persuade an increasingly restless population that they were better off within the empire. Within the same discipline, members of Dublin Corporation, as well as radical labor leaders and other officials who would later transfer their allegiance to the Irish Free State, saw in planning a means to visualize their own power. In the end, they would all attempt to make their mark by deciding who would get to live where, how urban improvements would take shape, and how communications might be rationalized within the new city.

Town planning had early promoters in Ireland. An article titled "Some Remedies for Overcrowded City Districts" appeared in the

1907 volume of the *Journal of the Statistical and Social Inquiry Society of Ireland*. Its author, a Miss Rooney, argued in Victorian and paternalistic terms that "the decentralization of industries, or removal of factories outside the city area, is to be advocated as a remedy for congestion, that is likely to benefit the deserving classes, and eliminate them by a gradual process from the lower strata of society.... Manufacturers and consumers would find work done in pure air, under improved physical conditions, would be of better quality" (Mooney 1907, 53). The *Irish Builder and Engineer* reported regularly on foreign developments, including England's 1909 Housing and Town Planning Act, which aimed to secure "the home healthy, the house beautiful, the town dignified, and the suburb salubrious" (Hall 1996, 53). In 1911 the paper commented extensively on Dublin Corporation's resolution to "give facilities for the erection of a Garden City at Marino, involving the expenditure of 50,000 pounds, the supplying of cheap and healthy dwellings for the people, and increased city revenue."[32] For some on the city council, the journal reported, the term "garden city" seemed like a "red rag to a bull... 'Give us working class dwellings,'" the opponents argued. The journal's editorial line, though, consistently supported town planning: "This is supposed to be a democratic age and it sounds strange to hear the representatives of democracy crying out for the perpetuation of the hideous artizans' dwellings of the past and the huge barrack-like 'model-dwellings.' Under a properly conceived scheme of town planning, and every town and city should be obliged by law to have such a plan, there would be no difficulty in providing garden cities or garden suburbs for the middle classes and the working classes. Even if the tramway companies had to be subsidized, the money would be fully saved in police, gaols, and workhouses."[33]

Dublin Corporation was the leading provider of housing in the city. During the decade that saw the arrival of planning and a series of nationalist revolts in the city, the political balance of the corporation would shift from moderate unionists and nationalists (the remnants of Parnell's party) to separatist and radical nationalists—most notably, after 1918, Sinn Féin. (So independent did Dublin Corporation become that the Irish Free State in the mid-1920s did away with it, seeing its exercise of local authority as potentially threatening to the fragile new government.) In 1910 the corporation dispatched two of its councilors "to visit Birmingham, with the purpose of obtaining information on the all-important subject of the housing of the working classes" (O'Beirne and Travers 1911). Their findings included a substantial section designed to introduce the principles of planning to Dublin city officials. The three ideals of planning, they reported, were "well-ordered harmony" of "the constituent parts of a modern town," the "co-operation between local authorities, landowners and all others concerned in providing homes...with modern hygienic conditions," and the limitation of "the number of houses per acre so as to provide...air, light and open spaces." More urgently, they recognized the political importance of urbanism to nationalist symbolism by stating that "should Dublin soon become the seat of a National parliament, the development of the city and all Irish towns on modern town planning lines should begin immediately" (ibid.).

Perhaps the most significant achievement during these early years was the exhibition on town planning and the series of lectures and events around it coordinated by Patrick Geddes in Dublin in 1911. The Royal Institute of Public Health held its annual congress in Dublin that year, and Lady Aberdeen invited Geddes to display his "City and Town Planning Exhibition" to "stir up public opinion on the subject" (Aberdeen and Gordon 1925, 188). Geddes's Dublin display was divided into sections: geographical and historical, and survey material on Dublin and other Irish towns, with particular reference to the connection of town and county. Geddes first developed his theory of surveying cities at Edinburgh's Outlook Tower, a regional museum in Scotland. Started in 1892, this institution had as its aim to illustrate the city's connections to an ever widening geography. Each floor of the museum displayed Edinburgh's links to broader spatial geographies: the region, the nation, the empire, and the world. If the goal of Outlook Tower was to relate a city to the world, the hope of the "City and Town Planning Exhibition" was to bring the world of cities to a specific locality. The exhibit opened in Dublin with a section on physical geography, followed by displays on "Ancient and Antique cities," "Medieval and Renaissance cities," and "the contemporary industrial city" (Ui Breasail 1911). It concluded with the garden city, which, for Geddes, embodied the latest ideas on the improvement of life in contemporary cities.

The idea of a public exhibition rested firmly at the center of Geddes's vision for town planning. Since traditional language proved inadequate to the originality of his ideas, Geddes was soon supplementing the term *town planning* with two others: *civics* and *applied sociology*. The concept of civics revolved around two basic issues for Geddes: first, the production of a regional survey by a body of experts, "the select few who could be made responsible for guiding the direction of the future" (Meller 1990, 74); and, second, public display of the survey, in order to promote the values of social responsibility, volunteerism, and citizenship. "How best can we set about the study of Cities?" Geddes asks. "Obtain more pictures and photographs; obtain statistics . . . so that every active citizen shall find . . . all he wants to about his city" (Geddes 1908, 74).

A survey, fundamentally, was nothing more than a conscious familiarization with the environment. The perspective it assumed was both a lofty and a technical one. Ideally, a civic survey began with an overview conducted from a point raised high above the ground—a tower or a hill—that allowed for objects to be seen in their context. Surveyed from above, towns were suddenly perceived as elements of a larger region. At the heart of Geddes's message lay the belief that social peace could be achieved through civic endeavor, and that a new cooperative spirit, somehow conjured up through collective acts of urban renewal (pageants, the creation of parks and playgrounds, public lectures), could offset the deep economic divisions that severed classes and interests from each other in the wake of economic modernization. In this, Geddes was largely influenced by the work of the Anglo-Irish aristocrat and landlord, Horace Plunkett, whose agricultural cooperativism in Ireland sought to wean farmers off home rule by turning their attention to "the means, outside politics, by which the material prosperity of Ireland might be stimulated" (Cherry 1981, 59).[34] Just as Plunkett refused to consider such basic issues as the system of landownership, rents, and unfair competition, so Geddes felt that his "applied sociology" could recapture the lost values of citizenship, which he believed existed in the preindustrial era, regenerate urban life, and sweep away the blind values of political nationalism (Fraser 1996, 133). Following this exhibition, Geddes helped establish the Housing and Town Planning Association of Ireland (HTPAI). In addition to recommending civic surveys, the HTPAI also urged all local authorities to record "any local customs, requirements, or prejudices" affecting the shape of towns (HTPAI 1911, 11). A survey encouraged attention to the discovery, documentation, and preservation of national uniqueness and specificity—those aspects of national identity that could exist within planning's modernizing framework.

The growth of town planning in Ireland has most commonly been read as an offshoot of what was occurring in England. Of the early planners who arrived in Ireland, critics have written that they put forward an intellectual structure that conceived the economic and social relations of housing design in explicitly British terms (Fraser 1996, 294). The reason Geddes's sociology and Unwin's garden suburbs never flourished, the argument goes, is that these reformers believed Dublin's problems were the same as Manchester's: industrialization, overpopulation, crime, and disease. But, this argument continues, Irish cities, with the exception of Belfast, did not have the same sociological histories that caused the rapid urbanization of English and European towns, such as factories and extensive rural-to-urban migration. The rural Irish poor emigrated not to Dublin or Cork, but to London and New York. Irish towns suffered not from exponential growth, but rather from economic stagnation and physical decay. Present-day commentators continue to contextualize Unwin's and Abercrombie's sojourns in Ireland in terms of the general international effort to remedy "the apparent disorder that threatened to overwhelm" the Victorian city (McManus 2002, 48). It is certainly true that early planners, such as Geddes and Unwin, were concerned with mounting a critique of the industrial revolution. In their early essays, in which they laid out their doctrines, these planners rarely, if ever, reference the concept of nationality. In "Study before Town Planning," Abercrombie defines the discipline's goal as "the systematic intention to control and direct the growth of our cities," and discusses ways to enhance the "health, beauty and convenience" of "dreary" towns (1916, 171). The subject is never framed as a national issue. Likewise, in "The Survey of Cities," Geddes's aim is to understand "industrial and other conditions, with their advantages and defects" (1908, 78). National identity, in the English context, is neither a concern nor a problem.

When it came to Ireland, however, planning rhetoric consistently highlighted the connections between town planning, development, and national identity. In the foreword to his 1914 *Dublin of the Future* plan, for example, Abercrombie states that his aim is "to arouse the historic and traditional spirit of Civic pride once so evident, and to revive that native genius which will place Dublin in its proper position as one of the World's best Capital Cities" (1922, vi). James Brady spoke in 1911 of the ideals of planning in language borrowed from the cultural nationalism of the Gaelic renaissance: "To those interested in the modern revival in Ireland, whether of her language, industries, commerce or arts, it must be apparent that there is great need . . . [for the] comprehensive . . . development of its cities" (1911, 237). Following the 1916 Rising, which destroyed much of central Dublin, R. M. Butler, writing in the Jesuit journal *Studies,* extended the patriotic claims of planning to include the materials with which Ireland's principal thoroughfare ought to be rebuilt: "Our fine street with its well-toned mellow walls is gone; we do not want to see it replaced with gaudy colours. . . . The traditional tone of our old Dublin streets is soft and somewhat sombre. Ireland is not a brick country. . . . It would be a disaster if the dominant note in the reconstruction of O'Connell Street were to be modern red-made brick. . . . The use of native materials is not alone patriotic, but aesthetically sound practice" (1916, 573).

Clearly, there was something at stake in these planners' attempts to evoke urban reform in the terms of national pride and sentiment. Inseparable from the time in which they operated, this mixture of planners, architects, and reformers was reading the psychological landscape of the country. While obviously not armed with knowledge of the future, they were hoping to forestall upheaval: the events that would, in spite of their aims, occur in 1916, 1922, and 1923, when crucial architectural symbols in the center of Dublin would be set aflame by forces eager to break the connection with Britain.

The HTPAI championed the cause of garden suburbs—new, small-scale communities for workers located in rural areas close, but not adjacent, to their place of work. In the aftermath of the 1913 Lockout, which foreshadowed, for reforming imperialists and moderate nationalists, the dangerous combination of Irish republicanism and militant socialism, advocates of planning had their best opportunity yet to present themselves as sociologists, as experts capable of diagnosing and curing the causes of Irish discontent. In 1914 the British government conducted an inquiry into the causes of the strike, which, officials believed, was largely the result of poor-quality housing. The report, in large part, blamed individual landlords who had "little sense of their responsibilities," thereby shifting attention away from economic and political issues (LGB 1914b, 14). The housing inquiry ended up firmly supporting the cause of population decentralization in Dublin—that is, the notion of transplanting sixty thousand people from the city center and relocating them to fourteen thousand new cottages situated on greenfield sites on the urban periphery: "We deprecate much work being undertaken... in the heart of the city, and would rather see such houses as may be built erected on virgin soil... on the outskirts" (LGB 1914b, 23). During the inquiry several experts gave testimony about the necessity of suburbanization. Charles Dwyer, speaking for the Dublin Citizen's Association, believed that the ideal house for the working man was a suburban one. Charles McCarthy, the city architect, argued against the rehabilitation of existing homes, lest they "become ruins in a few years" (LGB 1914b, 30).

Suburban expansion, in the minds of all these self-proclaimed reformers, was inherently connected to the cause of town planning. In his statements to the housing inquiry, E. A. Aston, a conservative Unionist businessman and founding member of the HTPAI, insisted on a general plan of city development, "incorporating topographical, geological and sociological considerations within the Dublin region." A regional survey of "the entire natural community of Dublin" was essential, as over a hundred thousand people, over the preceding decades, had moved south of the city's formal boundaries. Aston also wanted to encourage "industries to locate outside the densely populated areas of the city," and even suggested the creation of "plantations for city workers in convenient rural areas" (Bannon 1985, 210). Geddes also gave evidence to the inquiry, recommending that the British Town Planning Act (1909) be introduced to Ireland. In a prescient statement, he also insisted that new housing should be socially mixed. Convinced of their arguments, J. F. McCabe, one of the committee members overseeing the housing inquiry, added an appendix to the final report. In it, he urged the adoption of Geddes's core principle of documenting the totality of Dublin's landscape and population before any more concrete action took place: "If even the areas which have already been acquired are built upon before a Civic Survey is completed," he wrote, "I shall look upon it as a grave misfortune ... and without such information no Town Plan can be produced." It was just this kind of sociological, technical, and problem-solving language that would provide one practical means to imagine how power might manifest itself in any Dublin of the future.

Given the rhetoric of planning that often consciously appealed to nationalists' desire for self-government and material improvement, and given planning's potentially pragmatic ability to resolve entrenched political divisions in an apolitical and technical manner, it is not surprising to find that town planning trickled down to nationalist groups, both radical and more moderate. Increasingly, planning went from an imported, reformist movement to a system integrated into the platforms of political groups across the ideological spectrum. During the Dublin Lockout, the Citizens Housing League was formed out of the unusual union of business interests, represented by Aston and Larkinite socialists. Many of those who participated in the organization's demonstrations were leading socialist and nationalist campaigners, including Countess Markiewicz and James Connolly. Despite tensions within this organization between middle-class reformers and radical activists, the campaign itself sought to mobilize popular support for the construction of fourteen thousand homes on low-density suburban estates, to be subsidized by the British government. Cooperativist ideology and a residual attachment to the principles of guild socialism motivated leaders Captain J. R. White and George Russell (a central figure in the Gaelic renaissance) to create a movement that called for the building of a garden suburb for and by workers. Thus the Irish Builders' Cooperative Society was formed in 1914, born from the merging of militant strands of labor and nationalism (Fraser 1996, 130).

How are we to interpret the drive for suburbs in Ireland during the years that saw British authority increasingly threatened? Why did the town planning movement appeal to so many varied groups and interests? Suburbs today are often maligned as the site of insularity and conformity. They provide an easy target for those with a critique of the demise of lively and democratic urban everyday life and its associated values of communalism, cultural integration, and vitality. But the original motivation behind Ebenezer Howard's vision was an anarchist one. Howard imagined a self-sufficient urban community, one with no hovering landlords, thriving with full employment and pride of place, in opposition to the reality of the industrial city. The suburb offered an image of the idealized family, albeit one that functioned on strictly segregated gender lines. This nuclear family would be enclosed in a new private architecture, each surrounded by a plot of private land suitable for productive leisure-time cultivation. This newly located population would flourish in the midst of nature, not far from culture, neither isolated in the rural hinterlands nor caught up in urban chaos. Suburbs offered an ideology of harmonious modernization and balanced urban expansion. Almost every political group operating in the city could imagine the suburb as the geographic site of new social relations—a utopia on the edge of the city. At the center of garden suburbs were always communal spaces and halls; in suburbs, an actual emerging middle class could be dreamed as a population with the leisure time and civic focus to be good citizens of whatever new political order was in store, whether reformed colonialism or a new state. Suburbanization solved the problem of alienation. For socialists such as Larkin and Connolly, suburbs offered affordable housing connected to industrial zones via efficient means of communication. Free from the tenement, workers would lead healthier, more empowered lives. For moderate nationalists, suburbs offered a way to reconcile their obligations to a historically rural subject and a modern future. For imperialists, suburbs held the promise of a more contented citizen, removed from the problems that might produce rebellion. For all of these groups, garden suburbs and town planning offered a vision, suitably mutable, of a modern city with a well-informed citizenship. The suburb was, in a word, the frontier—a real and an imagined space onto which competing ideologies could be projected.

Over the next several years, planners in Ireland would continue to engage, and even try to steer, the tumultuous political upheavals that were overtaking Ireland and Europe. In 1914 the Third Home

Rule Bill received the royal signature. Self-government for Ireland became a legal, if not an actual reality. The same year saw the HTPAI organize a series of lectures and another conference on planning. Both events appealed to modernizing nationalists, whose time in the sun seemed just around the corner. John Nolen, professor of city planning at Harvard, presented a lecture, "Why Planning Pays?" in which he stressed the capitalist imperatives behind planning: "The doctors of cities, civic improvers, could do nothing for Dublin unless the ways and means were found through the medium of town planning to extend the character and business significance of the city."[35] Unwin urged Dubliners "to plan on a grand scale and to get to work as though no private interests were involved." Recognizing the "creative destruction" that the modern urban experience had so often wrought, Unwin warns Dubliners to hold their nerve: "Romance must not stand in the way of reform."[36]

The Easter Rising of 1916 destroyed much of central Dublin. Planning was one discourse that the British as well as nationalists employed as a way of comprehending what had happened and making use of the surprising occasion afforded by destruction. As R. M. Butler wrote in *Studies,* "Half of [O'Connell Street] now lies in ruins. Seven months have elapsed, and it is still a wilderness. It has to be reconstructed" (1916, 570). The significance of Easter, chosen by the rebels for its associations with death, rebirth, and sacrifice, was not lost on the architects and engineers: "It was now the duty of every level-headed Irishman," the *Irish Builder* opined, "to turn his attention to the future, and to treasure only such memories of the past few days as will enable him to approach the national and civic problems in a spirit of national toleration."[37]

Interpretations of the Easter 1916 Rising—what it represented, whether it was truly popular, and how it should be commemorated— have long been the subject of controversy in Ireland. Since the outbreak of "the Troubles" in the North at the end of the 1960s, politicians and historians have sought to either downplay or underscore the militancy of Ireland's nationalist past. As complex and as inflected with contemporary attitudes as these debates are, they are not anything new. Almost as soon as word of the Rising got out in 1916, local papers rushed to condemn or praise the events. The most popular interpretations were the "German invasion" and the "socialist subversion" theses. The *Connacht Tribune,* the paper of Galway's middle class, denounced the rebels as stooges of both Prussia and Larkin—that is, of international and domestic socialists (Lee 1989, 34). The *Cork Examiner* labeled the Rising a "communistic disturbance rather than a revolutionary movement" (ibid., 32). The *Daily Express* blamed the leaders who organized it, because they "were men of no position" (ibid., 35). In contrast, the *Irish Builder* took a broader view and argued that while the rebellion had the sympathy of only a small minority of Irish people, "it could not have reached the proportions it did but for the culpable negligence of the peace; for the menace of revolution has long been with us." Furthermore, while the insurgents were "mere youths," those who came into contact with them spoke "favorably" of their behavior: "They were under military control and do not seem to have caused any wanton destruction."[38] The *Builder*'s implication is that the British bombardment caused the damage.

Reactions to the rebellion, then, were far more varied and complex than they are currently portrayed. The *Irish Builder* not only shifts much of the blame onto the British, it actually praises the discipline of the rebels. Moreover, it reminds its middle-class readership of the potential material gains of the rebellion. While the Rising put the country through a "period of thrills, alarms and horrors more closely associated with South American Republics than with a sane and prosperous nation," the paper reported, "our city now offers a wide field, a mine of wealth to the architect and engineer and the contractor."[39] *Studies* reported on the chance to rebuild O'Connell Street as the physical center of a modern nation: "Dublin has need for many public buildings—an Art Gallery, a school for progressive Irish Art, a National Theatre... new offices for the Bank of Ireland, a new Parliament House.... These would form the salient features of a new noble thoroughfare bordered with trees and lined with stately edifices of private enterprise" (Butler 1916, 571). The projects associated with rebuilding—civic architecture, slum clearance, rehousing, and transportation—would be both economic and ideological. With regard to the former, Dublin commercial interests campaigned successfully to have the Rising labeled an act of war, so that the government would be required to provide compensation to individual property owners as well to pay for the overall reconstruction. For the latter, Irish and British interests put forward competing design proposals, hoping to influence what the capital of an autonomous state might look like. At its core, planning is a material project. Therefore, as an independent government grew more tangible, those who sought to physically rebuild the city focused their attention on town planning.

There were those who spoke for the radically shaken authority of the British state in Ireland. Represented by Raymond Unwin, chair of the Dublin Reconstruction Committee, this group sought to impose a uniform, linear, Haussmannesque style of classical architecture on Dublin's central thoroughfares. Some Irish parliamentary leaders, though, railed against the authoritarian ideas contained in Unwin's original Reconstruction Bill. Horace O'Rourke, for example, maintained that a uniform design was unsuitable, that the required legislation was cumbersome and the standardized measurements burdensome to businessmen. Then again, a third possible stylistic trajectory, one that imagined a new beginning altogether, was presented by Edwin Bradbury at his inaugural address to the Architectural Association of Ireland in 1917. Unadorned modernism, he put forth, would free space from the heavy weight of history, overcoming age-old social divisions in a new, simpler language that spoke to everyone equally and did not condescend to the majority. "The war is revealing and producing man at his best: natural and strong and rational," he declared. "Let us endeavor to help in producing a rational architecture—an architecture which excludes unessentials and which embodies only what is true and of unassailable worth" (Rothery 1991, 85).

The Dublin Civic Survey, carried out between 1923 and 1925 in anticipation of furthering the work of Unwin's Reconstruction Committee and of implementing aspects of *Dublin of the Future,* stakes the claim of the new state in determining priorities on behalf of the nation. "Our civic problems, physical and administrative, cry out for immediate resolution. In a progressive capital the want of modern educational facilities; the need for proper forms of juvenile recreation; indifference to historical associations, so valued elsewhere; the stagnation of industry and commerce; the inconvenience and costliness of transport; and the wretched habitations of the masses of the poor, cannot be allowed to remain as they are in Dublin" (Civics Institute of Ireland 1925, xvii). To implement the necessary changes, "the authorities need drastic statutory powers reinforced by State expenditure.... As the capital is a national asset, it is the work of the State, rather than the Municipality, to bring about its regeneration" (ibid.).

British town planning in Ireland had always reinforced the city's dominance over the rural periphery. This particular hierarchy would remain central in post-1922 planning: As the *Survey* states, "The importance of civic ideals—whereby all units essential to city life may co-operate and advance in an orderly manner—is not yet realized by the mass of our citizens. Within the past few years, the population of the capital has been augmented by a disproportionately large rural element. This accretion cannot be expected to possess civic ideals, for its notions are naturally primitive: with the lure of city life it becomes undisciplined" (Civics Institute of Ireland 1925, 3). Planning, in other words, would play a role in creating a civilized society and the citizens to populate it.

Through all of these political upheavals, from the Dublin Lockout through the Home Rule Bill and the Easter Rising to the founding of the Irish Free State, one text in particular reveals the allure of planning for those who sought to quell discontent as well as those who wanted to steer that restlessness to their own ends. In Ireland, the story of modernization can be read from the history of cities. During a time when colonialists sought to reform their imperial system, and nationalists came close to realizing their modernizing mission—obtaining the reins of state—*Dublin of the Future* brought together diverse aspects of urban life (housing and harbors, transport and theaters, architecture and allotments) in a single, complete vision for the city. There was, as Abercrombie argues in his introduction, no room for "piecemeal tinkering...Dublin requires overhauling right down to the fundamentals" (1922, 4).

Dublin of the Future

Dublin of the Future displayed in a single, sweeping technical document the means by which Dublin could be transformed from an underdeveloped regional city into a capitalist metropolis (Figure 2). The plan displayed the infrastructure required to modernize the state. The

Figure 2. New town plan of Dublin. From Abercrombie, *Dublin of the Future* (1922), 36.

solution to transform Dublin into a beautiful, rationalized entity was to occur within the context of industrialization and modernization.

The key requirements of the 1914 town planning competition were brief and listed under three headings: "Communications," in which the entrants were asked to reorganize the city's transport system, including the rail and canal system, while also addressing land use in Dublin and its environs; "Housing," where they were to provide fourteen thousand new dwellings, specifically relocating residents from the city center to the suburbs; and "Metropolitan Improvements," which called for ways to make better use of the city's rivers and bay for recreation and to preserve or expand the city's key public buildings. Eight entries were submitted: four from contestants in Ireland, three from entrants in England (two from Liverpool, one from London), and one from a contestant in the United States (Illinois). The competition was finally adjudicated by Patrick Geddes and

John Nolen in 1916. Abercrombie's winning entry was ultimately published, together with survey notes by the Civics Institute of Ireland, in 1922. It was then used by the Irish Free State as the basis for a new comprehensive city survey.

When Abercrombie's design was chosen, the immediate problem for both the administration and Dublin's middle class was the rebuilding of destroyed commercial areas, especially Sackville Street (now O'Connell Street), the city's principal shopping district. The destruction of the city center, wrote the *Builder* in May 1916, allowed the previously heterogeneous city — "old, of all shapes and sizes" — to be remodeled and "a uniform scheme to be adopted, like Nash's Regent Street or Haussmann's Paris."[40] Abercrombie's introduction mirrored this language, stating that his design sought "to replace the present planless and haphazard growth with a well-reasoned scheme" (3).[41]

As the title of the plan suggests, the city was to be the arena of the future, the locale of evolutionary progress. Abercrombie includes several maps of Dublin at different stages in its development: the medieval city, the city in 1780 at the height of its Georgian remodeling, and Dublin in 1836 as it entered a lengthy period of economic decline. Abercrombie's plan promoted a vision of the future that was committed to bringing Ireland into line with the rest of the industrial world. There was to be no return to a rural or Arcadian past. His plan made no secret of where town planning stood in relationship to the energy unleashed by nationalism: "Following the granting of power to Ireland to manage its own affairs from a national standpoint," his introduction states, "there can be no doubt that a tremendous industrial and commercial development will take place in the near future. The exploitation of mineral wealth, coupled with the natural adaptability for the enlargement of industries, will call for the greatest care being taken that these developments be carried out according to the modern conception of Housing and Town Planning. Every effort must be made... to stem the flowing tide of emigration, thereby conserving the forces of labor for the upbuilding of the new industrial Ireland" (5).

The first section of the plan, therefore, spells out the radical restructuring required to improve the city's, and hence the nation's, industry and communications. It contains three large-scale colored maps. All are overviews of the entire city. The first, highlighting the primary proposals of the plan—housing, industrial zoning, parkways, and roads—displays the degree of urgency associated with each major recommendation. In pink are those areas requiring immediate action, including the three new garden suburbs, located on the fringes of the city: Crumlin on the south side, Drumcondra and Cabra on the north side. In all, sixty-four thousand people were to be relocated. Also included in this phase are two broad, new avenues connecting the suburbs to the center, and a massive new traffic center spanning both sides of the river. In purple are those aspects of the plan to be completed within ten years, including the erection of a new Power Citadel on reclaimed land, "where the raw material of energy entering the harbor is converted into the motive force for the industrial activities of the whole of the community" (15). The Power Citadel would be six hundred feet high: "Architecturally, its effect at the entrance to the harbor and as the center point of the reclaimed Dublin Bay would be magnificent" (16). The establishment of the Dodder and Tolka river parkways were to act as the city's lungs, filtering air down from the Dublin mountains. Also emphasized was the expansion of the harbor and commercial railways. In yellow are those projects to be developed last, but which were still necessary for the city to grow. These developments included new suburbs at Clontarf and Ringsend, the latter on land reclaimed from the sea.

The second map belonging to the section on industry and communications proposed a whole host of new tram and bus routes, all of which notably begin and end in the city center. The third map illustrated the current rail routes to and from the city and called for their expansion, especially to the proposed new docks and the industrial zones. No doubt the emphasis on personal mobility and increased speed of movement were among the elements that appealed to residents of a city that had experienced a sizable military presence and surveillance. Alongside the maps runs a detailed description of those changes advocated by Abercrombie to develop the Irish capital for the future. Traffic flows overrode most other considerations. Fifteen new grand boulevards and radial roads linking the city core with the ring of new suburbs radiated outward from the new traffic center. To make room for this new traffic center, Abercrombie proposed to demolish the medieval core of the city, much as had been done to build Dublin

Castle. The removal of the population that lived there would then allow more of the central area for business and the expanding needs of the new national government.

The second section of Abercrombie's plan concerns housing, specifically the issue of how to reduce the density of the city center. Perhaps the greatest appeal of *Dublin of the Future,* for both its British judges and the leaders of the new Irish state, lay in its claim to be able to solve the problem of Dublin's notorious slums, which were widely construed as the bearers of disease, insurrection, and immorality. *Dublin of the Future* speaks directly to the fears of middle- and upper-class Dubliners, who dreaded the eruption of yet more violence in the city. Town planning, Abercrombie promised them, would solve the tenement problem in a scientific (read: apolitical) manner. To accomplish this, he divided Dublin into "intra-" and "extra-" urban areas. The intraurban area, enclosed by the Grand Canal on the south side and the Circular Road on the north side, had a density of 95.8 persons per acre. This was to be reduced to 75 persons per acre through the forced removal of ten thousand families. The free space opened up by suburban migration would leave more room in the city itself for street widening, public buildings, town squares and gardens, and business premises (21). This demographic pruning would produce 1,359 derelict sites "to be rebuilt or remodeled for commercial purposes, as the wave of prosperity [following the establishment of an Irish Parliament] rises high" (22). Abercrombie's plan also aimed to take ten acres of land away from the site of the Royal Barracks, no doubt to the delight of many. The reasons for clearing the center of much of its indigenous population were both financial and moral: land for rebuilding cost more in the city center than it did at the urban periphery, and also "the moral and exemplary effect of suburban planning would be incalculable" to the laborer (23). Suburbanization as "moral effect" was tied to Abercrombie's stated intention of creating "a satisfactory type of workingman" (30). "After the work of the planner," he continues, "the future race, brought up under hygienic conditions... will be able to afford larger and more capacious homes on the outer fringe" (30). Living in lower-density, single-family homes (nine houses to the acre) on the outer fringe, being closer to nature, would, it was hoped, have an ameliorative effect on the lower classes. Each family received a garden allotment for producing their own food, thereby instilling a sense of frugality and self-sufficiency, creating as well an environment of hard work and increased contact with the land. As the foreword to his plan mentions, "In many European cities the docker lives in a rural district and is thus enabled to take his unemployed time in the cultivations of his garden, or some other bread-winning craft. The docker is normally a peasant, who lends a helping hand to the ship; and the sooner he regains something of this status the better for the town and country everywhere" (vii). The three areas selected to be developed as garden cities, Crumlin, Cabra, and Drumcondra, were to be connected to the city center with "high speed electric cars" taking the workman "practically from the workshop to his own house door" (26). Extra-wide roads were to be constructed, and tree-planted footwalks would form recreation and promenade areas. In this way, *Dublin of the Future* offered nationalists a vision of a modern capital, complete with a mobile workforce, recreation schemes, and industrial infrastructure. Abercrombie even provided detailed financial estimates for his housing schemes, laying out in detail the enormous sums of money that state officials would have to both collect and manage. And it offered liberal unionists peace of mind.

The third and final section of *Dublin of the Future* concerns metropolitan improvements. A new national theater, gallery, stock market, and Catholic Cathedral—all in neoclassical style—were advocated (Figure 3). Abercrombie's designs were monumental, vast celebrations of a European civilization long gone. Comparing Dublin's potential to the grandeur of Paris, Abercrombie, through his designs, sought to situate Irish history within the context of European development and progress: "Dublin today," he writes in his introduction, "presents a similar spectacle to Paris prior to the operation of Napoleon III and Haussmann: it is a city of magnificent possibilities" (3). The use of classical architecture has always conjured up the qualities of order, proportion, equilibrium, and harmony (Boyer 1983, 50). In Dublin, a city that had so recently displayed disorder and chaos, the static, ceremonial civic spaces envisaged by Abercrombie nostalgically evoked the rigid social hierarchies of imperial Rome. In concrete fashion, these civic centers attempted to erase the remaining cluttered spaces within the colonial

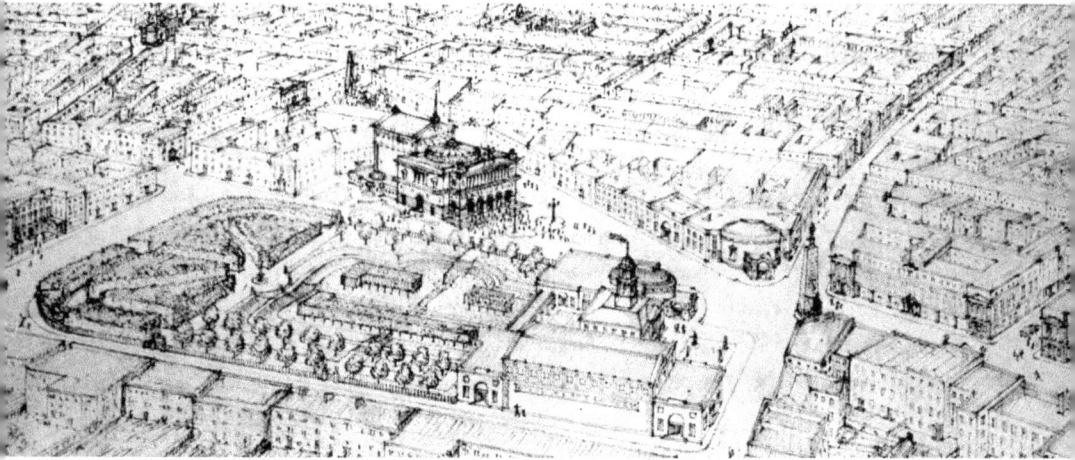

Figure 3. National Theatre. From Abercrombie, *Dublin of the Future* (1922), 38.

city. These buildings embodied state authority before which the individual, the regional, and the marginal appeared insignificant.

Abercrombie's improvements would visibly dominate the town. And yet his architecture also appealed to an official form of nationalist ideology. Engaging nationalism's sense of tradition, for example, a proposed five-hundred-foot campanile was to be placed in the courtyard behind the new Catholic cathedral on Capel Street (Figure 4). The monument was to be crowned with the figure of St. Patrick, its form based on an Irish round tower. The encircling arcade would contain medallion busts of the Irish saints in the spandrils of the arches, and below a series of cenotaphs to famous Irishmen.

While Dublin had the largest enclosed park in Europe, the two-thousand-acre Phoenix Park, *Dublin of the Future* placed great emphasis on providing more playgrounds and open areas for recreation and the improvement of pubic health. The city beautiful movement had already impressed on municipal leaders in America and Europe the importance of nature and parks for relieving tenement squalor and augmenting land values. Parks were seen as democratic spaces, sites where people of all classes and backgrounds mingled and came into contact. In Dublin, as elsewhere, there had long been a liberal reform effort to promote the construction of playgrounds and parks as a way to control children and supervise adolescents. Parks, the argument goes, were "an alternative to the centrifugal city. The playground

Figure 4. St. Patrick's Campanile. From Abercrombie, *Dublin of the Future* (1922), 39.

supplied the corrective for bad forms of recreation, illicit drinking, dance halls, theatres" (Wilson 1964, 82). *Dublin of the Future* proposed establishing many such open spaces: small playgrounds, neighborhood parks, parkways, city squares, and nature reserves. One of the best correctives to Dublin's problem was fresh air and exercise. Abercrombie's report identified over thirteen hundred vacant sites suitable for small playground development; no child should have to walk more than a quarter of a mile to play. This training would make the child more receptive to the discipline of work and teach the values of civic idealism and patriotism: both Geddes and Abercrombie admired the work of the Gaelic Athletic Association, a nationalist organization dedicated to promoting Irish games. In the aftermath of a nationalist settlement, there would be more land available for community uses, land vacated, for example, by the retreating British military: "Dublin has the opportunity of acquiring the ground of four barrack sites.... [T]hese sites closely parallel the town's fortifications, which, however crippling and strangling in the past, have proved by way of compensation wonderful assets, affording opportunities which English towns can merely wonder at.... What could be more fitting than that they should be used as playgrounds" (43). Each playground, Abercrombie calculated, would be used by hundreds of people: "the tennis courts would carry 50 members, the bowling green 100, the croquet lawn 50 and the putting green 50.... Add to this a large number of casual participants and spectators... and those who would use the newsrooms and promenade, and soon the park would rise to full capacity" (44). Clearly, the metaphor of the bourgeois public sphere organizes how space is to be perceived and lived: a site of civic virtue, pride, and genteel society. Dotted regularly over the city, Abercrombie writes, the amount of good that parks could accomplish, both physically and morally, is incalculable.

The metropolitan improvements proposed by Abercrombie in *Dublin of the Future* clearly represent the capital city as historical heir to the Enlightenment: classical, cosmopolitan, and rational. His plan claimed, through the production of a new kind of space, to be able to turn the suspicious subjects of British rule into bourgeois citizens. But Abercrombie's plan was also driven by a concern for efficiency. As the plan for the proposed new traffic center and central boulevards

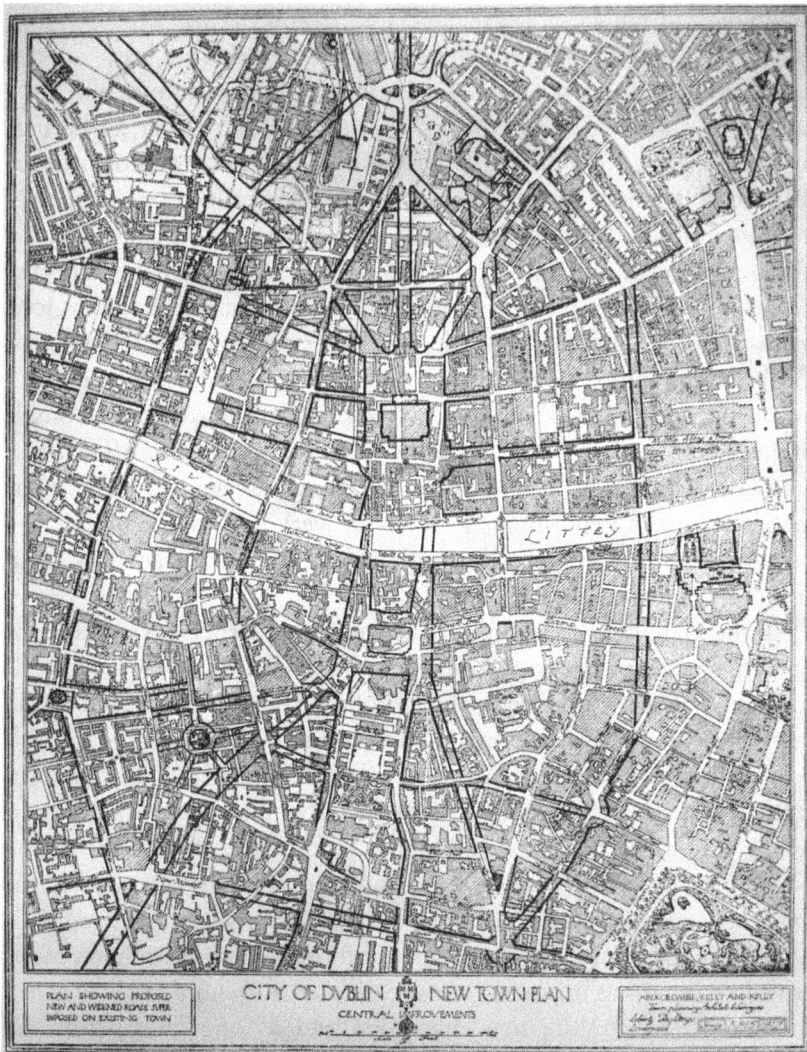

Figure 5. Proposed new roads in Dublin. From Abercrombie, *Dublin of the Future* (1922), 37.

demonstrates, *Dublin of the Future* placed a high premium on movement, on reducing the time that it took for individuals and commodities to move to and from the city (Figure 5). For planners, congestion meant failure; increased mobility is the key ingredient of modernization. Zoning also furthered the requirements of modern space; it homogenized land use, segregated public and private housing, and established a strict division between public and private life.

Central to the process of development and modernization proposed by *Dublin of the Future* lay the concept of fact gathering, so that reasoned judgments could be made about the allocation of resources and manpower. Abercrombie's plan called for the speedy passage in Ireland's soon-to-be national parliament of the latest town planning legislation. This would show the world "that [the nation's] first thoughts have been directed to the better housing and development of her people" (5). Such legislation would establish a series of local town planning boards, which would prepare schemes in consultation with a Central Commission. Each local board would consist of an engineer, an architect, a surveyor, a medical health officer, and a town planner (6). Such professions, long reserved in Ireland for members of the Protestant upper class, were now to be stocked by the educated native elite, who would help smooth the transition from colonial to postcolonial society.

In the magnificent buildings of the new civic structures, in the productive spaces of the industrial zones, and in the landscaped environments of the proposed parks, *Dublin of the Future* proposed the infrastructure required to build a new, modern city on top of the old. For nationalists, the plan displayed the architecture of the modern state, theirs for the taking, if they were only up to the task. The plan opens with a dramatic image, Harry Clarke's "The Last Hour of the Night." In that picture we see a city in flames, caught between a burning imperial past and a seemingly futureless present. During that revolutionary decade before the creation of the Irish Free State, modern town planning made its first appearance in Ireland. This was not a coincidence, for the new discipline had as one of its aims the pacification of a restless colony. The stories of the early planners make that clear. At first, the British authorities thought that town planning would demonstrate to the Irish how the path of modernization and industrialization was better, as well as more probable, under them. Imperial administrators hoped to convince indigenous leaders and the broader Irish public to remain in the United Kingdom with the promise of a new and rational city. But in so doing, these officials also offered indigenous elites an image of how nationalists would like to be seen, as masters of their own domain.

In the evolution of Irish nationalism, therefore, Dublin came to play an increasingly important role in the definition of state-centered nationalist politics. In the campaign for town planning and urban housing at the beginning of the last century, we see the beginnings of a postcolonial geography that nationalists hoped would help legitimate their own ideological positions after the foundation of an independent state.

2 | Postindependence Ireland: Beyond Tradition

A Challenge to Conventional Wisdom

In Irish studies, as represented by the writing of such authors as Declan Kiberd, Terry Eagleton, and David Lloyd, the postcolonial state, particularly during those years immediately following independence, is portrayed as a repressive and authoritarian regime. This state, it is said, presides over a deeply conservative culture, which has retreated to tradition, particularly religion, and "nativism" as a means of establishing a national cultural foundation, even a social uniformity with which to flatten the various regionalist identities that make up the country. This sentiment is echoed in postcolonial studies more generally in the writings of Frantz Fanon, Chinua Achebe, Benedict Anderson, Partha Chatterjee, and Ranajit Guha.[1] Writers such as Declan Kiberd often characterize the leaders of the new nation-state as products of a colonial training. This new class perpetuated the economic hierarchies and capitalist mentalities of the former colonizer, while ignoring the needs of the urban poor, the landless peasantry, and minorities—all atypical subjects of the nation. The postindependence period, the common story goes, is presented almost as if the population and their rulers were so weary from having overthrown imperialism that they had little energy left for reimagining or creating the conditions in which a new society might flourish.

This paradigm of the dark, almost feudal days of postcolonialism in Ireland is repeated across several disciplines. In literature, the shift from the pre- to postrevolutionary days is portrayed as a move from modernism to mediocrity, from the great satiric and hybrid works of Synge, Shaw, and Wilde to the modest short stories of Frank O'Connor and Liam O'Flaherty, with their rural epiphanies and tales of economic hardship. The three-volume *Field Day Anthology of Irish Writing* (Deane 1992), for example, offers a section on the immediate postcolonial period titled "The Counter-Revival: Provincialism and Censorship." The influential *Writing Ireland: Colonialism, Nationalism, and Culture* opens its section on the same years with the following statement: "If revolutions are what happens to wheels, then Ireland underwent a revolution between 1916 and 1922. Social and political institutions were turned upside down, only to revert to full circle upon the establishment of the Irish Free State" (Cairns and Richards 1988, 114). Referencing Samuel Beckett's phrase the "Victorian Gael," Kiberd in *Inventing Ireland: The Literature of the Modern Nation* emphasizes the new state's attempts to regulate public morals, including laws prohibiting divorce (in 1925) and homosexuality, for which the previous British statutes were carried forward (Kiberd 1996, 361, 484). Eagleton compares Joyce's *Ulysses* to Marx's *Eighteenth Brumaire of Louis Bonaparte*. For Eagleton, the theme of the disjuncture between the rhetoric and reality of bourgeois revolutions in Marx mirrors that of Joyce's text, "which appeared just as the heroic tradition of Irish nationalism was giving birth of the mouse of the Irish Free State" (Eagleton 1995, 257). Deane describes the Free State as "that little world," which followed the extravagant rhetoric of the Revival and the Rising, the War of Independence and the Civil War (1997, 162). "It is a world that has lost faith in the heroic consciousness of the heroic individual and has replaced it by the unheroic consciousness of the ordinary" (162).

The same story, not unlike that portrayed in *Angela's Ashes*, of a rain-soaked time after independence when the Irish people were mere children under the strict watch of a parental state, is to be found in other disciplines as well. In political science, Mike Cronin (2000) labels his work on the period, "Golden Dreams, Harsh Realities: Economics and Informal Empire in the Irish Free State." Mary Daly, an economic historian, suggests that the attempt by de Valera's postcolonial government to establish economic self-sufficiency was inseparable from a cultural program of "autarky, xenophobia, and the preservation of rural society" (1992, 63). The verdict is in, then, on the postcolonial state and society. It was a bleak time, and those who were not forced to emigrate suffered in silence, as they rarely did in the days under British rule.

Such views of Irish society in the 1920s, 1930s, and 1940s rely on a particular theory of the state, a theory that I seek here to complicate and question. Despite the mixed ideological tendencies—liberal, conservative, and radical—of the critics who write about this moment of Irish history, the general view of the time period is rather one-dimensional. The theory of the state that is implied, I suggest, derives from that offered a century and a half ago in *The Communist Manifesto,* which describes the "executive of the modern state" as "but a committee for managing the common affairs of the whole bourgeoisie" (Marx 1998, 53). The commentators I have mentioned, such as Kiberd, Lloyd, and Daly, along with others, see the policies and officials of the new Ireland as expressing a singular ideological viewpoint, and a rather narrow, essentialist one at that. They view the leaders of the new state, Cosgrave and especially, later, de Valera, as representative of a rather generic nationalist elite that sought to impose its will, often through repressive and authoritarian measures, such as censorship, prison, and doctrinaire pedagogy, on a battle-weary, somewhat naive population.

I aim not to contradict such views, but rather to situate the early trajectory of the postcolonial state, and the moment of its founding, in a broader and more nuanced context, one that takes into account international influences on the new regime, as well as the domestic limitations of the particular time period. I argue, too, that the view one gets of a historical epoch is largely determined by the discipline through which one approaches it. For the most part, Irish studies has been governed by a literary paradigm, which has itself been dominated by the figures of Yeats and Joyce, each of whom represented one of the two opposing poles of European and Irish modernism: the avant-garde and the allusively dense. From a literary perspective, the view of the early years of independent Ireland is dominated by these two men. Given Joyce's, Beckett's, and O'Casey's self-imposed exiles, and Yeats's attacks on censorship and nationalism, literary critics might be excused for having a theory that sees more repression than hegemony in the organizing and stabilizing practices of the new state. They saw in Ireland a place from which thinkers and writers were compelled to flee in order for their artistic integrity to flourish, a country that had no room for imagination or creativity, a place hostile to experimental modernism. The danger of the literary paradigm—indeed, the pitfall of any discipline—lies in what it excludes. The association of Ireland with the literary not only perpetuates the stereotype of the talkative, entertaining, and charming Irishman, but it overlooks the contribution of so much other cultural production, such as painting, music, and architecture, that can be used to better understand Irish history and subjectivity. Here I will focus on the built environment as a means of presenting a different interpretation of this period.

My argument has two primary goals. The first is to demonstrate how and why contemporary cultural and literary critics represent the postcolonial decades in the ways that they do. Today's writers evaluate the early years of the independent state from a narrowly contemporary perspective that has as much to do with the politics of the present as with the complexity of the past. In reevaluating these early years, then, I hope ultimately to call into question the present-day emphasis on neoliberalism, which seeks to undermine economic interventions and regulations. In short, I wish to understand the various legitimating projects of the early Irish state, in order to argue that early nationalism—flawed though its execution might have been— was not a failure: the leaders of the postcolonial state *were* engaged in a modernization project, a project that, like nationalism, cannot be dismissed out of hand as simply nativist and reactionary. To do so would be to misread many of the progressive or libratory impulses that were embedded in the official discourses of postindependence Irish culture. For example, Ireland did not retreat from international politics and debates at the moment of its founding. From the outset, the government pursued an active foreign policy, playing a leading role in the League of Nations and in the Commonwealth. The legitimating projects of the 1920s and 1930s reveal some of the important inner contradictions that existed in Irish society, such as rural/urban, middle class/working class, traditional/modern. I will read these projects in an attempt to underline these contradictions and to show how the new state struggled to ease the tensions; ultimately, this struggle was doomed to fail, but in the attempts we see the complex inner workings of a fledgling government aiming to reconcile the ideals of nationalism with the hard realities of a functioning state.

I will distinguish the postrevolutionary decades and reinterpret the time as a more experimental and progressive one, an era that must be judged in the fullness of its own complicated, diverse, and often contradictory context. My reading suggests that, far from being a moment of stagnation and isolation, the years between 1922 and 1945 were a time of cultural gestation and expansion. Many city developments—garden suburbs, social housing, industrial projects, and urban designs—were undertaken by leading state figures and other private institutions during these years. Their locations, styles, and materials were influenced by broader trends of international politics and economics. Irish architects and developers were aware of and participated in international debates over urban development. In architecture, for example, the deployment of a stripped-down classical style in several new and large-scale commercial buildings foreshadowed the later arrival of the international style in Ireland. The construction of new suburban estates in the 1920s and 1930s in Dublin was a local manifestation of broader transatlantic developments aimed at reconciling the ideals of industrialism with the values of a "civilized" national population.

Many of the urban and infrastructural developments constructed in Ireland during these years maintain several competing interpretations at the same time. Nothing, in other words, is ideologically pure. State planners, architects, and politicians were forced to move beyond their immediate supporters and integrate, even control, elements of Irish society that had the potential, especially after a lengthy period of militarism, to undermine the state. Although the immediate post–Civil War years lacked some of the internecine intensity associated with other, more fraught decades, each government of the period—whether the cautious and conservative regime of William Cosgrave in the 1920s, or the more populist and Catholic regime of Eamon de Valera in the 1930s—had to contend with different elements within its own regime as well as different public factions. The state, inasmuch as we can identify such a singular entity, had, therefore, both to manage its allies and to assimilate potentially hostile forces unto itself. Those efforts were attempted in part through the production of space.

With regard to literature, the suggestion that Irish writing fell into a period of provincialism and censorship is equally misguided. Numerous writers engaged contemporary world and European developments. Peader O'Donnell, a renowned international socialist and campaigner for the rights of small farmers, wrote a book about the Spanish Civil War, as did Kate O'Brien. Liam O'Flaherty traveled to Soviet Russia and documented his travels. His novel *The Informer* (1925) displays a range of modernist techniques: an acute awareness of literature's emerging relationship to film, the inability to separate parochial Irish nationalism from the internationalist trends of European socialism, and the rapid and constant switch between competing literary genres—melodrama, gothic, naturalism, and expressionism.[2] The Irish tradition of producing works of high literary modernism did not stop with the departures of Joyce and Beckett to the continent. Flann O'Brien's novels, beginning in the 1930s, echoed a style that would later, in the context of decolonizing Latin America, be called "magical realism." They wove folklore, fantasy, and political commentary together into a nihilistic and self-referential text. In the more realist and caustic form of the short story, Frank O'Connor, Sean O'Faolain, and Liam O'Flaherty reveal the tensions of class, of rural-to-urban migration, and of family and generational conflict. Declan Kiberd (1979) has argued that the structure of the short story, with its limited outlook and minor epiphanies, was the narrative form best suited to portraying the claustrophobic world of postindependence Ireland. But the work of these short-story writers can just as easily be read as affirming the grander themes of life: passion, ambivalence, and struggle. With regard to censorship, it is true that many authors fell victim to the state's moralizing, but this was not unique to Ireland. In almost every other European country, the insecure conditions of the time produced official attempts to shape public discourse. The idea that the world of postindependence Irish literature was stunted and isolationist flies in the face of the facts. And, while much pornographic material was edited or banned, there was little stricture against ideas as such; socialist, communist, and other overtly political literature remained unaffected (Fallon 1988, 4–6).

What an updated interpretation of these years reveals, therefore, is the inherent modernism of Irish nationalism in the immediate post-colonial period. I wish to highlight the contradictory messages emitted by the range of construction projects and building styles during the 1920s and 1930s. I will argue that, in a housing estate such as the one built at Marino, one can see a conservative agenda in aspects of the symmetrical, neo-Georgian layout and in the rental prices; at the same time, one can also identify a wish, a liberal hope that a traditionally impoverished working class could be raised, materially and culturally, to a new level of heightened citizenship and economic well-being. Also in the 1920s, a time constantly noted for the frugality of its ministers—Ernest Blythe (finance), Patrick Horgan (agriculture)—the government in its first year created a "million pound" scheme to subsidize urban housing development.

Postcolonial Ireland, the period up until 1945, is normally divided into two phases. The first is the period from 1922 to 1932, when Cumann na Gaedheal, under the leadership of William Cosgrave, controlled the reins of the new state. Compared to the 1930s, the initial post–Civil War years are regarded as direct descendants of their British predecessors: economically conservative and rooted in the policies of free trade, low taxation, and the promotion of large agricultural interests over smaller peasant farms. The emphasis was on the avoidance of more violent conflict and the creation of working state institutions such as a civil service and a parliamentary system. Taken on their own merits, these were not insignificant achievements. The new regime cautiously implemented an urban agenda in Marino, Fairbrothers Fields, and, later, in a more ambitious and populist move, at Cabra. It also enacted small measures of slum clearance that would later be adopted wholesale by de Valera's Fianna Fáil party. The Cosgrave government also embarked on the Shannon electrification scheme, damming the country's largest river to bring electricity to the masses. Conventional wisdom defines these years as moments of stagnation, but clearly they were not.

The 1930s differed from the 1920s as the more populist administration of de Valera embarked on a series of symbolic and real attempts to merge some of the former ideals of Irish nationalism—

rural iconography, Catholic rhetoric, and Gaelic naturalism—with the accepted reality of the state as it had developed. He introduced a social welfare package, subsidized the Irish language, undermined trade with Britain, elevated Catholicism, and paid lip service to a nationalist image of frugality, self-sufficiency, and pastoralism. He also increased significantly the program of slum clearance and, during his term, Dublin Corporation initiated the building of inner-city apartment blocks. De Valera's government also supported public industry, such as Aer Rianta, which nationalized the airports, and Bord na Móna, which oversaw the extraction of natural resources (Lee 1989, 190).

It is worth noting the differences between the two decades, but for the purposes of my argument, I want to suggest the links and continuity between the time periods. In general, I will refer to the 1920s and 1930s as one era, because in the longer sweep of postcolonial Ireland, the country's leaders set out to accomplish the same important goals: to stabilize Ireland, to build a functioning democracy, and to naturalize a modernist agenda, one that partook fully in its local and international conversations. That is, while there are differences between the two eras, both are considered by contemporary critics to have been repressive and traditionalist. I aim to illuminate the complicated truth of a more progressive early nationalism, and thereby defend some of its better underpinnings.

My second goal is to offer an approach that investigates these years of national consolidation through a different discourse than literature, namely, through an examination of architecture and urban planning. Such an approach exposes an alternative picture of these supposedly bleak years, one that shows the state as consisting of competing tendencies. The government aimed to industrialize and modernize its economy and workforce, as demonstrated by the deployment of a stripped-down classical style in architecture, garden suburb housing, slum clearance schemes, and the construction of new apartment buildings in the latest styles available from Amsterdam; it looked to an official compromise between the imperial classicism of the past and functional modernism in order to, literally, appear less ideologically extreme; it oversaw the construction of several state buildings that featured art deco details, a style noted for its evocation of glamour, consumerism, and popular culture. This avenue of investigation—that is, an analysis of material space—also highlights some of the ways in which the new state sought to persuade and assimilate skeptical citizens and groups into accepting its authority and legitimation by actually *building* for them (public housing, libraries, parks, and so on). In short, I argue that the postcolonial state, when viewed from the standpoint of cultural geography, put more thought into winning consent than demanding it.

Town planning, I suggested earlier, arose in Ireland largely as a response to a series of colonial crises—strikes, insurrection, and a legacy of underdevelopment. Examining the Irish context, I also reflected on a broader, more general problem: the relationship between the built environment and social control. The growth of planning discourse in Ireland at the beginning of the twentieth century revealed two aspects of that relationship. First, planners saw their work as playing a key role in maintaining social order. The ultimate goal of *Dublin of the Future,* for example, was to regulate not just *where* but also *how* people lived, worked, and relaxed. But built space does more than define and police social relations. The second way in which planning is positioned between space and control is as "an exploratory genre for addressing new problems and challenges" (Archer 2002, 147). The Wide Streets commissioners in Dublin, for example, at the beginning of the eighteenth century, did not just operate amid the changing nature of colonial rule. Their "modern" and novel urban strategies—wide boulevards, large civic buildings, and neoclassical architecture—were an innovative part of the solution to a larger political problem: how to convert a military victory into a cultural one. And Abercrombie and Geddes, in the decade before independence, deployed the new tactics of the survey, the civic exhibition, and the garden suburb, in part as a response to the problems associated with the rise of nationalism. It is in this spirit that I approach the architecture and planning of the Irish Free State. Implicit in the idea that planning innovations emerge out of a change in social conditions is the converse: that a new social arrangement will produce experimental physical changes. The Irish Free State was a new political situation: what, then, are its spatial equivalents? And what social problems and challenges did these spatial transformations seek to solve?

Hegemony and Space in the Irish Free State

When the last British infantryman departed Dublin Castle in 1922 and made his way back to what Unionists in Ireland like to call "the mainland," the new Irish state faced enormous problems. It had, most immediately, to begin the task of repairing the country's infrastructure after a decade of violence and upheaval. Much of central Dublin, for example, needed to be cleared of rubble and its thoroughfares reopened. The Dublin Reconstruction Act (1924), for example, allowed the corporation to enact a series of urban renewal measures, including street widening (North Earl Street) and street creation (Cathal Brugha and Sean MacDermott Street).[3] Public housing also needed to be constructed, and many former colonial structures— military barracks, police posts, and government offices—needed to be remodeled and put to other, more popular, uses.[4] In 1924 Dublin Corporation converted the former British army base, Keogh Barracks, into two hundred flats (Bennett 1991, 170). The Linenhall Barracks was converted in 1925, and the corporation leased Marshalsea Barracks in 1932.[5] Military structures were not the only buildings targeted for conversion and renewal. The Greater Dublin Reconstruction Committee, a voluntary group of parliamentarians, businessmen, and architects, sought to maintain the interest in modern town planning, which had begun with the pioneering work of Abercrombie and Geddes a decade earlier. In the hope of replanning Dublin "as a national capital and seat of government," this committee made a host of recommendations aimed at implementing "a unified scheme of physical reconstruction" for the purpose of solving the new state's inherited urban problems (Moran 1923, 43): shortage of housing; a lack of government space, given the destruction of major public buildings; poverty; and major traffic congestion, given the destruction of the city's main bridge. Initial proposals called for the conversion of the Four Courts into the Municipal Art Gallery, and the turning of Dublin Castle into the site of the new parliament (ibid.). The changes were both pragmatic and symbolic.

Along with the immediate physical needs of the capital, the economy demanded urgent attention. When the British were in control, they had subsidized the Irish economy heavily. Paying the wages of Dublin's civil service, for example, required a massive subvention from Westminster. From the mid-nineteenth century onward, the British had also hoped to appease nationalists by providing national education and underwriting loans for farmers, both of which depended on large sums of money. In 1922, however, these subventions were abruptly withdrawn, and the Irish had to go it alone financially.

The new regime had its own pressing financial problems. The size of the Free State Army, the victors in the Civil War, had swollen to sixty thousand, and payment of its soldiers and officers had to be a priority to prevent further unrest. (The biggest threat in the early years of the state was a narrowly averted mutiny by the military after the government attempted to halve its size.) There was also the burden of large Civil War debts owed to Britain. The terms of the treaty demanded, as well, that Ireland pay "land annuities" to Britain as a form of compensation to English landlords and banks. More mundanely, state employees had to be paid, pensions had to be honored, and transport kept running. And yet, despite the loss of revenue from the British Exchequer, the lack of a lively indigenous industrial sector, and the flight of much British capital, the financial situation of the new state was less dire than that of many later decolonizing societies.[6]

Ireland entered independence with some relative economic and social advantages. Per capita income, while not anything near that of Britain, was in line with the rest of Western Europe (Lee 1989, 70). The new administration had the institutional help of the Catholic Church. If there was no indigenous state in Ireland during the nineteenth century, the Catholic Church was the next best thing: it ran a large educational system, a hospital system, and a rudimentary welfare system. After independence, in return for ideological and political support from the new secular leaders, the Church continued to train and recruit a large number of doctors, teachers, and nurses. Initially, it might also be claimed, partition helped the southern regime, allowing, as it did, for the temporary shelving of the "national question," which centered on the issue of how to accommodate two hostile populations into the one state.

At the moment of its inception, therefore, the Irish Free State, it appeared, had inherited some of the preconditions of political stability: a statewide education structure, a relatively modernized society, and a homogeneous population (Lee 1989, 77). In an empirical sense, the outlook for the new state seemed quite hopeful. In another sense, however, the future looked much more uncertain. Where would the country go from here? And how would reconstructing Dublin help consolidate the power of a newly independent state? "We are now entering upon a new era and it is the national duty to ensure that the national capital shall naturally reflect the spirit of a free Ireland."[7] Thus proclaimed the editorial of the *Freeman's Journal,* a leading nationalist newspaper. In 1923 Ernst Blythe, the minister for local government, felt that "the character of the capital will have a very important influence upon the progress and development of the state.... If Dublin is not as good a capital as we ought to have, the State will suffer" (Campbell 1994, 43). But, again, how was the "character" and "influence" of the capital to be defined? As a movement, nationalism has rarely had a coherent voice. Rather, as I have previously suggested, it is made up of a range of competing individuals, groups, parties, and classes, each striving in its own way to grab hold of the reins of discourse and normalize the meaning of inherently abstract words and phrases, such as "the people," "the land," "the nation," and even "Ireland" itself. This was the case before the Rising and during the whole revolutionary period. Debates over how to define the basic terms of identity did not stop with the formation of the Irish Free State. As at other watershed moments in Irish history, efforts to shape the physical growth of Dublin and to regulate its architecture were attempts to define what nationalism was, what the function of government ought to be, and whom the state should aid. A cultural reading of the physical landscape of Dublin in the years after independence, therefore, reveals much about the priorities of the new state. This analysis exposes not just the prejudices of the new regime, but also the way in which it functioned not merely as a repressive apparatus, the instrument of a single class, but as a bridge on which various factions would meet and often find consensus.

The critical attitude that prevails regarding the Free State extends to all aspects of Irish culture, including architecture and planning. According to Terence Brown, when de Valera took power in 1932, "Fianna Fáil's bucolic Utopianism struck a chord in a society that considered urban life an essentially alien intrusion on Irish civilization and this militated against architectural innovation in the cities" (Brown 2000, 22). To strengthen his claim that architecture played little role in the life of the new state, Brown quotes R. M. Butler, editor

of the *Irish Builder and Engineer*, as saying that "few buildings, ecclesiastical or secular, have been erected in more recent years in Ireland" (ibid.). In his article "Irish Architecture," in the 1932 *Official
Handbook* of the Irish Free State, Butler's original quote read, "Few
buildings, ecclesiastical or secular, *of very outstanding merit,* have been
erected in more recent years in Ireland" (Saorstat Eireann 1932, 256;
italics mine). Brown's subtle misquoting serves his larger agenda: the
characterizing of independent Ireland as an architectural wasteland.
What's more, Butler was one of the leading defenders of classicism
in Ireland, and in his capacity as editor of the *Builder,* he often opposed the spreading influence of modernism and art deco. Indeed, a
purveyor and booster of classicism might choose to define the period
in terms of monumental, civic architecture; *his* agenda was to show
not that little was built, but that what was constructed did not fall
into the worthy European tradition he supported.

Thousands of structures were erected in Dublin during the 1920s
and 1930s. To dismiss domestic architecture and a whole range of
other, smaller projects, from inner-city apartments through cinemas
to government buildings, is unimaginative. Rather than pointing at
all the structures that were not realized, it is more useful, I suggest,
to focus on what actually was produced, and to read the styles and
locations for what they tell us about their own historical context.
Hugh Campbell further argues in *Interpreting the City* that Dublin,
because of its anomalous urban position in the history of a rurally
based nationalism, "was generally ignored" by the postcolonial governments. "Urban Ireland," according to Campbell, "was a phenomenon which nobody seemed to want to examine too deeply. The capital city had come to engender a feeling of alienation in its own
citizenry" (1994, 42). Both Brown and Campbell accept the still pervasive myth that Dublin was passed over in the quest to fashion a
particular vision of Irish identity: "rustic, ascetic and spiritual"
(Becker, Olley, and Lang 1997, 85).

The social reality of the 1920s and 1930s was more layered. While
lip service was paid to rural Ireland and its culture in official statements, thousands of new units of suburban housing and high-density
apartments were built. While the Church and older Anglo-Irish elements exercised a degree of control over the economic and ideological agenda of the new regime, Dublin Corporation often clashed

with these dominant forces: in Cabra, for example, Dublin Corporation issued a compulsory purchase order to the Catholic Church in order to lay down its popular housing program. As part of the same development, it also demolished a lived-in Anglo-Irish estate.[8]

When we turn to examine what leading architectural commentators were saying about their own postindependence environment, the official record reveals a segment of the population deeply committed to urban matters, such as slum clearance, the relationship between architectural aesthetics and economic progress, and the physical and psychological health of the citizenry. For example, Darrell Figgis, a nationalist, writer, and co-drafter of the Irish Free State's Constitution, argued that the best stylistic choice for new building ought not to be historicist or ornamental. His address in 1922 to the Architectural Association of Ireland echoes the strongest appeals by international modernists for a functionalist aesthetic. In *Planning for the Future,* Figgis writes, "First of all we must cleanse our minds of imitation, and, disengaging ourselves of antique manners, bring our work to simplicity and truth, shaping each building to necessity, and look for beauty in chastity and proportion. That is the task before all Irish art, and it is especially the task before Irish architecture" (1922, 34). Figgis's plea for modern European standards was an early example of the postcolonial quest for newness and experiment. Simply put, it was the opposite of an easy retreat into an essentialized notion of identity. Figgis, furthermore, defines the architect as a "worker of miracles, a creator... who does not compromise with his fellows, but by the faith which is in him imposes his decisive will on them" (9). Figgis's language not only rejects the idea of an Irish style, but also celebrates the modernist myth of the architect as hero, a colossus who can impose order on cities and shape brave new worlds.

Three years after Figgis's address, one of Ireland's leading town planners and architectural commentators, Manning Robertson, argued in *Laymen and the New Architecture* that Ireland's "architecture cannot live a self-contained life" (1925, 166). In typical modernist fashion, he sees in Ireland a new start, a possibility for an old civilization to begin anew. "We may be sure that the coming Ireland will not rest content with the Puritanical frugality of its older cottages and streets; for inspiration it would do well to turn again to the South European spirit of selective exuberance from which it can learn so much, and thus enliven the old work as well as enrich the new" (ibid.). Robertson presents his call for new architecture as a means to achieve a historical goal: "'Let us try to build appropriately, and national expression will look after itself; character and worthy craftsmanship . . . whether hand or machine rendered . . . will forge the unconscious link with race and tradition'" (quoted in Rothery 1991, 119).

Modernism enacts a split between the old and the new. In that sense, it has no inherent social content; it is a temporal construction that "valorizes the new" and in so doing, "produces the old" (Mulhern 1998, 20). Modernist works often tout themselves as staging innovation in order to give expression to a new cultural moment. In literature, the years surrounding World War I are most often thought of as producing, at least in the West, the physical and psychological disillusionment required to break with historical precedent. Nineteen twenty-two, in particular, with the publication of Joyce's *Ulysses* and Eliot's *Wasteland,* is seen as a watershed moment: these works are experimental and rooted in a new kind of urban experience, one that is highly individualistic yet alienating. The high priests of modernist architecture also conceived of their theories and practices around the idea of rupture, a breaking-away from traditions and conventions. Le Corbusier says that architecture "is stifled by custom" (Le Corbusier 1946, 132). Mies van der Rohe argues, "It is hopeless to try to use the forms of the past in our architecture" (Rowe 1994, 25).

Ireland experienced a moment of rupture, of course, also in 1922: the founding of the independent state (and the violent years that surrounded it). While Robertson, Figgis, and others would self-consciously fashion their arguments for a new kind of space, they also relied on the rhetoric of history to pitch their claim that the nation required a new aesthetic to make the ideals and hopes of nationalism come true. In Europe and the United States, modernist architectural manifestos saw history as a burden to shrug off, a weight that dragged on the possibility for a new international, universal, and egalitarian kind of space (the old, consequently, was produced as parochial and repressive). Robertson and Figgis, in contrast, wrote in a postcolonial context in which recent events, loaded with historical significance, were the cause of the present situation—immediate and inescapable. The motivating factor behind the search for new architecture was an attempt to rectify historical wrongs: for Figgis, the denial of "distinctive political genius" (1922, 24). Figgis here, in 1922, is highlighting what is now a commonplace idea—that in blocking the "natural" development of native culture, colonialism produces a double alienation among the colonized, who become distanced from their own as well as from the imposed culture. Inevitably, this also meant that Ireland had been left "without a distinctive architecture . . . [O]ur ancient manner may have been lost; and for all I care it may be irrecoverable" (30). Figgis and Robertson recognized that there could be no architectural "return to the source." For Robertson, any "reproduction" of native Irish style, such as Irish romanesque, "could lead nowhere" (1925, 12). Likewise, for Figgis, "Truth and Sincerity in Architecture" in Ireland could only be achieved through the pursuit of aesthetic simplicity, function over form, and lack of ornamentation. "We must not be in fear of extreme severity of form. Only by such severity can we be assured that later exuberance will be sincerely our own, and not simply derivative" (1922, 34).

Debates over the meaning, applicability, and modernity of international trends and local developments were not limited to professional planners and politicians. Popular and academic journals in Ireland also frequently reported on architecture. In 1927 the *Irish Statesman,* one of early twentieth-century Ireland's most important magazines, ran two articles that explored the quirky linkage in American popular culture between jazz and the skyscraper. The energy of jazz, the author argues, cannot be separated from the life of the city. The pulse of jazz was finding its way into other arts: into Carpenter's *Skyscraper Ballet,* Dos Passos's *Manhattan Transfer,* and the buildings of urban America. The author describes jazz as laughing "with the humour of life . . . [T]he intricate mathematical rhythm . . . [is] like the mind of an inventor . . . the beating of the drum ties the whole to earth."[9] This he compares directly to "the towers of Manhattan rising in sheer joy from the waters of New York harbour." Implicit in the argument here is the suggestion that Ireland ought to follow the innovative lead of modernist architecture in rebuilding itself.

Another leading journal, *Studies,* also contributed to the ongoing debate about architecture in Ireland, again disproving the myth that Dublin—its population and its housing crisis—did not feature in the minds of the Irish postcolonial intelligentsia. Fergal McGrath, a respected Catholic priest, wrote consistently about the crisis of urban overcrowding in the capital. In a 1931 article, "The Sweep and the Slums," he acknowledges that the government and Dublin Corporation "are undoubtedly alive to the magnitude of the problem" (530). While it remains true that not enough units of new housing were instantly created at the onset of independence, McGrath, unlike many critics today, recognizes the difficult economic circumstances of the new state during the 1920s, not the least of which was a worldwide recession. In the midst of these early years, however, McGrath praises the "million-pound scheme" that the government instigated for the completion of two thousand dwellings a year. "It is true," he concedes, "that since 1922 about 6,000 houses have been built in Dublin with State...assistance" (535). This clearly was not enough, and the purpose of McGrath's article was to push for the already tested program of a national lottery to fund reform. Dublin in 1930 had inaugurated an internationally famous Hospital Sweepstakes, based on the outcome of horse races, to financially support hospitals. There was an immediate postcolonial context for the Irish Sweepstakes: Irish immigrants in New York or London, it was hoped, would buy tickets not only with the dream of instant wealth, but with the goal of supporting a fledgling social welfare system back home. In "Homes for the People," another article that appeared in *Studies,* McGrath weighs in on the longstanding debate over the best location for new subsidized housing, arguing for suburban homes built on "virgin soil" (1932, 269). When one goes, he wrote, to Cabra or Donnycarney, one sees houses surrounded by "garden[s] bright with flowers or stocked with useful vegetables and the patch of grass where the smallest children can play in safety" (271). Against this image, he painted a picture of rental accommodation as the breeding ground for insurrection, "weakening throughout the State that... respect for property that is the expression of man's desire for liberty" (272). For McGrath, housing was central to any effort to consolidate the authority of the new Irish state and prevent insurgence.

Another overly ambitious but fundamentally misguided urban proposal was proffered by John McBride, a member of the new parliament, in 1924. In a Dáil debate, he stated that Dublin's "streets... speak of the foreigner and the foreigner's power. The capital of this

country should be removed from the atmosphere of Dublin city. . . .
We are going to have to start from the beginning" (Campbell 1994,
48). On the back of these nationalist and admittedly Gaelic senti-
ments, he suggested moving the capital from Dublin to a new city, to
be built in the center of the country. This was not a totally new idea.
The *United Irishman* newspaper, founded by Sinn Féin's Arthur
Griffith in 1899, told its readers in 1902 that the old Gaelic "city of
Tara was best suited to represent the country, and that Dublin was
really terribly planned" (Garvin 1987, 160). D. P. Moran's *Leader*
argued, as a later generation of modernizers would in the 1960s,
that Georgian Dublin ought to be destroyed, and that the city should
develop modern suburbs, connected to the center by ample new roads
for cars (ibid.).

Yet another engagement with the changing nature of the urban environment was seen in conservative complaints against urban sprawl.
The *Irish Builder* ran an editorial, "The Spoiling of the Suburbs,"
complaining that Dublin was an "object lesson of the evils that flow
from the lack of zoning."[10] During the eighteenth century, the writer
of the editorial opined, the Wide Streets Commissioners "gave us
splendid thoroughfares and dignified architecture." In the aftermath
of independence, though, Dublin's population grew rapidly, with the
result that suburban architecture had become "blatant and vulgar."
Instead of dignified housing, "weird attempts at picturesqueness are
made . . . [through] bits of terra-cotta here and there, a lavish display
of moulded brick, or corbels under eaves and bays." The *Irish
Builder*'s call for aesthetic and architectural control in the suburbs
was wrapped up in a plea for town planning. On account of "the
large amount of housing done in the Free State during the past couple
of years . . . [the editors hope that] a Town Planning and Zoning Act"
might be passed soon. An anonymous author (writing under the name
Artifex) argued that the new, privately built "garden suburbs at
Killester, Foxrock and Mount-Merrion . . . presage a type of expansion which was undreamt of even ten short years ago" (Artifex 1930,
41). Horace T. O'Rourke, who became Dublin Corporation's city
architect in 1922, had long championed the cause of planning. In
1929 he got his wish when Thomas Johnson, leader of the Labour
Party, introduced a bill into Parliament; in 1934 this bill became

law. The act, influenced by the pioneering work of Geddes and Unwin a decade earlier, encouraged, but did not mandate, each local authority to conduct a civic survey and to "make provisions for the orderly and progressive development of cities."[11] The act listed all the concerns that a drawn-up planning scheme ought to contain, including roads, parks, historic preservation, lighting, compensation, water, rights of way, and advertising.

The Town and Regional Planning Act was an important early state intervention in postcolonial Irish politics. Physical planning helped establish the state as the ultimate arbiter over geography. A planning survey, after all, declared what the objects of planning were and, hence, what matters were subject to government regulation. Given the range of potential material to be surveyed, it is no surprise that politicians were attracted by the lure of planning: land use controls could regulate population growth and migration, steer investment toward specific locations, and reward constituencies and clients. Planning had always been an integral part of colonialism, but the rhetoric of physical improvement and progress now operated in a postindependence atmosphere, in which the government was eager to display its democratic credentials. Planning law required consultation with citizens: public inquiries were built into the statute, individuals were allowed to appeal decisions, and compensation was offered. While planning may ultimately have been an ideological state apparatus, a nonrepressive means to further official ideology, that ideology itself was ambiguous and was reflected in planning rhetoric. The 1929 planning bill was an attempt to mediate between an industrializing economy and a traditional culture (that which planners defined as needing improvement); between a robust, free-market economy and social welfare; between a strong central administration and local and regional authorities; and, ultimately, between modernization and national memory. Planning attempts to rationalize modernization, but it cannot repress its contradictions.

From suggestions that Ireland look abroad to modernist international trends for its architectural inspiration, to proposed lottery schemes for the funding of mass public housing, to legislation that sought to grant planners new powers to regulate urban areas and lives, the vast majority of contemporary commentators on postcolonial Ireland have got it wrong. Fresh, creative, and energetic discussions about the legacy and future of urbanism were taking place in Ireland during the 1920s and 1930s. I revisit the 1920s and 1930s precisely to challenge the stereotypes associated with them. When we look at these decades, we see that their urban initiatives—suburbanization, attempts at inner-city renewal, and statist claims on planning—helped to produce, often in circuitous ways, our own present.

"Siberia" or Green Fields? The Suburbs

Dublin in the 1990s and early twenty-first century is a vast, sprawling city. Its population currently accounts for over one-third of the state's total. It was not always this way. During the nineteenth century, suburban development was concentrated on the south side, in the leafy suburbs where the Protestant middle class relocated to avoid the deteriorating physical and political climates of the urban core. As Protestants moved out, they were accompanied by a growing number of middle-class Catholics. The bulk of Dublin's population, however, remained between the two canals, that congested yet compact area that formed the nucleus of the city. This is the part of Dublin that was celebrated in *Ulysses,* a novel premised on the idea that a few people from the same city will inevitably cross paths during the course of an average day. Dublin, as Joyce once remarked, was the world's biggest village. During the first three decades of independence, however, that dense and knowable town would begin to lose its shape as the trend toward low-density suburban housing intensified. In 1925 work began on the Marino estate, north of the city; when completed, it would have 1,262 houses, built at 12 to the acre. By 1929 state ambitions were grander. To the west of the city larger, denser schemes were being developed that made cheaper and smaller homes available to the city's working class and lower middle class. Dublin Corporation initially zoned Cabra for 641 houses, but during the 1930s this number more than doubled. Beginning in 1934, the biggest western suburb, Crumlin, was launched, with plans for over 3,000 new homes; by the time it was completed in 1944, 5,391 houses had been built (Craft 1971, 69). Of all those who relocated to these new areas, one particular literary representation has come to serve as a stand-in for the complexity of new suburban lives: the image of the suburbs as a wild hinterland. Dominic Behan describes his family's relocation to Kimmage, one of these new estates, as a move "to Siberia" (Behan 1965, 16). New ribbon developments were branching out in every direction. Long before the words *modernization* or *globalization* became fashionable, these years pointed toward the kind of urban expansion that would feverishly take hold in Dublin during the 1960s and 1990s.

In the aftermath of independence, Dublin, like many other postcolonial countries, experienced a large upsurge in the number of people coming to the city in search of work. The built-up area of the city increased by 50 percent during the first two decades of self-rule. Between 1911 and 1936 the population rose by over 100,000 (Horner 1992, 328). The 1929 Town Planning Bill was one example of contemporary concerns over the pace of development. In a commentary on the bill, planner John O'Gorman railed against the uncontrolled expansion of the city: "There has, evidently, been a spate of building during the last five years. But when one sees the suburbs one realises that the proper word is 'orgy.' Here is building gone mad, pretentiousness supreme, vulgarity rampant.... There is nothing, nothing whatever, so horrible, so stupid, so utterly tragic as the mess that this city has made of its suburbs within five short years" (O'Gorman 1936, 131). Many of the new arrivals who were destined to be the new suburbanites were recruits to the burgeoning civil service; a steady, pensionable government job was the best reward for services rendered to the new state during its troublesome and formative years. Others were poorer, peasant victims of the land policies pursued by the new state, which offered loans to more profitable farmers at the expense of those less viable subsistence producers (Lee 1989, 71–72).

Certainly, the thought of a Dublin swamped with rural migrants who had little or no training in the arts of urban living threatened the imaginations of some in the postcolonial administration, especially those who viewed the capital as the civic and cultural center of a new, modern, and independent Ireland. Many of these liberal reformers had been members of the Housing and Town Planning Association of Ireland, now renamed the Civics Institute. Rooted in the ideals of philanthropic reform, constructive unionism, and beaux arts architecture and planning, these individuals represented the Irish wing of the city beautiful movement. This aesthetic and political movement was based on the principle that a magnificent neoclassical downtown required a suitably educated, civilized, and financially viable citizenry. Its idealized formula depended on concentrating healthy businesses in a core downtown, around which new suburbs would house a comfortable and cosmopolitan population, which was as far removed from its reality of slum and tenement life as could be imagined. Proponents of this reform scheme aimed to change the form of the city without altering its substance; they wanted to attain greater equality and provide more opportunity without undermining the fundamental economic and social structures that produced the need for reform in the first place.

The *Dublin Civic Survey*, published in 1925, suggested that the new arrivals required a degree of social control and ought to be placed in surroundings that would suit their rustic, unrefined manners. "The importance of civic ideals—whereby all units essential to city life may co-operate and advance in an orderly manner—is not yet realized by the mass of our citizens. Within the past few years, the population of the capital has been augmented by a disproportionately large rural element. This accretion cannot be expected to possess civic ideals, for its notions are naturally primitive: with the lure of the city life it becomes undisciplined" (Civics Institute of Ireland 1925, 3). The survey deplored the lack of "civilization" in the new migrants to the city, a deficiency that could, in part, be ameliorated through housing, primarily garden suburbs. There, each family could live in a "natural" environment, could cultivate a plot of land and raise their children free from the dangers of inner-city urban life: crime, pollution, and poverty.

Another group that needed rehousing at the onset of independence was Dublin's inner-city population. Through the nineteenth century the once grand, but now derelict houses of the city's former aristocracy had been subdivided and occupied by the city's poor. By the 1900s thousands of families lived in dank, one-room dwellings.[12] Many of those who lived in these slums were receptive to the radical messages of militant nationalists. The Irish Citizen Army, which had played a significant role in the Easter Rising, recruited from this class.

It is hardly surprising, therefore, that the expansion of the housing industry was a top priority for the new government during the 1920s and 1930s. For the British, these slums had housed disease, crime, and rebellion; urban improvement had provided an ideological rationale for a range of colonialist interventions. In the new Irish Free State the construction of suburbs was, for some, motivated by many of the same urban fears. The conditions that were seen as producing urban discontent had not been solved by the formality of handing over power. As Fergal McGrath wrote in his polemic advocating suburban home ownership over inner-city rental: "If a more even distribution of property is to be the keynote of our national economic policy, is it a good start to deprive thousands of workers of that most primary belonging, a home in the fullest sense of the word? If a communist organizer wished to lay plans for the development of communist cells throughout Dublin or for the building of 'red forts' for revolutionary purposes, could he do better than dot the city over with large barracks of propertyless men?" (1932, 272). While there was some debate over how best to proceed on the housing issue, few doubted its urgency and importance to the project of state consolidation and legitimation. The head of the new state, William Cosgrave, a one-time councilor of Dublin Corporation, spoke in 1924 of how the housing question "directly or indirectly affects every aspect of national life, and until it is settled there will be no genuine peace or contentment in the land. For no populace housed as so many of the people of Dublin are, can be good citizens, or loyal and devoted subjects of the State, no matter what the State may be."[13]

During the 1920s more than 9,000 new houses were constructed by urban authorities in Ireland (26,000 homes were erected in total across the country with state and local aid). In Dublin the majority of the 4,248 units that were built between 1923 and 1931 were located in new suburban estates to the north and west of the city: at Marino (1925, 1,262 houses), at Fairbrothers Fields (1923, 416), at Drumcondra (1928, 535), at Emmet Road (1929, 702), and at Cabra (1931, 641).[14] One of the primary goals of the new initiatives was the dispersal of many of Dublin's inner-city population to the outskirts, which would in turn relieve urban densities in the core. Freeing up central space would also aid in the replanning of Dublin as "the national capital and the seat of Government."[15] The Greater

Dublin Reconstruction Movement, which had originally been set up with the help of Raymond Unwin in the wake of the Rising, had now, in the aftermath of the War of Independence and the Civil War, the task of finding homes for the new government ministries and most of the city's major civic institutions. In a 1923 report on the committee's progress, Senator James Moran stated that "three of the greatest, most important, and most imposing buildings in the city—the National General Post Office, the Custom House, and the Four Courts—have been reduced to ruins.... President Cosgrave has announced that the difficulties of setting up and carrying on the business of National Government are greatly increased by the lack of suitable buildings."[16] A state that had just won independence, and one that looked unconfidently to the international world for approval, needed a modern cultured capital—a representative space—that showed no evidence of weakness. Its leaders therefore sought to repress and displace those elements that gave lie to the notion that independence would be a cure for colonial ills.

Fairbrothers Fields, the state's first foray into new housing, was designed in 1916 according to the garden suburb principles suggested by Geddes and Unwin in their 1914 "Dublin Housing Report." The scheme was shelved in 1918 due to the outbreak of the War of Independence, but was picked up again in 1922. It was funded by the new regime's "million pound scheme" for housing.[17] Construction was done in part by the Dublin Building Trades Guild, a coalition of workers put together by the Irish Labor Party and Sinn Féin, and completed in 1927.[18] The project consisted of four hundred houses, three hundred of which had four rooms, and one hundred with five rooms. Architectural features, such as pedimented gables with keystones, columned porticos, and a plinth to separate a brick lower floor from a concrete upper, reveal the influence of Patrick Abercrombie's classical Liverpool School on Irish housing (Civics Institute of Ireland 1925, 60–64; Fraser 1996, 285). The Anglo-Irish proclivities of the first phase of the Irish Free State were reflected in this scheme: indeed, the Irish were implementing the actual construction of housing estates that the British had designed but not enacted. (It would take a number of years of mounting criticism before government policy would move toward the provision of smaller, cheaper housing that was less imitative of British colonial architectural styles. When de Valera attained power in 1932, there was a decisive shift toward populism in politics and its correlative in architecture: smaller, less ornate suburban homes and blocks of inner-city flats.)

The Marino estate also had its origin in the heady days of town planning in Dublin in the years running up to the Rising. Geddes had drawn up proposals for a symmetrical neo-Georgian suburban lay-out consisting of 550 houses as part of his "Dublin Housing Report." In 1922 the independent state enlarged the area of the site, in part through compulsory land acquisitions, and by 1926 had built over 1,200 houses (Bannon 1988, 139). As in most schemes of the time, only families with four or more children were considered for place-ment (McManus 2002, 192). The houses were for sale only, at 400 pounds each, well below market value but still not affordable for most.[19] Catering to the "aristocracy of labor in Dublin," as the *Irish Times* reported, Fairbrothers Fields and Marino reflected the initial cautious nature of the new state and its privileging of middle-class housing over slum clearance.[20] This, in many ways, was to be ex-pected. As I have argued previously, the housing "question" had ini-tially been framed in Ireland a decade earlier by British reformers in such a way as to yield only one possible answer—that the light, health, and air available in suburbs would solve urban poverty and disease. The leaders of the Irish Free State who had inherited the prob-lem, men such as O'Rourke, Blythe, and Cosgrave, were moderate and modernizing nationalists who, even before 1922, had accepted the environmentally determinist argument that social problems could be solved by reorganizing spatial relations along suburban lines. These politicians, like most planners, were middle class in their out-look and, consciously or unconsciously, saw suburbs as capable of promoting the values—property ownership, self-reliance, and financial frugality—that they believed were necessary for the nation to pros-per. Suburbs were a means to instill those values in what they saw as a reluctant, somewhat ignorant working-class population.

For the leaders of a new state eager both to appease their middle-class power base and to rally others to their mission, housing was a key instrument to demonstrate the state's immediate ability to improve lives. The new government proclaimed a commitment to free trade, but the standard belief, then as now, with regard to a government-financed building industry, was that it would trickle down and provide many construction-related jobs. So, beginning in 1924, this laissez-faire government subsidized the economy by launching the million-pound scheme. Furthermore, slum clearance itself suggested suburbanization. Clearance in central areas, the alternative to suburban housing, was slow and costly. As had been argued in earlier housing inquiries, it created, at least initially, a surplus population that would migrate to another area, leading, in turn, to that area's degeneration. At some point construction on a large scale would be necessary. The intellectual history, as well as the accepted economics of the problem (land was much cheaper in the suburbs; construction jobs would be created), added up to suburbanization.

For a fiscally frugal regime, homes for purchase, as opposed to houses for rent, also provided a quicker and greater monetary return. The emphasis on larger homes, such as those at Marino and Fairbrothers Fields, was also part and parcel of the young state's attempt to show natives and foreigners that it could build better than the previous colonial administration had done, and that it could compete favorably with its neighbors in Britain—a fact that some architectural historians acknowledge. Marino, writes Fraser, "was not merely a second-string application of Unwinian garden suburb design, visually indistinguishable from hundreds of schemes in Britain, but was in fact superior certainly in terms of housing standards" (1996, 289). In the final analysis, over four thousand dwellings were completed by Dublin Corporation in the first decade after independence.[21] This number is not as insignificant as contemporary commentators would have us believe; it represents a quarter of all the buildings that had ever before been built by Dublin Corporation. What we see in these projects, as in the early town planning movement in Ireland more generally, is a wish—a desire to create a well-funded, healthy, refined middle class, something that the country had traditionally lacked, but which was the prerequisite for Irish nationalism's entrance onto the world stage.

As the postcolonial economy refused to flourish during the 1920s, and the limits of expensive and nonrental housing were realized, state policy shifted toward smaller, three-room houses, constructed for rental purposes. Beginning in the late 1920s and early 1930s (Cabra 1929; Crumlin 1934), we see a shift in policy toward building larger housing estates. The corporation planned Crumlin originally for

3,000 houses, but in 1938 zoned 2,400 more at Crumlin North. The scale of these projects was unlike anything the authorities had undertaken before.

Crumlin was removed from traditional sites of industrial employment and initially lacked many public facilities, such as schools, churches, and public transport (Craft 1971, 73). A subgenre of Irish literature was thereby spawned, reflecting on the lives now led on the urban fringe. Some of these narratives expressed diffuse resentment, along with nostalgia for the urban community their inhabitants had left behind in the inner city; others were sympathetic to this monumental transition. Brendan Behan, referring to his family's migration, calls the new location the "wild west" (quoted in Behan 1965, 14). In contrast, Elaine Crowley, in her memoir *A Dublin Girl: Growing Up in the 1930s,* describes her time "exploring the countryside which surrounded our estate," and speaks of her family's garden full of "potatoes, heads of salad and cabbage, scallions and beetroot" (1996, 127).

In Cabra, as in Crumlin, the land for development was acquired by Dublin Corporation using compulsory purchase orders. At the time, the corporation had 2,400 families of seven or more members on its waiting list for new housing. Fourteen hundred houses were to be built on 162 acres at Cabra West, with another three hundred to be constructed by private enterprise. A further 22 acres was set aside for industrial purposes, sites for churches, a vocational school, a library, and a shopping center.[22] The majority of corporation houses were four-room, two-story, terraced houses, each with a front and back garden. Houses consisted of, on average, 850 square feet. All concrete, the government was proud to say, was of Irish manufacture. In a sign of the new regime's commitment to modernization, all older streets in the area were widened. To link the new, modern housing estates to a suggestion of ancient Irish strength and depth of history, new roads laid down were given rural-sounding, mythic names: New Grange, Monasterboice, Clonmacnoise, Armagh. Street lighting arrived in the 1940s.

The development of Cabra West revealed some of the contradictions that existed within Irish society at the time. On the one hand, the government wished to provide a new kind of space that previously had only been available to the city's elite: leafy, salubrious, well-maintained, hygienic houses and streets. This would provide a semi-rural environment for an expanding and, it was hoped, an industrial workforce; trams were to be provided to these communities to allow residents faster access to their jobs in the city. It was also anticipated that new factories and businesses would develop close to these new neighborhoods. In this environment, productivity and health would be paramount.

On the other hand, the plans also highlighted the rural, peasant origins of many of the new residents. Cattle paths were factored into the original designs for transporting animals by foot through residential areas to the local abattoirs. New dairies were built in the neighborhood to process milk from the cows in surrounding fields. Letters to Dublin Corporation regularly complained about farm animals "running amuck." Gardens in the newly built houses were spacious and allowed room for growing vegetables. Some residents kept pigs. In *A Dublin Girl,* Crowley writes about her family's move from a city tenement to a house in one of the new suburbs: "The house was an end one on a block of four. My mother was delighted with its outwards appearance, the steps up to it, the front garden and long side gardens. The green hall with its brass knocker, handle and letter-box" (1996, 116). She describes how her father "dug and hoed and dipped seedlings into liquid manure" (127). The persistence of folk ways and rural traditions could not be repressed. State architects were obliged to incorporate the rural into the urban, as much as they tried to bring the city out into the countryside. Dublin was, in many ways, a city of urbanized peasants.

As developments at Cabra progressed under de Valera in the 1930s, Dublin Corporation issued a compulsory purchase order for the land owned by and surrounding the local Dominican Convent. The Catholic Church fought the confiscation, objecting that the seizure "disturb[ed] the proper administration of our Charitable Institution." Nonetheless, the corporation proceeded with the transfer of land. In a country that was overwhelmingly Roman Catholic, and that had been forced, historically, to identify itself in ethnic and religious terms, it was perhaps inevitable that a Catholic ethos would dominate the new state. When they felt it was necessary, however, the authorities were ready to oppose religious authority and to show that the state was neither in thrall to the Church nor in psychic debt to it.

During completion of another suburban housing project at Crumlin North (now Drimnagh) in 1937, Dublin Corporation butted heads with the local remnants of the Anglo-Irish class, a group whose political influence had diminished significantly, but whose economic importance was still greatly valued. In order to build 450 new houses in Crumlin, the council purchased the lands and estate of the Honorable Kathleen Lawless and demolished the family home, Mount Shannon Lodge.[23] Given de Valera's move toward greater Irish economic and cultural self-sufficiency, it suited his populist and nationalist principles that such a relic of British presence in Ireland would be demolished to make way for so many new homes. But this symbolic and pragmatic destruction also demonstrated that the state was capable of acting in a reformist manner: while it was intent on maintaining power and expressing its ideologies, it managed to put the interests of the city's poorer families above the rights of inherited privilege and landed wealth.

Suburban housing development, such as occurred at Cabra and Crumlin, was also used by the state as a means to appease marginalized groups. Large state grants were provided by the government to private construction companies to hire and train local workers. At Cabra West, for example, a sum of ten thousand pounds was set aside "for the relieving of unemployment."[24]

The push for garden suburbs suggests that their construction is most necessary during times of potential social crisis, when governing forces sense an urban threat, a restless and discontented population. This would explain the moment of arrival of modern town planning in Ireland in the years before the Rising, when Abercrombie, Unwin, and Geddes lobbied intensively for suburbanization. It would also help account for the continued pursuit of a peaceful suburbia in the 1920s, in the aftermath of independence, when the leaders of a shaky new state had to stare down former nationalist allies, as well as disgruntled labor and peasant groups. As the roots of the state took hold, de Valera brought his anti-treaty forces with him into the establishment. When he grasped the reins of state for Fianna Fáil in 1932, therefore, de Valera had fewer worries about subversive military challenges to this government. For his administration, suburbs did not play the same role they had for the British, and initially for Cosgrave, of appeasing radical challenges to the state's authority. But there was a continuing crisis that needed to be solved: the country's economic strife. De Valera believed in moving the country toward industrial self-sufficiency, one of his many significant attempts to further decolonize Irish culture and economics.[25] Suburbs played an important role in solving the perennial crisis of Irish industrial under-development, a legacy of colonialism. During his years in power, "an average of 12,000 houses a year were built with state aid between 1932 and 1942 compared with fewer than 2,000 a year between 1923 and 1931" (Lee 1989, 193). In Dublin, the corporation completed 13,026 dwellings during the 1930s. The housing industry provided much-needed employment, an obvious measure to win over the city's working class. De Valera's suburbs were also, quite simply, "a marked improvement on the foul slums that had for so long disgraced Dublin" (ibid.).

Garden suburbs, both in Ireland and elsewhere, were simultaneously progressive and conservative. On the one hand, they attempted to solve the worst symptoms of poverty in late Victorian cities. They provided new homes and sought to establish "healthier" communities in previously undeveloped areas. On the other hand, their sponsors' focus on decentralizing inner-city areas meant that less energy went into restoring already existing, yet impoverished, neighborhoods. Moreover, in spite of their planners' intentions, suburbs ultimately did little to address the causes of distress, such as unemployment and a lack of health care, that produced the need for such housing in the first place. Suburban developments were Janus-faced: they were romantic, in that they imagined a city in which class struggles and oppositions of interest had no place; yet they were modern, in that they pointed to a time when industrialism and social emancipation were harnessed together. In Ireland, garden suburbs also attempted to reconcile the ideals of nationalism—community, equality, and progress—with those of industrialization. Garden suburbs were not without their critics, even their bourgeois and conservative ones. During the time of suburban construction, some establishment commentators took issue with the patterns of growth. P. L. Dickinson, a regular commentator in the moderate *Irish Builder* and an active promoter of modernism and international style, argued in 1927 that "around our cities and even into the heart of the country, the new bungalow is becoming a menace to beauty" (Bannon 1989, 34).

J. F. McCabe, in the *Dublin Magazine,* wrote: "In the years since 1900 the motor car commenced a social revolution, the culminating point of which is not even in sight.... The centrifugal tendency in Dublin has been apparent for years. Every motor car or 'bus is a stimulus thereto and the progress towards the mountains and the sea should be thought-out and orderly, rather than haphazard as heretofore" (McCabe 1925, 676). The problem with suburbs, then, for some purists, was an aesthetic one. But aesthetics is always politics. While protesting the advance of new housing under the guise of harm being done to the scenery, these writers were also attempting to maintain the demographic and class geographies of a previously colonial and segregated city. For conservatives, suburbs were seen as representing too much democracy; for radicals, they offered too little.

If garden suburbs were themselves the distortion of originally anarchist and socialist ideas about how to create cooperative, worker-owned, self-sufficient rural communities (as represented by Ebenezer Howard's *Garden Cities of Tomorrow*) away from the excesses of industrial life in London or Berlin, then Cabra and other such developments in Dublin reflected these trends. They were part of an ambitious attempt to build a better capital city for a new, independent state. The leaders of the new state were engaging the same issues and debates that were being fought elsewhere, about how to reform aging cities in such a way that citizens might reap greater benefits from the government in power and, therefore, be less likely to seek to undo it.

Modernist Architecture and Postcolonial Nationalism
Inner-City Renewal

In 1932, having realized the futility of remaining on the political sidelines, de Valera led his former rebels, now the Fianna Fáil party, into government. The policies he and his government promoted of protectionism, state-owned industry (fuel, sugar, alcohol, and banking), self-sufficiency, and the dissemination of the Irish language and culture were viewed by opponents as quasi-socialist and threatening to individual rights to private property (Daly 1992, 59). These policies were part of an effort to stabilize the economy and to give economic clout and reality to the espoused ideals of de Valera's brand of pragmatic nationalism, which sought to reconcile cultural and economic independence. These protective programs were also not unusual during the worldwide economic downturn of the 1930s, a decade that gave rise in the United States to President Franklin D. Roosevelt's New Deal. By 1936 de Valera's government, primarily under the influence of Sean Lemass, minister for industry and commerce, had imposed over nineteen hundred tariffs on imported products. According to one economist, between 1931 and 1936 taxes on these goods quadrupled (Daly 1992, 66). Lemass's argument that "the agitation for the protection of industries is identical with the struggle for the preservation of our nationality" received strong backing from John Maynard Keynes (ibid., 64). Keynes delivered a series of lectures in Dublin in 1933. Playing to de Valera's nationalism, he praised the new government's attempt to bring industry under native control: "Experience is accumulating that remoteness between ownership and operation—what is historically symbolized for you in Ireland by the absentee landlord—is an evil in the relations between men. . . . Ideas, knowledge, science, hospitality, travel are the things which should of their nature be international. But let goods be homespun whenever it is reasonably and conveniently possible, and, above all, let finance be primarily national" (Keynes 1933, 180–81). Rather than seeing Ireland as retreating into economic isolation, Keynes locates the country at the "centre of economic experiment" (178).

But the era of de Valera has been consistently depicted as a period of irredeemable intransigence, cultural and economic repression, and rampant traditionalism. Critics denounce Fianna Fáil's reinforcement "of a puritanical code . . . and [its] attempts to insulate the people from Anglicization" (Fitzpatrick 1988, 260). "The 1930s deepened the conservatism of Irish life. . . . To cultural and religious protectionism . . . was added economic nationalism as a force sustaining the structure of an essentially rural society" (Brown 1985, 117). "Self-sufficiency was a key Fianna Fáil objective, close to de Valera's heart because it represented a rejection of the modern world" (Daly 1992, 90). Such evaluations, possible with hindsight, serve a modern ideological function: they define the time as parochial in order to highlight the relative openness, pluralism, and grandly flourishing international economy of today's vastly improved modern, liberal, cosmopolitan culture.

As always, history is more complicated than these one-sided portrayals would admit. De Valera was not a simple promoter of rural life: during his administration, Dublin Corporation inaugurated a large-scale construction project of inner-city apartments. In the first decade after independence, the state funded the completion of five thousand dwellings in the city, of which only 8 percent were flats. By 1939, however, almost eight thousand new homes had been built, with blocks of flats accounting for a quarter of the total (McManus 2002, 213; Fraser 1996, 291). Some conservative critics deemed inner-city flats "un-Irish," not least because they conjured up the specter of socialists all living in the same space. The notion was prevalent that a large, concentrated urban population would inevitably become unruly. "But they [Dublin's underclass] already constitute a social danger which might easily grow to uncontrollable dimensions," argues a 1945 article on slum clearance (Dillon 1945, 14). As well, this urban type of accommodation was considered unnatural: "Flat life . . . hits a smashing blow at a fundamental instinct of humanity, the instinct to guard the family by isolation. Surely it is a momentous step to decide to box up 50,000 citizens of Dublin" (McGrath 1932, 272).

Clearly, the fear existed that Dublin might fall victim to the political trends of the 1920s and 1930s in Europe, where battles between the forces of the left and the extreme right were destabilizing fledgling democracies. In spite of these fears and arguments, during the 1930s Dublin Corporation constructed thousands of units of high-density apartments, many of which were inspired by currents within European modernism, in particular, the Amsterdam school (Conroy 1997, 56; Rothery 1991, 19). This inner-city work counters the Catholic and essentialist image that critics have imposed upon de Valera's Ireland. The continued policy of suburban housing, in particular at Crumlin, as well as de Valera's push for urban renewal, reveals his government's commitment to speaking the language of different demographic groups and interests, which won him the support of Dublin's working class. Other ideological aims and attempts to accumulate different loyalties were implicit in the mass urban schemes: Dublin's infamous red-light area would be destroyed to make way for new, modern apartments; left-wing republican and socialist ideologies would be less appealing; Labor Party support in the Dáil would be maintained. Furthermore, expressionist features deployed in the new

Dublin flat complexes, such as rounded corners, block-length façades, the use of brick for texture and detail, and internal courtyards, bespeak a liberal vision of the city. Such architectural traits reveal a dedication to urban place, history, and community in their deliberate gestures toward a balance between public space and individual expression. The location of the complexes in key central areas, close to traditional centers of employment—the docks, the railways—indicates a dedication to traditional industrialism. Indeed, the complex at Bridge Street, designed by Herbert Simms, the City Housing Department's primary architect, is centered on a clock tower, one of the most prominent reminders of the shift from a rural to an industrial economy (Figure 6). Its collective entrance is the symbolic antithesis of the private doorway of the suburban home.

In 1936, thirteen acres of land were acquired under compulsory purchase in the area around Newfoundland Street. On this site, twenty-four blocks of flats were constructed, at a density of fifty per acre. Thirty-two shops were placed at the ground-floor level of several of the buildings, and playgrounds and other amenities were provided. In total, 640 flats (32 with four rooms, 384 with three rooms, and 224 with two rooms) were constructed in one of Dublin's most notorious tenement districts.[26] There were two sizes of apartment blocks, one that contained sixteen units of housing, and another that held eight. The area around Newfoundland Street, which was at the center of this renewal effort, had also been the city's red-light district. The region was commonly referred to as "The Monto," after Montgomery Street, and between 1800 and 1900 it was recorded that the area housed sixteen hundred prostitutes (Finegan 1978, 9). For the new government, the district had stood as an impoverished and immoral symbol of all that was wrong with the previous order. The tenements symbolized the decline of Dublin under the Union, while British barracks throughout the city were blamed with supplying the brothels' clients. It fell to a Catholic zealot, Frank Duff, founder of the Legion of Mary, to articulate the campaign to close down the district, whose exploited population and crime- and disease-ridden streets were a blight on the image of the new national capital (ibid., 19). The topography of the area, long before its clearance and redevelopment, had worked its way into literature, a metaphor for the unhealthy city unable to support a viable (national) community. In

Figure 6. Bridge Street flats, built in the 1930s. Photograph by author.

Ulysses, published the same year that Ireland achieved autonomy, Joyce concludes the "Nighttown" section with a description of the region: "A drunken navvy grips with both hands the railings . . . lurching heavily. At a corner two night watch in shoulder capes, their hands upon their staff-hoisters, loom tall. A plate crashes; a woman screams; a child wails. Oaths of a man roar, mutter cease. Figures wander, lurk peer from warrens" (1986, 351). Liam O'Flaherty's novel, *The Informer,* employs expressionist techniques—a landscape of shadow and fog—to describe the neighborhood and to capture the intensity of the civil war: "He walked quickly along a narrow passage into a dark lane. The lane was empty. So it appeared at first.

But as Gypo stood hidden in the doorway of an old empty house, piercing the darkness with wild eyes, he heard a footstep. The footstep made him start. It was the first human footstep he had heard, the first sound of his fellow human beings, since he had become an informer... and an outcast" (1925, 22).

Contrary to the notion that de Valera's government was tight-fisted and hostile to the interests of urban workers, it acted as a pragmatic and genuine funder of urban housing. Many previous attempts had been made to tackle bad housing—the 1890 Housing of the Working Classes Act, the 1914 housing inquiry, Cosgrave's million-pound scheme—but none was quite as effective as de Valera's housing drive. Herbert Simms, during his tenure with the corporation, completed the enormous quantity of seventeen thousand units in the city of Dublin (Conroy 1997, 56). The generous loan terms offered by the national government to urban councils made the difference. De Valera's 1932 Housing Act provided a 67 percent subsidy on each unit built, with a maximum of 500 pounds per flat (Roche 1982, 225). Trade union wages were included in the new schemes. The entire project played into de Valera's ideological agenda of placating the grass roots, which meant the industrial working class as much as any mythic, rural, Catholic base.

The Newfoundland Street scheme demonstrated, in a local sense, those modernist energies of "creative destruction"—a phrase coined by Baron von Haussmann and commonly associated with upheavals in contemporary urban life. In 1936 the chief housing officer of Dublin wrote, "The completed scheme provides with dealing with the entire site.... All existing roads, back streets and alleys will be obliterated." To prepare legally for the demolition, a team of health inspectors was called in to declare the district unfit for habitation. Their notes detail the "piggeries, sheds, cottages, and outhouses" that made up the area. Newfoundland Street contained mostly very old two-story cottages, while older Georgian houses, which were woefully overcrowded, needed to be "acquired and cleared." The area was also prone to flooding. The total cost of the clearance was 382,000 pounds. Ambitious in its reach and hopeful in its aims, the scheme to renew these areas, which included providing each new apartment with hot and cold water and electric light, as well as building new schools and playgrounds, demonstrates once again the state's modernizing vision of the city. The dream of nationalism is sovereignty over territory, where a community is brought together and made to thrive through the reorganization of space. In the eyes of officials, by constructing inner-city housing, the state was not only doing away with the rural and impoverished vestiges of the past but abolishing the legacy of colonialism itself.

Newfoundland Street was not the only inner-city redevelopment scheme that was undertaken during these years. On James Street, in the heart of the oldest part of the city, 152 flats were built in 1934 on a site of just under three acres (a density of 53 per acre). In Newmarket, 97 apartments went up. In most of these, we can see the influence of new European public housing, in particular those designs associated with the urban planning ideals of Hendrick Berlage and the architectural expressionism of Michel de Klerk and Piet Kramer in Amsterdam. As Sean Rothery points out, members of Dublin Corporation visited Amsterdam several times during the 1920s and 1930s to learn more about the housing policies of that city. The most significant of these visits occurred in 1925, when Horace O'Rourke, city architect; T. J. Byrne, chief architect with the national Office of Public Works; and W. C. Dwyer, commissioner of the County Borough of Dublin, traveled to Rotterdam and Amsterdam, "at the request of President Cosgrave . . . for the purpose of inspecting different systems there" (Rothery 1991, 150). Between 1875 and 1900, the population of Amsterdam had doubled as a result of migration to the recently industrialized city. A 1902 Dutch Housing Act, introduced by the newly ascendant Social Democrats in Holland, was passed in order to get a grip on the housing crisis and to provide, on a mass scale, housing for those who had come to the city in search of work (Stieber 1998, 20). That housing act allowed Dutch municipalities to intervene in the real estate market—to support, launch, and control housing programs on public land. By 1919, ninety projects had been approved as part of this new legal setup, comprising fourteen thousand flats (ibid., 21). Out of the new constellation of forces in Holland (the rise of mass political parties, the formation of a socialist-oriented government, and the emergence of cultural modernism) came a new generation of modern architects—Oud, Berlage, de Klerk, and Kramer—who were dedicated to the creation of architecture that expressed, as they saw it, working-class consciousness.

The postcolonial Irish administration saw in these European plans an alternative to garden suburb densities and values, and a style of building that embodied nationalism's embrace of both aesthetic and social urban improvement.

The work of Hendrick Berlage in Holland was as much town planning as it was architecture. His designs, as in the case of the New South area of Amsterdam, were conceived as whole neighborhoods as much as individual blocks (Curtis 1982, 162–64). He deplored the deurbanizing tendencies of the English garden city. To the apparent chaos and growth of Amsterdam, Berlage attempted to bring order by creating grand avenues, which in turn were penetrated by secondary systems of roads and squares containing shops, schools, and public institutions. The main units of collective dwelling were organized into "perimeter blocks," which ran around internal courtyards that contained recreational areas and gardens. The buildings were finely detailed in dark brick; arches, windows, and corners "conspired to give the whole area a unity of theme and sobriety of effect, offset by a looser order of trees and pathways" (ibid., 162). The streetscape was tightly regulated. Berlage argued in favor of unity and cohesion. "A beautiful city is not composed of separate entities, but is itself a single entity that becomes a total work of art only when both the plan and the buildings on it have been designed as one" (Stieber 1998, 219). Berlage invested the aesthetic with social power and, in his own words, sought to promote "unity in diversity."[27] Writing in 1908, Berlage linked the pared-down formal language of emerging modernism (he was associated with the functionalist, machine-inspired De Stijl movement) with a politically driven communitarianism. The growth of the workers' movement, he wrote, will mean that "the rational can become the basis" of the new architecture (Whyte 2003, 8). Working through various drafts of his Amsterdam Exchange, he reduced the number of turrets and gables, and eliminated every trace of banded stone. It was this sober modernism that made its way into many of Dublin's flat schemes in the 1930s.

The features of many of Berlage's Amsterdam apartments impressed the visiting members of Dublin Corporation, argues Rothery, and encouraged the promotion of similar modernist techniques at home. Dublin's Thorncastle scheme, for instance, shares the rounded corners of many of the Dutch schemes, and is topped with flat blanket

Figure 7. Thorncastle Street flats, built in the 1930s. Photograph by author.

roofing, synonymous with modernism's quest for uniformity and objectivity (Figure 7). Aligned along the length of a street, in a solidly working-class district of the city adjacent to the docks, the strongly horizontal weight of the structure suggests communal living and socialist rationalism. In Thorncastle, few features are superfluous to the function; no ornate details clamor for attention. The only two breaks in the façade are reminiscent of defensive towers or entrances to a walled city, again demonstrating a strong, historical urban style. Several of the new flat complexes, including Townsend Street (1934–36), are organized around a central internal courtyard.

Against the more monumental and functional architecture of Berlage, a second generation of Amsterdam architects, notably Piet

Kramer and Michel de Klerk, designed still functional but now more fanciful public housing units. They took care to add idiosyncratic aesthetic features to the streamlined façades of Berlage. De Klerk, for example, in one of his housing blocks (nicknamed "The Ship") carved out rounded, organic shapes and added peculiar features, such as a superfluous tower with no entrance, to create a more sculptural and even personalized approach to workers' housing. The expressionist branch of the Amsterdam modernists sought to create workers' community, stability, and solidarity through a more sensuous approach to place. These architects tried to mediate between the oncoming wave of international-style modernism and a sense of history that was not imitative of former medieval or romantic styles, which, they believed, had been co-opted by the far right (Stieber 1998, 202). They attempted to express a class consciousness through architectural detail, but in a less heavy-handed way than they saw in their predecessors and in their contemporary colleagues from De Stijl. They broke up the formal street façade with curved windows, projecting eaves and cantilevers, rounded corners, and ornamental brickwork. In Dublin, this strand of aesthetic appears, for example, in the flats at Chancery Place and Henrietta Place. At Chancery, an expressionist, flat-topped archway with art nouveau ironwork greets visitors. A parabolic brick tower and staircase soften the angularity of the buildings. The use of both brick and plasterwork shows how the Dublin projects combined elements of expressionism and modernism. The two-toned brickwork at Henrietta Place, along with the braided effect of the corners, is an attempt to dignify the inhabitants, to acknowledge both aesthetics and a larger social project: the building of working-class community.

The movement for mass housing in Europe catalyzed new patterns of public architectural patronage. The postcolonial Irish state was also keen to participate in this most modern of projects—modern in the architectural sense (as in its material features) and in the political meaning (via its legitimating agenda). The apartment buildings that went up in the historical center of Dublin during the 1930s were intended to instill a sense of pride and continuity in the oldest areas of the city. They remain among the most popular flats in the city, well built and better located than subsequent 1960s public housing. That the southern Irish state remained a relatively stable democracy during the 1930s and 1940s, with few of the demonstrations of militarism that ripped other countries apart, was the result of many factors. But one important element among those reasons was the role played by architecture in trying to win over Dublin's working class, a group that had often been among nationalism's most ardent supporters.

Other architectural forms and urban designs, apart from garden suburbs and modernist-inspired apartment blocks, are a lens through which we can see the ways different social interests projected their values onto the physical landscape, creating a varied topography based on their diverse demands. De Valera's postcolonial nationalism held to a liberal theory of the state, the function of which, he argued, was to avoid "state absolutism, to preside like a father as the dispenser of social justice, to see that the natural resources of the nation were so distributed among private individuals and among the various classes as adequately to secure the common good" (Bew, Hazelkorn, and Patterson 1989, 73). Fianna Fáil sought to fashion a populist hegemony, one that found its spatial corollary in a range of architectural styles. Art deco, full-blown international-style modernism, and variants of neoclassicism further reveal this complicated truth.

Classicism

The classical tradition lived on in Ireland after independence. But even with regard to this most celebratory and monumental of architectural styles, a more subtle reading than has generally been offered is required. Unlike the official buildings of the new northern Irish state, many of the classical structures that were erected in southern Ireland during the 1920s and 1930s were not designed in a full-blown neoclassical style, but rather adopted a stripped-down, more austere version of it. They lacked the decorative and exaggerated motifs—statues of national or mythic figures, large domes, and rows of columns—that characterize traditional neoclassical buildings. In Northern Ireland, for example, the new state, which had been created to guarantee a unionist and British majority, crowned its foundation by constructing the epic and neoclassical Parliament building at Stormont (1927–32). Stormont, impressively placed on a great axial site plan, stamped an air of permanency and historical pomposity on what was, in the eyes of many, an illegitimate and minor statelet. As if compensating for its own insecurities, Stormont, together with its sister building, Belfast City Hall, was a triumphalist statement by its Protestant rulers.

Unlike the northern Irish state, however, the southern administration had a major influence in encouraging a more modest, more functional, and more modern form of classicism. The stripped-down classical style adopted in the first new government building (1935–38) and in Cork City Hall (1935–36), for example, along with several new commercial premises in the center of Dublin, looked as much to the future as to the past (Figure 8). Their flat and plain-stoned faces, more reserved scales, and almost entirely unornamented surfaces point to the development of international-style architecture and, more generally, to modernism, and they refuse to engage in the language of traditional neoclassicism.

In addition to new government buildings, in the construction of the Gresham Hotel in 1925 and the remodeling of Clery's Department Store in the aftermath of the Rising and during the War of Independence, we see the emergence of a new "corporate" classicism that marks the evolution of "imperial" neoclassicism, forming a bridge between it and modernism. Clery's Department Store, which stands at the center of Dublin's primary thoroughfare, had been destroyed during the Rising. Its rebuilding, begun in 1918 and completed in 1920, echoed Daniel Burnham's Selfridge's Building in London (Rothery 1991, 76). The broad, showcase glass fenestration encouraged window-shopping, greater transparency between the street and the interior, and the increased public display of commodities. Standing opposite the General Post Office, Clery's combined classical features, such as Ionic columns, a roof balustrade, and wreath moldings, with the new rationalism of the Chicago style: cast-iron glazing, reinforced structural framing, and a tripartite-storied division consisting of a glass-encased ground floor, a pillared midsection with decorative beaux arts railings, and a top-floor attic for office space and industrial equipment. The building has a flat roof. Clery's international lineage, linking Dublin, Chicago, and London, again highlights how domestic and international histories continued to overlap and fashion an urban space in Ireland, one that combined elements of far-flung modernism with local traditions and patterns of development. (Meeting under Clery's clock has for generations been a

Figure 8. Department of Commerce and Industry, built 1935–38. Photograph by author.

Dublin, indeed an Irish, tradition.) Also constructed on O'Connell Street in a toned-down classical style was the Gresham Hotel (1925), designed by Robert Atkinson. Symbolic of new economic hopes, of consumerism and of tourism, these two buildings, both new and updated, reinstated a mark of grandeur and unimposing elegance at the heart of the nation's capital. The Gresham's façade minimized ornament and blended into the scale of the buildings on either side. It was a confident yet functional statement during a time when the nation was recovering from a period of ideological extremism and militarism. Moreover, the Gresham, long a symbol of Protestant culture in Dublin, represented at least some of that group's commercial commitment to the new regime. These architectural developments were reflective, therefore, not of postindependence Ireland's reactionary tendencies, but of its progressive, even dispassionate, temperament.

In the 1930s the Irish government commissioned its first new office building since independence, notably to house the Department of Industry and Commerce. The structure combined a simpler version of classicism with more upbeat and fashionable art deco elements. The building avoids the monumentalism of many state buildings in other postcolonial countries. The four upper levels of the five-story structure are modernist in their flat, planar, uncarved limestone walls, which are broken only by unobtrusive windows, and the flat roof is modernist as well. An art deco doorway, with its stepped, symmetrical porch, elongated windows, and decorative, angular carvings, is the focal point of the edifice (Figure 8). In the building's centralized location, the government was advocating industry and commerce (carved, expressionist panels along the length of the building detail important Irish industries, such as tobacco, leather, textiles, and mining). And through its blend of architectural styles, the building suggests a view of an era that has several different ideological trends working through it at once. Art deco speaks to an emerging consumerism and leisure-oriented popular culture; stripped classicism connotes authority, history, and tradition; and modernism indicates the search for efficiency, rationality, even technology. A carved keystone of Saint Brendan, who, legend has it, traveled to America in a skin-clad boat in the seventh century, sits above the stretched entranceway. Above the porch lintel is another carving, this time of Lugh, the Celtic sun god, releasing airplanes into the sky: a timely image, since Ireland's first airport was under construction north of the city (Office of Public Works [OPW] 1999, 77). Rather than interpreting this building as others have done, as an exercise in *conservative* classicism, ignoring its modernist elements in favor of its symmetrical, imposing strength, we can more accurately read it as an attempt, expressed through art deco leanings and *streamlined* classicism, to move beyond traditionalism. The building evokes an updated national image, one informed by industrialism, consumerism, and internationalism, and is clearly not cut off from cultural movements elsewhere.

The appearance of a stripped-down version of classicism during the 1920s and 1930s did not mean the death of its grander counterpart—a fully self-conscious and ornate neoclassicism. The remnants of the ascendancy who stayed in Ireland after 1922 saw in classical Georgian architecture a means to preserve and make visible what they regarded as their cultural and historical values: a respect for the principles of the Enlightenment, a distrust of innovation, and a moral assuredness. In several architectural schemes, this weakened class attempted to use the language of classicism, long their signature style, to maintain their presence and influence in changed circumstances. In the politics and planning of the Greater Dublin Reconstruction Movement (GDRM), for example, as well as in the architecture of the World War I Memorial at Islandbridge, one can perceive this former elite's desire to continue to shape the ideology and memory of the postcolonial nation. Both of these plans, to varying degrees, failed. Their failures served to highlight the waning of ornate classicism and the decline of those who had traditionally sponsored it.

The GDRM was organized to oversee the rebuilding of Dublin after 1922. Its members included many of those who had been associated with Patrick Abercrombie's 1914 *Dublin of the Future* plan. After the return of a national parliament, many of the liberal Anglo-Irish figures interested in town planning, along with some more conservative nationalists, continued to push for a major, neoclassically inspired reorganization of the city. The driving forces behind these initiatives were Ernest A. Aston, a leading Dublin businessman; Senator James Moran; Lady Aberdeen; and Frank Mears, Patrick Geddes's son-in-law. In December 1922 the group unveiled their proposals, which received "the general approval" of the government, which regarded them as "a very valuable achievement" (Moran 1923, 43). In the middle of the ongoing Civil War, Aston argued that "young Dublin—young Ireland—literally overflows with energy and ambition. You can then take your part in directing that energy and that ambition from violence and destruction to the noble conception of building up a greater and a better city—at once the symbol and the centre of the new Ireland" (Bannon 1989, 16).

Following the advice of Abercrombie, who was acting as a consultant, the GDRM suggested reallocating all former colonial state buildings to the new administration, rebuilding the destroyed structures in their original Georgian splendor. Dublin Castle was to house the judiciary; the Royal Hospital at Kilmainham was to be the seat of the new Parliament. In a time of continuing unrest, much of it locally coordinated guerrilla attacks, the Reconstruction Committee urged the dismantling of local councils and the centralization of power in the hands of a strong national government: "One problem! One authority," they insisted. "Without central control," wrote Senator Moran, "it will be impossible to prepare or execute a unified scheme of physical reconstruction" (Moran 1923, 43). While elements of the committee's proposals read like an ascendancy wish list, there was also an attempt to broker a compromise of sorts with the new nationalist realities and to integrate Anglo-Irish culture into the larger political framework. The result, however, was a "nativist" and essentialist understanding of what nationalist desires were. Moran pointed out that Kilmainham, an inner-city neighborhood of Dublin, had been the site of an ancient Celtic village and would therefore be an excellent location for the new government (Campbell 1994, 44). Mears felt that the new Catholic cathedral should be placed on a high point overlooking Dublin Castle as a symbolic victory of one regime over the other. The initial enthusiasm about the symbolic and imperious possibilities of Dublin soon dissipated, however. As the movement ran low on funds, government support, too, dried up. It would be wrong to conclude from this, as one critic has done, that "the government lacked empathy with urban culture, which was necessary to invest the city with a new significance and purpose" (ibid.). To suggest this is to promote the singular perspective of a stubborn, unconcerned, and detached regime. Rather, early suburbanization, flat construction, and the appearance of an array of architectural styles reveal a more flexible and open state, one whose officials, although working to maintain government authority, sought to promote a modernizing and nationalist agenda, which, they hoped, would forestall the possibility of dissent. The example of the GDRM indicates the demise of traditional neoclassicism, rather than its persistence. A stripped-down classicism came to prevail over full-blown classicism. This style of architecture, far from looking back to a conservative imperial past, gazed forward to modernism and to international style.

Neoclassicism in Ireland, since the Georgian era, had been adopted to celebrate and demonstrate the link with Britain. After partition in 1922, the northern Irish state maintained this link in a clear and obvious way. In the Irish Free State, this style was more repressed and, when it did appear, more controversial. The new government building in Kildare Street, with its art deco and expressionist features, and new commercial premises such as Clery's and the Gresham, with their flatter, more modernist façades and commercial orientation, express a less impassioned form of classicism, one that highlights the state's more functionalist, corporate, and pragmatic ideology.

Art Deco and International Style

A look at the architecture of art deco during these years suggests a society caught in an interesting space, between provincialism and modernism, between rediscovering its own heritage (language, literature, and history) and exploring the pleasures of imported cultural commodities, most notably film. During the 1930s in Ireland, art deco dominated in the construction of many ornate cinemas and theater halls and lent an international elegance to the state's ongoing project of building schools, post offices, and libraries (O'Leary 1990).

The art deco movement, named after the 1925 "Exposition Internationale des Arts Décoratifs et Industriels Modernes," added glamor and ornamentation to what were often, at base, stripped classical structures. The distinctive stylistic trademarks of the movement were stepped doorways and archways; angular, zigzag chevron carvings and etchings; polished, smooth surfaces; unusual and exotic materials, such as black marble on exteriors and teak and ebony for interiors; elongated windows and columns; metallic lettering; and often superfluous decorative motifs, such as sunbursts and flames. Many influences are brought to bear, critics argue, in art deco: art nouveau (against whose organic and flowing shapes art deco was a reaction); Bauhaus (to whose boxy and rectilinear shapes were added superficial ornament); the world of jazz and cinema (in whose theaters and venues art deco expressed an atmosphere of insouciance). Art deco also echoed the look of contemporary industry—ships and machines. But its buildings often housed the emerging commerce of white-collar business: media conglomerates, hotels, and department stores. Ireland, while never a center of art deco, made its own uses and appropriations of this modernist style, producing a local variant of it.

The most successful rendition in Dublin of art deco was produced by the architectural firm of Robinson & Keefe, well known for its execution of the style. The Dublin Gas Company structure (1928) featured polychromatic tiling and metalwork; stepped, angular ornamentation; and metallic lettering, all of which gives an up-to-the-minute feel, a sense of newness well matched with the building's function—that is, it evokes a sense of cleanliness, functionality, and convenience. In a new nation, driven by dreams of self-sufficiency and progress, the harnessing of natural resources to fuel the country—its industries as well as its parlors—represented confidence. Art deco features were also adopted to ornament and add lightness to institutions of mass democracy. The post office at Rathmines (1934) was commissioned by the Office of Public Works, and it combined stripped classical dimensions with art deco ornament, most significantly the tiered doorway and decorative bronze panels between the vertical windows. The building was constructed of granite, concrete, and marble, while the interior woodwork is teak. A number of libraries constructed during the 1930s to a common Dublin Corporation architectural design again employed extravagant entranceways; the effect is hopeful and negates the current prevailing wisdom about these years.

The primary application of art deco style was in the building of cinemas. Escapist by their very nature, art deco cinemas were lushly ornamented. The ostentatious, jazzy, and exotic traits of art deco were most visible in the interiors of some of Dublin's new cinemas. By the mid-1930s, just about every small town in Ireland had a cinema. Dublin's Theatre Royal seated almost four thousand people, and more notable than its outer art deco features was its famously glamorous interior. Arches and balustrades and a starlit sky on the ceiling produce a lavish, oriental effect as extreme art deco lapses into kitsch. The embellishments, catering to a new mass public, were devoid of highbrow pretensions. The dozens of cinemas built in Ireland during the 1920s and 1930s, along with the romanticism of their interiors and the popularity of cinema-going itself, suggest that postcolonial Ireland was far from puritanical and censorious.

Certainly there were those who complained that the cinema trend was leading toward "moral, artistic, and intellectual degradation" (Fallon 1938, 250). For one Catholic commentator, "the carpeted floors," the "plush" seats, and the "soothing" atmosphere evoked effeminacy, and existed to menace the harder minds of the "nationalist, the economist and the sociologist" (ibid., 248). Such moralizing tirades demonstrate, I suggest, less the accuracy of the conception of a puritan Ireland than the reaction of a minority to the integration of Ireland into a still emerging international order. The use of art deco in the decades after independence in Ireland shows the country's eclectic mixture of tradition and modernity, localism and internationalism. (The Theatre Royal, owned by the Rank Organization, boasted its own version of the Rockettes, the Royalettes.) As with drawings and designs of cinemas elsewhere, images in the Irish press depicted the new buildings at night, ablaze with light, which evoked the modern spirit of a world of nighttime urban leisure. In a whole series of projects, then, Irish architects and developers, both public and private, engaged art deco and its emergence from American popular culture, modern French design, and the growing world of global commerce.

In the 1920s a new approach to architecture and urban planning burst onto the scene in Europe and America. The architects who employed international style, as it came to be known after 1932, prided themselves on a rejection of previous national and historical styles. (The use of the term *international* represented a widening of communities and an end of nationalism.) Led by Le Corbusier, Walter Gropius, and Mies van der Rohe, a new generation of politically motivated architects strove, between the wars, to create a functional, pragmatic, and socially committed architecture. Their brand of design stressed volume rather than mass, standardization of parts, regularity of surfaces, and function instead of ornament. The straight line was the new source of beauty. Flat roofs, white planar walls, cubist forms, large areas of glazing, and open planning became their signature. The use of reinforced concrete, steel frames, and prefabricated elements revealed the movement's embrace of industrialism.

"The house is a machine for living in," Le Corbusier states at the beginning of *Towards a New Architecture*. Apartments—"cells," he would call them—would be mass-produced in his ideal city: "We must arrive at the 'house-machine,' which must be both practical and emotionally satisfying and designed for a succession of tenants" (1946, 13). He had little time for idiosyncrasy, and the paternalism and arrogance of such statements are, today, hard to bear. International-style modernism was not just architecture and urban planning, it was sociology. The practitioners of international-style modernism saw themselves as objective social critics who believed that their architecture was capable of solving inequality by approaching the production of space with a new set of principles: functionalism, industrialization, and a universal aesthetic stripped of all regional references.

Ireland stood amid these developments. International style was covered in the architectural press and was favorably received; lively debate surrounded this radical form. In a 1938 review of an exhibition by the Modern Architectural Research group (the British equivalent of the Congrès Internationaux d'Architecture Moderne [CIAM]), architectural critic John O'Gorman commends both the political underpinnings and material execution of international style. "Architecture has been liberated from those purely artificial considerations of 'style' which had dominated it since the Renaissance."[28] Architects such as Mies, Gropius, and Le Corbusier, O'Gorman writes, "take this ugly muddled world . . . [and] endeavour to build Utopia." Manning Robertson, another noted Irish architectural critic, commented regularly on the "new architecture." His 1925 book, *Laymen and the New Architecture,* appeared two years before the English translation of Le Corbusier's *Towards a New Architecture* and made note of contemporary trends in Europe, from Dutch expressionism to Nordic romanticism. In a chapter called "Ireland's Mistake," Robertson condemns the aping of British suburban housing—"villa architectura"—in Ireland, and asks that architects bear in mind an older, "freer native style," which included the "castle keep: the compact rectangular block . . . plain, uncompromising . . . blunt and Puritanical" (1925, 163). Irish vernacular, he seemed to be suggesting, was modernist all along. In the 1930s Robertson's book was attacked by the British critic Reginald Blomfield for describing modernism as "youthful." Robertson, in Blomfield's view, proposes that the architect be "a purveyor of thrills" and that he is free "to follow the notorious example of the cubists, the vorticists... anything to startle" (1934, 6). "Robertson," Blomfield continues, "says that the new architecture should be efficient... that it should aim 'at the sensational and dramatic... and that there should at present only be one style, that of the present'" (4). But modern architecture, Blomfield insists, is nothing but a "gigantic box... erected for the purposes of trade.... It assumes that there can be an architecture which cuts right adrift from the past... an idea about as valuable as Esperanto. We cannot dissociate ourselves from the past" (11–14).

Page Dickinson was Ireland's foremost defender and promoter of the style. Soon after independence, he expressed fear that Ireland would retreat into a simple, essentialized world, in terms of both culture and architecture. During his architectural training, he states, "round towers were discussed at length; the Irish Romanesque given a great deal of consideration... and everything of a Gaelic nature given great prominence in the young energies of our time."[29] (He sardonically suggested that abusing cormorants, something he had watched young boys do when he was growing up in the west of Ireland, be integrated into the national games, for it was "a more national sport than Rugby.") By 1937 Dickinson had focused this diffuse anxiety into a positive embrace of international style—a potential guarantee that his fears would not be realized. "There is to-day in the new architecture a cry for straight lines and simple masses—a cry for an honest expression of purpose and material. This seems to be an excellent thing," Dickinson writes.[30] At the same time, his early fears were proven to be naive and one-dimensional: the construction of a host of new buildings in the international style in Ireland during the 1930s, including many new state hospitals, suggests an eagerness on the part of the government to present a modern, functional, and efficient image (Figures 9 and 10). Some of the most famous and dramatic examples of international-style architecture and urban planning can be found in postcolonial countries, most notably Oscar Niermeyer's design for Brasília and Le Corbusier's plan for Chandigarh. In countries where recent and painful colonial legacies give rise to a dual desire to remember and forget, international style shouts boldly and unsubtly that forgetting will prevail.

Figure 9. Portlaoise Hospital, front view. Photograph courtesy of Gandon Editions.

But in doing so, it draws attention to the very act of erasure. It is not surprising, therefore, that international style found a ready home in Ireland in the 1920s and 1930s, since it is a material symptom of the deeper anxiety of a country caught between the yearning to be normal, modernized, and developed, and the equally powerful emotional pull not to escape its cultural roots and identity.

A private home, constructed adjacent to Joyce's Tower at Sandycove, has come retroactively to symbolize the "introduction of modern architecture to Ireland" (Olley 1997, 114). The building, called Geragh, was completed in 1937 by Michael Scott and was one of the first structures in the country to use mass concrete throughout. The three stories evoke the maritime imagery of luxury liners, which Le Corbusier had hailed as a model for modern architecture. If people were happy to pay to live in such streamlined, efficient, and standardized units at sea, Le Corbusier thought, then surely these conditions were good enough for life on land. Geragh's flat rooftops and planar, white walls are treated like a series of decks, each with railings and portholes. One end of the structure, with a descending series of circular bays and crescent balconies, resembles the ship's stern. True to

Figure 10. Portlaoise Hospital, rear view. Photograph courtesy of Gandon Editions.

Le Corbusier's fetishization of *pilotis,* the whole building stands atop stilts. Scott, who designed the home for his family, went on to become Ireland's most famous architect and the country's leading proponent of modernism. In 1937, as president of the Architectural Association, he brought Gropius to Dublin. "The Bauhaus," Scott believed, "was a remarkable event in the history of architecture and it had a dramatic effect on the whole creative world. When I became aware of it I really began to understand what I was doing. It was a marvelous period with Le Corbusier, Gropius and, of course, Mies— it was the re-introduction of classical architecture in our time."[31]

In Europe, the architects of the international style (and Bauhaus) were preoccupied with the social aspects of design, attempting to find an architectural form that could express the ethos of the time: objectivity, progress, and industrialization. Gropius and Le Corbusier made no secret of their avant-garde tendencies. With the dissolution of the Bauhaus in 1933, proponents of international style went either to England or America. Gropius and Mies ended up in America. There, by contrast, international style tended to reflect more capitalist tendencies: office buildings (Seagram Building) and upscale homes (in California). In Ireland the situation differed. The country neither enjoyed a wealthy client base, commercial or individual, nor possessed the violent ideological extremes of Europe in the 1930s. International style became a state-sponsored movement, as the postcolonial government used it for the construction of a series of public projects, including factories, hospitals, and Dublin airport. In the combination of large, state-funded public works and rational, efficient, modern architecture, one can see the populist hopes of a postcolonial government attempting to make up for decades of underdevelopment. The majority of the work the government commissioned Michael Scott to produce was for public bodies: the state-owned transport company, state theaters, and the Irish exhibit at the New York World's Fair in 1939. Under de Valera's strict guidance of the economy, international-style architecture was an attempt to build what the free market had failed to produce in Ireland's historically stagnant economy. One can see in de Valera's ambitions both an authoritarianism that never fully slipped into the dictatorship of other countries at the time, and a kind of corporate socialism that attempted to import and impose a brand of modernization that would provide mass employment; efficient, industrial production; and an entrée into the burgeoning world market. Culturally, too, international style is a self-confident form, an attempt to overcompensate for a postcolonial national psychology of self-doubt, insecurity, and the attendant failures of the country to solve emigration and underdevelopment.

Many structures that went up in Ireland in the 1930s demonstrate this combination of design and ideology. In 1935 de Valera's government commissioned the Dutch architect, J. D. Postma, to construct a series of alcohol factories across rural Ireland as part of its commitment to decentralize industry, modernize the countryside, and establish national self-sufficiency. Built between 1935 and 1938, Bauhaus-style structures—large, cubic masses with white-paneled walls, flat concrete roofs, and narrow horizontal windows—became symbols of the machine age in rural Ireland (Rothery 1991, 204). Also during the 1930s, the state constructed eleven new public hospitals, all of which are still used today; their designs employed the language of international style, including sun balconies to produce a bright, clean, and contemporary image (O'Sheehan and de Barra 1940). Vincent Kelly, Joseph Downes, and Scott were the main beneficiaries of these large state contracts. Scott's hospital at Tullamore (1934–37), while strongly horizontal and symmetrical, is fronted with limestone and lined with arched windows on its lower floor. A glass, industrial stairwell contrasts with the building's more traditional massing material. A round entrance bay is reminiscent of Dutch expressionism. Indeed, Scott describes his travels to Holland at this time and recounts how he was inspired by J. P. Oud and his "use of brickwork" (1995, 71). It was only after this trip, Scott writes, that he "became aware of Le Corbusier, Gropius and the Bauhaus." The modernist trend in hospital architecture was repeated across the state, at Tipperary, Kilkenny, and Monaghan, reinforcing the movement toward modern state welfare. Another large state project that drew heavily on international style was Dublin airport.

Commissioned after the establishment of a national airline, the terminal building is considered the most important prewar modern building in Ireland: its convex shape functions to serve the maximum number of planes with the least space, while the curved arms of the plan sweep backward, expressive of flight (Figure 11). Designed by a team of Office of Public Works architects, led by Desmond Fitzgerald, the airport, true to the Bauhaus spirit, was a work of "total design." All furniture, fittings, even forks and spoons, were created specifically for this venue. The 1939 New York World's Fair provided another opportunity for de Valera's government to promote Ireland on the world stage. The theme of the exposition was "A New World of Tomorrow," and it was dedicated to displaying "a fuller, happy existence for the average man."[32] The government approached Scott again to create the design. He was keen to design "a modern building of our time," and one that "25 million Irish-Americans could connect with" (1995, 95). Scott rejected obvious allusions to indigenous architecture, which, he said, did not exist after the twelfth century: "all the rest was influenced one way or another by outside

Figure 11. Dublin airport, built 1937–41. Photograph courtesy of Robert Allen.

sources" (ibid.). "At first," he stated, "I honestly did not know how to portray Ireland through a building. . . . What, I thought, is a 'national' style? As far as I was concerned the only thing that makes a style national are the materials, the climate, and the function. I mean, can you have a national medicine?"[33] Scott later hit on the idea of a three-story structure in the shape of a shamrock, which could be recognized from the air, in keeping with the exhibition's theme of "the world of tomorrow." Consisting of glass curtain walls and beams of steel, with flat gables and roof, the building took a traditional Irish symbol and updated it in the international style for a global audience of consumers. Scott's work beat out competing designs by Alvar Aalto of Finland and Niemeyer of Brazil.

The arrival of international style in Ireland during the 1930s proves that postcolonial Ireland was not in thrall to a simple, essentialist interpretation of culture and history. Rather, international-style architecture, along with simultaneous urban developments such as inner-city housing that drew on Dutch expressionism, as well as garden suburbs and art deco, reveals the hopes and tensions in the political, and literal, landscape. That these innovative architectural forms were made concrete in Ireland during the 1920s and 1930s exposes the most literal of agendas: the government sought to build a bridge between the rhetoric of traditionalism and idealism, and the pragmatic urgency of building a state and winning the consent of its citizens.

It may currently be popular to see only the negative cultural and economic effects of independence in the Irish Free State. After all, the contemporary success of the Celtic Tiger highlights how long it took for today's confidence, entrepreneurialism, and internationalism to appear after a long, dark, bleak period. Such a view, however, ignores the complexity of the time, overlooking potentially progressive attempts to win hegemony from different social groups and classes in favor of interpreting these decades one-dimensionally. This perspective offers a one-sided theory of nationalism, which, from the standpoint of the present, sees in its rhetoric and actions only the cause of current sectarianisms and economic failures. In evaluating not the traditional arts and areas typically used to understand this time, but rather its architecture, I have argued that Ireland stood squarely in the midst of international debates over the appropriate mode of expression for living in a new and modern time. Ireland engaged European and American debates over the hopes and limitations of an industrial present, but its leaders, thinkers, architects, and citizens were also forced to contend with the legacy of colonialism on top of these usual debates.

What distinguished Irish modernity from its European counterpart were the ways in which, in Ireland, European culture and discourse clashed with colonialism and its nationalist counterforce. When international architectural influences were used in Ireland, they were justified in terms of nationalism. When the postcolonial state experimented with suburban housing, it was a deliberate and self-conscious attempt to rectify the evils of the tenement system, which had always been perceived as a direct legacy of nineteenth-century colonial government. The postindependence Irish state was a product of nationalism. And nationalism was not, as more recent critics have asserted, a purely sectarian and atavistic ideology. Like modernity itself, nationalism is caught in its own contradiction. Its purveyors look to the future, to progress, while often conjuring romantic and historical images. The past inspires the future, and the future is fought for to rectify the wrongs of history. In Irish architectural modernism, we see this ambiguity reflected in style, location, and purpose. Irish modernity is a suburban housing estate constructed in 1929, with ancient Celtic street names such as Monasterboice and Clonmacnoise, inhabited by an eclectic mix of new residents—Dublin's indigenous working class and newly arrived rural migrants. Irish modernity is the new government office built for the Department of Industry and Commerce in 1939: St. Brendan the Navigator looking down over an art deco porch. And Irish modernity is slum clearance: tenements replaced by ambitious inner-city housing flats that run the length of the street.

The government that came into being in 1922, and which de Valera inherited in 1932, was born in violent and unstable circumstances. But Ireland, unlike many of the new nations that would claim independence from Britain in later decades, remained a fairly stable democracy. In the production of space through the 1920s and 1930s, we see the concrete manifestation of the hopes and perils of a new democracy. Architecture played a role in attempting to reconcile tensions within that new society, to heal fractures that existed along class, religious, regional, and ideological lines. In suburbanization, we see the hope of creating a civilized and prosperous middle class, one that would provide a better life for newly arrived rural immigrants and for Dublin's traditionally poorly housed inner-city working class. Suburbs were also an attempt to heal the rift between country and city, creating a city in the garden. Likewise, each of the other styles that found concrete expression in Ireland during these years spoke to an immediate need. International-style architecture, born out of the German Bauhaus movement, found a ready home in Ireland in the new factories and hospitals built by de Valera's populist government, eager to make amends for centuries of underdevelopment. The use of art deco by the state, and its large-scale employment by private contractors who built cinemas across the country, reflects an engagement with leisure, wealth, and American popular culture: a whole way of being that contradicts contemporary conventional wisdom about the era. Architecture shows us in a most material manner that the "bleak" years of postcolonial, postindependence Ireland were a time when conflicting and varied interests found their needs met and their hopes expressed via a literal claim on a contested landscape.

3 | Revisionism in Ireland: A Historical and Spatial Project

Ideological Shifts and Urban Change in 1960s Dublin

Nineteen sixty-six marked the fiftieth anniversary of the Irish Revolution. That year also saw the erection of Ireland's first residential tower blocks at Ballymun, an open and windswept site on the outermost northern fringes of Dublin city (Figure 12). The construction there of more than three thousand units in seven fifteen-story structures was, at the time, Europe's largest industrial contract, and the planned population of sixteen thousand was bigger than most regional Irish towns. When the Royal Institute of British Architects held its annual conference in Dublin in 1966 (two years before the collapse of Ronan Point in east London), government officials and private industry promoted Ireland's first modernist housing project as the exciting solution to the city's housing needs. The minister for local development, Neil Blaney, accepting the advice of the National Building Agency, agreed that Ireland had to build at least one tower block-housing estate.[1] This would be crucial if the country were to take part in the postwar European program of modernization. Ballymun, begun in 1965, was to be completed in three years, showcasing the ability of the latest industrial technology to provide cheap and accessible public housing.[2] Although attempts had been made throughout the 1930s and 1940s to eliminate Dublin's tenements, slums still

Figure 12. Ballymun. Photograph courtesy of National Library of Ireland.

persisted. This project, which would produce 3,021 units, would eradicate the problem once and for all, while simultaneously freeing up space in the city for the ever-expanding offices of the state.

To rationalize production and minimize cost, the British contractor Cubitts Haden Sisk established a factory on twenty acres adjacent to the building site. There, Irish workers mass-produced the prefabricated concrete slabs—floors, panels, and walls—which were then easily transported, moved into place, and connected together. According to the original plan, drawings of the final product displayed a happy, communal scene: well-dressed children in school playgrounds, landscaped grounds; "the town centre will be only a few minutes walk from the dwellings along the pedestrian paths. It will be designed to include within one complex . . . shops, . . . meeting halls, dance hall, clinic, library, swimming pool, bowling alley and perhaps a small cinema" (Cubitts Haden Sisk 1966, 1.1). It was a daring symbol of improvement in a city pursuing progress and attempting to compensate for years of underdevelopment. In May 1966, as part of the official commemoration of the Easter Rising, in a patriotic flourish, Dublin Corporation decided that the seven tower blocks would be named after the signatories of the original 1916 Proclamation of an Irish Republic. Of course, nobody imagined then that the great leap forward in housing would turn out to be an enormous failure. In one twelve-month period in the late 1970s, the corporation had to deal with twenty-five hundred complaints due to vandalism, equipment failures, and crime. A decade earlier, however, the future had looked bright: the international style of architecture—flat, concrete, rational—had successfully been harnessed, it seemed, to a new national narrative of economic and state modernization. A younger generation of indigenous planners, bureaucrats, and economists had begun, through the 1960s, to attract foreign investment to a country that since independence had emphasized the primacy of native control over economic life. Once again, architecture and urban planning were at the forefront of these attempts to produce a new national project, more viable, industrial, and cosmopolitan. The production of space would mirror the major rewriting of nationalist history that would take place along with this architectural overhaul.

Critiquing Postcolonial Nationalism

The 1960s are said to have been the moment when the Irish republic first embraced foreign capital and opened up to international cultural influences. In 1959, the state launched a series of five-year plans aimed at industrializing and urbanizing the still predominantly rural Irish economy. In 1961 the government applied for membership in the European community. In 1962 television became nationally available. These modernizing forces required and produced not only a refashioning of urban space and a move away from national sovereignty, but also a push toward bigger and more cosmopolitan cities and a retelling of the nationalist narrative.

Many commentators—journalists, economists, state officials, and others—with the perspective of later decades have regarded the 1960s as watershed years in the transition of postcolonial Ireland from an isolationist, conservative, monolithic nation into what is now commonly referred to as "modern Ireland," an Ireland that is by implication different from an old, or at least not-so-modern, Ireland. Francis Mulhern, for example, argues that "the phrase 'modern Ireland'... began to take shape from the sixties, after the abandonment of autotelic nationalism" (1998, 21). David Lloyd points to "Ireland's rapid transition through the 1960s and 1970s" (1999, 86). Luke Gibbons charts cultural changes during those years "against a wider economic backdrop which saw a shift from agriculture to industry" (1996, 83). Joseph Lee, in his best-selling work, *Ireland, 1912–85,* heaps praise on Seán Lemass, who became Taoiseach in 1959, for initiating a series of five-year plans (1959–73) aimed at attracting international capital and companies to Ireland, promoting the growth of industry, and creating a new entrepreneurial class. For Lee, the Lemass years signaled a break with the policies of self-sufficiency that had been pursued by the Irish state since 1921. His book assaults the achievements of postindependence Ireland, a revisionist move that, by the time he was writing in 1989, had become increasingly fashionable.[3] In the course of six hundred pages, Lee purposefully focuses on the postcolonial state's inability to stem emigration, its reinforcement of Unionist fears and its acceptance of partition, and, most of all, its failures in economic policy (consistent low growth, high unemployment, few exports). He stresses these failings in order to highlight the era of Lemass as the first serious attempt by the state to move beyond the jaded rhetoric of autarkic nationalism, the cultural language of Gaelic nativism, the frugal fiscal policies of self-reliance, and the territorial notions of sovereignty that had defined the postcolonial state. These isolationist aspects of the national project, according to Lee, were traditional and outmoded ideologies. He, along with a new generation of thinkers who had not grown up in the shadow of the revolution, saw them as irrelevant, even dangerous, for a modernizing society, which, from the 1960s on, had decided to embrace global capital as the solution to its economic woes.

To solve Ireland's persistent woes, Lemass chose to pursue the development policies advocated by the banking and academic proponents of what, by the 1950s, had come to be known as modernization theory: Western promotion of urbanization, mass consumption, and industrialization in the decolonizing nations of Africa, Asia, and Latin America. Lemass, who had served as de Valera's minister of finance for many years, was, by the late 1950s, intent on reversing his former leader's policies of protectionism and tariffs. "It is unlikely," he said in 1957, "that we will get...development on a significant scale without linking up with external firms with ample financial and technical resources and established connections to the world's markets" (Bew and Patterson 1982, 120). Citing Asian economic growth and development, he argued that "the swift advance of Japan to be a modern industrial state is a striking example of what can be achieved by standing on other people's shoulders....But this exploitation of foreign brains is made more difficult by the nature of Irish nationalism" (Bew and Patterson 1982, 122). Lemass's answer to the perennial problem of how to create a viable Irish industry was, accordingly, a fairly predictable, Keynesian one: greater state investment and planning (overseen by the United Nations and other supervisory institutions), tax concessions to foreign financiers, and government grants to those companies engaged in manufacture and export.

Lee's perception was that Ireland had, since independence, become hopelessly cut off from the European mainstream, that it had gotten stuck somewhere between the first and third worlds and needed, at all costs, to find its way back into the family of developed, capitalist nations. For the advocates of modernization theory, the reorganization of the city—involving development planning, international-style corporate architecture, and a vast new program of suburbanization— was a key element in the effort to industrialize and to reshape the attitudes of a reluctant and inward-looking population. David Thornley, an up-and-coming political scientist who was closely associated with the new generation of modernizers, hoped, as much as predicted, "that the depopulation of the countryside will continue...and that our social habits and our politics will take on a flavour that is ever more urban....And this in turn will sound the death-knell of the attempt to preserve any kind of indigenous Gaelic folk culture in these islands" (1964, 16). During the 1960s and 1970s the state poured massive amounts of money into planning and redeveloping an urban infrastructure in Dublin. These new roads, towns, and industrial renovations, it was hoped, would provide the kind of space capable of (re)producing an urban workforce and, as a consequence, an ever more cosmopolitan society exposed to outside cultural influences. The theory pursued by Lemass and his administration relied, as modernization theories always have, on the contrast between traditional/rural and modern/urban values.[4] The United Nations played its necessary reformist role, too, in promoting this physical and psychological shift from rural to urban life. Beginning in 1960, Lemass's government requested UN help in the process of "redeveloping cleared central areas" (Abrams 1961, v). By 1964 a team of UN officials, working in conjunction with the state's new planning agency, An Foras Forbartha, was producing reports on everything from tourism to heritage to urban renewal and the location of new towns. "If Ireland is to become increasingly [a]...liberal trading nation," wrote one of these New York–based developers, "her economy must inevitably be based on manufacturing industry. . . . [T]he prosperity in any region is a function of its urban centres" (Copcutt 1967, 18).

Refashioning an economy always requires reshaping personal attitudes and social values, and the changes to the collective national psychology sought by Lemass are what Lee finds appealing about attempts to "open up" Irish society in the 1960s. Throughout this period Lemass and his supporters would often fault the lack of initiative shown by the Irish bourgeoisie: "I am not satisfied that native enterprise has made an all out effort to expand and develop industry," stated J. Brennan, a parliamentary ally of Lemass (Bew and Patterson 1982, 125). Lee's own book concludes with a discussion of national character, those moral values on which the state is built and citizenship constructed. Given the lack of social and economic mobility in Ireland during the nineteenth century, he argues, it is little wonder that a disposition toward stability, security, and social ritual should have persisted until quite recently. The combination of economic, marital, and mobility patterns, Lee explains, meant that Ireland had more than its fair share of individuals suffering from thwarted ambition, frustrated hopes, and shattered ideals. Envy, jealousy, and spite were rampant in "traditional" Ireland, he maintains. There was nothing unique to Ireland in that. But these qualities were now perceived to be so central to the Irish way of life that the Irish devised their own word to describe the resultant personality type, the begrudger. In Ireland, "winners could flourish only at the expense of losers" (Lee 1989, 646). So it comes as no surprise to learn that what the Irish have lacked, and what has held back their economic development at home, is a work ethic, or, as Lee puts it, a "performance" ethic. This is to be contrasted with the distinguishing feature of a traditional society, the "possessor principle"—that is, the prizing of security above all. The objective in Ireland, Lee reminds us, was, until recently, the landing of "permanent and pensionable" employment, the achievement of an institutional position, most often the civil service, in which seniority, not individual initiative, became the criterion for promotion (ibid., 394).

The possessor principle, the distinguishing trait of postcolonial Irish society, is a "direct inheritance from traditional Ireland," with its obsessive attachment to the land and security of tenure (Lee 1989, 395). The persistence of traditional values, however, has led to an abhorrence of risk taking, innovation, and ambition. Acting as a drag on modernity, tradition—the indigenous propensity for mediocrity and tenancy at all costs—has held Ireland back from developing an entrepreneurial middle class, which, as Lee believes, Lemass worked so hard to build up during the 1960s. In Lemass, Lee sees a leader who insisted that the Irish would have to change their sense of injured innocence if they were to have a better future. "The economic survival of this country depends entirely on our own efforts," Lemass said (Lee 1989, 400). The essentialist critique of postcolonial society Lee offers was, by the time he was writing in 1989, quite commonplace in parts of the decolonizing world (V. S. Naipaul in India; Camus in Algeria), but Lee was a primary purveyor of this message in Ireland.[5]

In tracing the evolution of Western societies, sociologists from Durkheim to Weber to Parsons all set up the basic juxtaposition of particular social roles and assumptions based on the difference between traditional and modern, a difference that, as they see it, manifests itself as rural and urban life. Durkheim phrases this as the comparison between "mechanical" and "organic" solidarity (Williams 1983, 229). In other words, there are two opposing cultures: one is rooted in the stability of small-scale, communal, village-like life, in which one's social status is defined by one's birth; the other is a more multilayered environment, mobile and merit-based. For Max Weber, rationalization became the dominant principle under industrial capitalism, with the values of profit and efficiency turning "peasants into labourers" (1985, 67) and idlers into frugal earners (68). *Gemeinschaft* and *gesellschaft* are Ferdinand Tönnies's key terms for this concept. In his preface to *The Modernization of Irish Society, 1848–1918* (1983), Lee suggests that modernization ought to be immune from the "parochial preoccupations" that are implicit in the "more emotive concepts" of "gaelicization and Anglicization." The main attraction of "modernization" is the "decline of deference based on inherited status, and the growth of functional specialization" (ibid.). He begins his later book, *Ireland, 1912–1985,* with a defense of his historiographical approach. The present generation of scholars, he writes, has been given the responsibility to "inculcat[e] a more mature attitude" in the population toward Anglo-Irish relations. Quoting other historians to support his quest for a more up-to-date brand of history writing, he advocates "exorcis[ing] passion from the study of the Irish past," which had so often been used merely to "stir old grievances" (1989, xiv). Such an approach will not satisfy everyone, he acknowledges, for "the market for truth is a finite one" (xiii). Lee's language clearly opposes former emotion, naïveté, and ideology to contemporary objectivity, maturity, and truth. His commercial metaphor further reveals a series of connections, which, for the modernizers, is a truism: that the mutual overhaul of economic, historical, and national principles is required for an individualistic and liberal culture to emerge from a history defined by a "protracted struggle for sovereignty" (xiii).

Lee is not alone in constructing the 1960s in Ireland as the decade during which an official critique of the social trajectory of postcolonial Ireland began to develop. If the focus of Lee's analysis is the economic policies of modernization proposed by Lemass, then Terence Brown, in his book *Ireland: A Social and Cultural History, 1922 to the Present,* draws our attention to concurrent social changes and cultural advancements that exposed Ireland in the 1960s to foreign influences and pressures. By 1967, 80 percent of households owned televisions. While two-thirds of the original programming was home-produced, by the mid-1970s this pattern had reversed itself, with the vast majority of shows being of American and British origin.

Brown argues, accordingly, that this created "a sense of Ireland as firmly within the British commercial sphere of influence" and helped to spread the "new attitudes and values of urban consumerism" (1985, 200). (Ireland's first shopping mall opened at Stillorgan in 1966, the same year, as we shall see, that the state promoted another round of mass suburbanization on the city's northern and western fringes.) Brown also highlights other momentous changes that took place and that, for him, signaled the demise of "traditional" Ireland and its constraining ideologies. Applying for membership in the European Community in 1961 linked "economic resurgence within the economic orbit of the United Kingdom and Europe to Irish patriotic instincts" (Brown 1985, 189). The religious reforms of the Second Vatican Council—the stressing of social teaching, the restructuring of the Church's hierarchy, and the promoting of religious tolerance—were implemented between 1962 and 1965. Planning, the managerial buzzword of the period, had become a synonym for rational, efficient, and standardized industrial production for many countries reconstructing their economies in the aftermath of World War II. So, in Ireland, Brown tells us, the Economic and Social Research Institute was founded in 1961 to provide state functionaries with the latest data on employment, the market, and national economic performance.

The 1960s saw not only the advent of increased state intervention in the planning of the economy, but also the rise of a closely related physical planning—a site of revisionist activity overlooked by most commentators. The production of rational and efficient space was seen as central to the formation of capital and, hence, to the creation of a commercially thriving bourgeoisie. Developers, architects, corporations, and government departments reorganized Dublin during the 1960s and 1970s to implement their own brand of modernization, one that took on the legacy of populist nationalism for being old-fashioned and threatening to the demands of international business. In 1959 the National Building Center opened with Michael Scott, Ireland's leading modernist architect, as chairman. The aims of the founders of the new center, as stated in the first editorial of its magazine, *Forgnán*, were to encourage the use of "new materials and labor-saving building equipment and machinery."[6] The editors continued: "An old nation, a new state, squeezed into part of a small island, dominated by its agricultural industry, has begun to build, to expand its cities, to think in terms of factory production, processing and assembly of goods. The Common Market is providing the drama. The tariff walls are being undermined: nations are going to learn that the only effective substitute for Protection is Attack." In the same issue, one of Ireland's leading economists and a future Taoiseach, Garrett Fitzgerald, wrote of how the bulk of construction during the whole postwar decade was "unproductive": "We built houses, hospitals and schools,—but not factories or offices. . . . We succumbed to the malady to which democracies are prone—over-emphasis on 'social' investment at the expense of productive investment."[7] The 1960s were to change all that.

In 1963 the Local Government (Planning and Development) Act became law, creating eighty-seven planning authorities, each of which was required to prepare development plans for its region, dealing with zoning, traffic, circulation, and the renewal of obsolete areas. In May 1964, An Foras Forbartha, the National Institute for Physical Planning and Construction Research, was established as a state agency with UN assistance to "undertake research into and provide training in and advance knowledge of the physical planning and development of cities, towns and rural areas" (Bannon 1989, 132). (In 1960 Charles Abrams, the American planning expert, was appointed UN consultant to the Irish government.) The moves toward a more free-market economy heavily dependent on international capital saw two concurrent planning discourses emerge and mutually support each other. The first was the rise of economic planning, forecasting, and statistics gathering. A whole series of books produced during the 1960s espoused a new kind of managerial and technocratic approach to analyzing Ireland's economic infrastructure: *Planning in Ireland* (Fitzgerald 1968), *Development Planning in Ireland* (Donaldson 1966), and *Spatial Planning in the Small Economy: A Case Study of Ireland* (O'Neill 1971). This new discourse elevated its thinkers into experts who performed the dual role of intellectual and state functionary—ostensibly outside the realm of emotion and ideology. David Thornley, for example, wrote that the "science" of statistics was flourishing, and advocated a social and economic program formed "deep below the surface of politics, in a creative dialogue between a group of first-class non-partisan administrators and a handful of politicians who had enough courage and commonsense to recognize stark necessity when they saw it" (1964, 17). The second planning discourse was the growth of new trade journals. *Forgnán,* along with *Build,* whose subtitle distinguishes it as the "Journal of the Industry Incorporating 'Irish Architect and Contractor,'" promoted the latest in technical and functional approaches to the new corporate and business headquarters in Dublin. These pseudoscientific, supposedly nonideological, and highly pragmatic discourses soon began to make their physical mark.

In 1961 Ireland got its first new town at Shannon, a remote townland on the western seaboard. Initially consisting of thirteen apartment blocks, the development also included ten "American-style" houses—a group of identical wood-frame boxes with attached garages, arranged around a horseshoe-shaped cul-de-sac, that constituted a parody of suburban America. Their two stories and high eaves bizarrely contrast with the adjacent stone cottages dotting the wind-swept Irish coastline. Ten matchboxes stuck awkwardly and artlessly into the bog, this development is nothing more than a contrived attempt to yank Ireland into the twentieth century. The population soon grew to ten thousand people, drawn there by the expansion of Shannon airport and its associated industries. Beyond the laying out of a new town, the government pioneered several initiatives in Shannon aimed at promoting free trade—notably, the creation of a custom-free zone, the first in the world to lift taxes on the importation of raw materials for the manufacture of goods in the area, and the building of a new, grid-patterned industrial estate to accommodate foreign companies. The Shannon scheme further grew in size as the number of transatlantic tourists to Ireland increased. Tourists were lured by the ever greater marketing skills of Bord Fáilte, the Irish tourist board, which promoted the remote West as a beautiful and unspoiled paradise. Of course, this image contrasted, as the artist Robert Ballagh pointed out, with the other picture of Ireland, represented by the Shannon scheme itself, of the country as a "modern, progressive, go-ahead capitalist society," at the cutting edge of international trade (Gibbons 1996, 86). The two notions could be reconciled, however, if one thought of Ireland as leading the way in the postmodern economic model of industrialization without urbanization. For Brown, though, Shannon, with its experimental attempts at fostering international free trade, was "another primary symbol

of the new Ireland" and a welcome addition to the arsenal of ideologies and new practices ready to condemn traditional Ireland and
its outmoded philosophies (Brown 1985, 201).

The 1960s saw the establishment of new towns in Ireland (especially on the western outskirts of Dublin city), the building of hundreds of modernist office blocks in the capital, the destruction of
many of Dublin's Georgian houses, and the construction of vast,
low-density suburbs around Dublin to cater to an expanding and industrializing economy. The state's adoption of modernist planning
and architecture had international as well as local motivations. The
international context was that of the Cold War, postwar economic
expansion, and the creation of a network of new international alliances—NATO, the EEC, and the UN. If Ireland were to participate in some or all of these initiatives, the national economy would
have to be modernized. The local motivations behind urban change
in Dublin during the 1960s and 1970s were questions about the
achievements of nationalism, posed fifty years after independence.
Such reconsiderations of nationalism were not new, of course. They
had been lodged, notably by Irish writers, since the 1930s and
1940s. But the fiftieth anniversary of the Irish revolution, along with
Lemass's drive toward internationalism, as well as the outbreak of
the Troubles in the North toward the end of the decade, helped popularize these debates.

Interestingly, architectural magazines and building journals weighed
in with evaluations of postcolonial success and failure. In 1966, for
example, an article in *Build* magazine reflected on the "continuous
decline" of Ireland "relative to the rest of Europe."[8] This critique,
however, did not point the finger at the legacy of Ireland's long history of underdevelopment and the difficult circumstances out of
which the new nation was born. Rather, it blamed Irish social and
economic problems on nationalist ideology itself: "The little fracas
in 1916" did not accomplish much. And any so-called progress that
had been attained would have occurred regardless of Irish independence. In fact, "it may well be argued that we would enjoy more
progress technically by being left to deal with a whole island." In
other words, had Ireland remained within the United Kingdom, like
Scotland or Wales, development would have flourished. Nationalism
was a hindrance. The adoption of modernist architecture and devel-

opment planning promoted by these and other journals during the 1960s was the spatial version of a consciously critical attitude toward received versions (primarily nationalist, but colonialist too) of the past—what would later be called revisionism.

Tradition, for its critics, is to be located in the regional (rural) and religious (Catholic) structure of Irish society as it came to be constituted in the aftermath of independence. For Brown, nationalism was a monolithic, unified, and ultimately sectarian ideology, the effect of which was the perpetuation of a culturally and economically conservative Gaelic ideology, one deeply imbued with Catholicism and that was, therefore, narrow-minded and inward-looking. Such a nativist mindset hindered the development of a secular, urban society; this advance, the modernizers believed, was necessary if Ireland were to have a pluralist future. To blame the economic and social problems of the country on the tenacity of rural values is to build a straw man: the "rural tradition," against which critics rail, is largely of their own making. As more recent critics of Irish nationalism, those working with cultural and postcolonial theory, have shown, the portrayal of a singular, national tradition is most often a move initiated by those in the present who require a caricatured version of the past in order to promote their own vision of modern Ireland. The more malign rural, Catholic Ireland appeared, the more an industrial, urban Ireland seemed appealing. To judge the conservatism of the past, after all, is to testify to one's own maturity and objectivity. Modernity and its social enactment (modernization), therefore, would be a simple, rational solution to Ireland's troubled histories.

The Loss of the Dialectic: From Modernity to Modernization

But the concept of modernity is inherently paradoxical. The dialectic of Enlightenment combines opposing themes: modernity gives us the promise of science, for example, but it also gives us the horrors of technological warfare. Myriad thinkers from Marx (capitalism has been the best and worst thing that ever happened)[9] through Freud (to be modern is to endlessly dredge up the past)[10] to Foucault (liberatory science oppresses us all)[11] have analyzed the contradictions that lie at the heart of modern life: destruction and renewal, crisis and consistency. For Marx and Freud, urban life in the nineteenth century provided the context for imagining universal categories of social analysis and global geographies of shared experiences. Beneath the chaos and complexity of daily life, they proposed the notion that everyone partakes in the same story: for Marx, as actors in class struggle; for Freud, as bearers of common neuroses. For both, history all over was a repetition of the same old story. And yet, the term *modernity* itself—signifying that there is a distinctly new way of doing things—is merely a temporal designator, an endless rearrangement of the present, past, and future in a way that works to endlessly valorize the contemporary moment.

While the notion of being modern—the idea that society and individuals can radically change their inherited histories—dates back at least to the Enlightenment, the term *modernization,* according to Jürgen Habermas, was introduced only as a technical term in the 1950s (Habermas 1990, 2). The term comes down to us from Max Weber's analysis of capitalist modernity as a process of secularization and rationalization, a bearer of bureaucracies and state informalities. The concept of modernization refers to a bundle of mutually reinforcing processes that have their end point in the bureaucratic state: the establishment of centralized political power, the formation of capital, an increase in the productivity of labor, and the proliferation of urban forms of life, formal schooling, and secular values and norms. Modernization is largely a state-administered project, and is the first half of the project of modernity, the less questioning side that accepts the progressive claims of science, industry, and technology as capable of shaping a better future. The other side of modernity, modernism, is a set of experimental, avant-gardist cultural tendencies that are critical of, if not hostile to, industrial modernization. Modernism is troubled by the similarities of experience and cultures that modern life seems to produce, and responds, as in the works of high modernists like Joyce, Picasso, and Beckett, with a call to disrupt accepted modes of understanding and representation. Aesthetic modernism is associated with rebellion, fluidity, resistance, struggle, and ambiguity. It seeks out alternative historical traditions, those disrupted or expunged by the seemingly unstoppable advance of capitalism.

When advocates of change in Ireland argue for modernization, they are propounding the official version of modernity. But we must understand the term *modernization* itself in each of its specific contexts. In the 1920s and 1930s, for example, the creation of suburbs, inner-city apartments, and inner-city renewal was legitimated by the use of nationalist rhetoric, defined by the need to create economic self-sufficiency and build on the recently achieved political sovereignty. When international trends in architecture, such as art deco and Amsterdam-style expressionism, were introduced, the result was an uneven, pluralist architectural landscape in which no one style dominated completely. The architectural aesthetics of modernization in the 1920s were more multifaceted than the monotonous repetition of the corporate office block that was transplanted to Ireland in the 1960s in great numbers. In the 1920s one sees playful decoration, rounded corners, and detailed brickwork, a balance between garden suburb and inner-city housing; even the functionalism of international style was new and experimental. The 1960s, in contrast, saw the deliberate depopulation of inner-city neighborhoods, the destruction of historic buildings, and the completion of dozens of high-rise blocks in an international style that had metamorphosed, by way of volume and function, into the overreaching blandness now commonly associated with the style. The modernization of the 1960s reflected a new political and economic culture that embraced a post-nationalist ethos. It was an irony that just as Ireland was adopting the forms of modernization that had brought prosperity to Britain, the United States, and other states in the years after World War II, the same forms of modernization were being discredited in those places for their authoritarian approach to social planning, their patriarchal presuppositions, and their ugly, condescending cloning of buildings, cities, and their inhabitants.

Those who presented the "achievements" (education, language, and employment) of postindependence Ireland in their worst, most undialectical light pinned the economic and social failures of postcolonial Ireland on the legacy, indeed history, of nationalism itself. This critique of nationalism was not launched in order to recover alternative social solutions to Ireland's economic problems (and certainly not to encourage socialist, republican, or other tendencies), but rather to pave the way for a Keynesian, later a neoliberal, economic agenda. Brown, Lee, and their ilk, however, never set the claims they made about the inherent ideological conservatism of nationalism within the larger context of postcolonial British-Irish relations. For example, the post-1922 Irish Free State, given its high hopes to build up a flourishing economy and culture, had had need of international loans, aid, and support. This required that they impress their old masters, and the world, by demonstrating the wherewithal to run a new state.

While not condoning the inherent conservatism of the nationalist imitation of imperial symbols (the adoption of the colonial court system, right down to the wearing of powdered wigs, for example), one must also consider the tragic, rigid, and inherited circumstances in which decolonization occurred. The history out of which decolonization and the postcolonial state emerged forces us to at least acknowledge that postcolonial Ireland, through the 1930s, 1940s, and 1950s, achieved some notable successes, as I have argued: it produced a stable democracy, elected by proportional representation; it participated with distinction in international affairs; it built the first national electrical grid; it had a balanced budget; it provided thousands of units of public housing; and it built schools, hospitals, and state-run factories. When a new generation of historians looked back at those early decades, however, they saw a gloomier picture, one of failed promise (and they were right, of course), but one for which they have no ready explanation, other than blaming the victim's lack of initiative (Lee) or the essentialist, reactionary politics of nationalism (Brown). Given the evidence that they amass, the conclusions they draw about the need to modernize Ireland appear logical enough. For them, that project began in earnest with state efforts in the 1960s to adopt a form of modernization that had been the foundations on which the post–World War II program of reconstruction and reorganization in Britain, Europe, and America had been built. In Ireland, which had sat out the war, the postcolonial economy, Lee argued, had failed under a system of tariff protections, just as, for Brown, a culture drunk on the remembrance of idealized histories had failed to sustain the national imagination. The 1960s were, then, for these critics, a response to years of "stagnation and crisis" (Brown

1985, 162), to the "politics of drift" (Keogh 1995, 214), and to the "morass" (Lee 1989, 271) that was postwar Irish society. The solution proposed by Lemass, and supported by a host of academics, historians, planners, and architects, was to propagate the gospel of modern capitalism.

For more left-leaning critics like Declan Kiberd, the 1960s marked the moment when the native elite identified their objective as middlemen for multinational companies and modeled their lifestyle according to international styles and tastes (Kiberd 1994, 95). As these conservative critics were writing, Lemass's hoped-for urban revival looked like a dismal failure—a factor that may account for their reluctance to address the urban in their endorsement of Ireland's 1960s modernization. But in the 1960s this urban project involved the creation of new towns and suburbs encircling the city center, which would, it was hoped, free up the city for administrative and business purposes and provide a new, more mobile workforce. The lack of a mobile workforce within the country, as opposed to one oriented toward moving to Boston or London, was a primary theme in the first five-year plan promoted by Lemass and his financial guru, T. K. Whitaker (Fitzgerald 1968, 30). (The new architecture looked even more appealing when, in June 1963, three Georgian buildings collapsed: two elderly residents of a house that caved in on Bolton Street were killed, and two young girls were buried under the rubble of two tenements in Fenian Street.) The renewed energy for urban regeneration promoted the demolition of many of Dublin's Georgian buildings (what the preservationists were then beginning to call "our architectural heritage"). Their culling made room for new buildings in the austere style of corporate modernism (a style some were beginning to label "new brutalism"), the material manifestation of the new, outward-looking Ireland.[12]

The Rise of Modernism: An International Project

An updated, corporate version of international style architecture, broader in scope and ultimately serving different interests than its predecessor, would burst on the Irish scene during the 1960s; Ballymun was but the most dramatic example. This ascetic style, along with its location and the methods and materials of its construction, was not, of course, merely the product of local or national history. Rather, it proudly staked its claim in the wider urban vision of state-sponsored architecture and planning that had swept across Europe and America in the decades after World War II. During the 1940s and 1950s Western governments searched for ways to build and legitimize the welfare state, a social system designed to assume responsibility for the well-being of the people, and to prevent a return to the prewar conditions of slump and unemployment, of slums and poverty, and of political and social unrest. In Britain in 1945, for example, the population voted overwhelmingly for a Labour government. If postwar politics were to remain capitalist and democratic, then Western leaders had to swiftly address the problems of unemployment, poverty, and lack of opportunity. With millions of demobbed soldiers returning to bombed cities and a devastated economy, there was, in England as elsewhere, an immediate need for affordable housing, well-paid jobs, and social security.

In the great reform project that followed the end of the war, Clement Atlee's British government nationalized many key industries, restored the power of the unions (integrating them into the postwar bureaucratic state), and undertook the major task of rebuilding those towns that had been badly damaged by German air raids. In 1946 the Bank of England was taken into public ownership. In the next two years the mines, railways, and electric and gas industries were absorbed. In 1948 the National Health Service was initiated. In 1950 the iron and steel industries, the economic and cultural backbone of working-class communities across Scotland, England, and Wales, were taken into public ownership, and their workers' interests tied to the fortunes of the Labour Party. But it was, perhaps, with the provision of vast numbers of new units of mass-produced public housing, erected quickly and containing the latest conveniences, that Britain's Labour party sought to win the legitimation of a tired yet expectant population. (In America, a different version of urban renewal was adopted: rapid and weakly regulated suburbanization, underpinned with massive subsidies for mortgages and highways.) Between 1953 and 1972 some 400,000 high-rise dwellings were built in Britain (Glendenning and Muthesius 1994,

333). In London alone, 384 residential tower blocks went up between 1964 and 1972 (Hall 1996, 225). As in his 1914 design for Dublin, Patrick Abercrombie's 1943 *County of London Plan,* largely implemented, opens with a striking frontispiece: a bombed-out East End street, in which groups of children, along with their families, search through the rubble; pausing momentarily from loading their meager possessions onto a truck, the young boys stare accusingly at the camera. Underneath is a quote from Winston Churchill promising that "London, Liverpool, Manchester and Birmingham...will rise up from the ruins, more healthy and, I hope, more beautiful....In all my life I have never been treated with so much kindness as by the people who have suffered most" (Abercrombie and Forshaw 1943, frontispiece). Abercrombie's London plan restricted suburbanization, imposed greenbelts, cleared slum areas, and developed new towns (eight in all). New modular homes, factories, schools, and hospitals— universal education and health care were cornerstones in Labour's reconstruction program—were built using the techniques of mass production and rational planning, so well developed during the war (Harvey 1989a, 69–70).

The postwar state's assumption of a huge variety of new tasks— from directing fiscal and monetary policy, through regulating transportation, to running public utilities and health care—secured millions of jobs. Greater financial stability led to increased consumption. The new economy was internationalist by design. The passage from nationalist, internecine Europe to internationalist, capitalist West depended on the massive expansion of world trade and the inauguration of large-scale international investment, exemplified by the Marshall Plan, the Bretton-Woods agreement (1944), and the founding of the United Nations (1946). The new internationalism—pushed for by the United States—required structural changes to the European economy. These included the integration of the economies of Europe (represented by the Coal-Steel pact of 1957, forerunner and prototype of the European Economic Community); the homogenization of wants and desires (typified by the rise of television, mass advertising, and American popular culture); and the standardization of production (seen in the expansion of Fordist assembly line techniques to European industries, such as cars, steel, and electrical goods). These social and economic changes were reflected in the search for a rationalized urban space, an aesthetic that demonstrated and served the power of the new economy.

It was out of this struggle to revitalize the war-torn (and aging) cities of Western Europe, suggests David Harvey, that the project of modernist architects and planners—Le Corbusier, Mies van der Rohe, and Frank Lloyd Wright—became welded to the technocratic and positivist vision of the postwar bureaucratic state (Harvey 1989a, 70). As the new social welfare state sought to spatialize itself, a new landscape of power appeared—a highly functional, corporate architecture, symbolized by a bland cubic structure, made both private and outward-looking by shiny walls of reflective glass. These buildings, anonymous and repetitive in their construction, began to make clones of the urban landscape. Their rejection of ornament and retreat from tradition sought to create a unified, unspecific, and controlled landscape, one that regarded citizens as equals and offered favoritism to no one. Their lack of intimate scale repudiated regionalism, while their imposing presence spoke the language of power, strength, and durability at a time when states were restructuring their foundations after a long war.

If the semiotics of modernist architecture (skeletal, linear, spacious, and functional) strove to create an "objective" and "universal" aesthetic, then its rejection of cultural specificity was a reaction, in part, to the overblown rhetoric of a variety of ethnic, regional, and class ideologies (racial nationalisms, militant imperialisms, and fiery socialisms), which threatened the early days of European democracies during the 1920s and 1930s. During those years, social democracy proved unworkable in many countries, such as Germany, Italy, and Spain, and almost in Depression-era America. The search for a well-regulated built form was but one response to the crisis-driven question of how best to organize the political chaos and to fashion stability in societies that seemed on the verge of collapse. In this context, caught in the tension between nationalism and internationalism, between universalism and elitism, modernist architecture has its origins. From the beginning, however, the rational and streamlined designs of Le Corbusier and Wright were open to competing interpretations. The architects of this new style sought to be ideologically impartial, to repress national styles and any obvious references to the past. In an age of fascism, communism, and fledgling democracies, it is difficult to advocate a neutral position; what is offered as above the fray, neutral, or in the realm of the universal always turns out to be just another partisanship. Le Corbusier's infamous conception of cities and houses as machines for living in, for example, while clearly derived from a positivist sociological stance, was never far removed from the fascist elevation of efficiency and speed at all costs, or the futurist fetishization of power, technology, and war. Likewise, Mies's understanding of "truth as the significance of fact" fed the emerging corporate principle, and its architecture, that what is insignificant or small must also be false (Frampton 1980, 161).

The development of modernist architecture before World War II, then, must be approached dialectically. It was both radical and conservative: radical in its spatial effort to build a new, less historicized future; and conservative in its attempt to ignore the unfinished business of history, its belief that one could build anew on virgin or leveled ground and not repeat the mistakes of the past—inequality, racism, poverty, and prejudice.

After World War II Western economies internationalized and grew rapidly, nations were forced quickly to take sides in the Cold War, and state bureaucracies attained unprecedented levels of power and influence over the everyday lives of their citizens in education, health, and employment. Cities expanded and reflected these changes. While in America private speculators developed new suburbs, in Europe, where class was still the major electoral category and often structured along urban/rural lines, city councils erected high-rise units of public housing in core city areas, hoping to maintain their power bases. When it came to building state and corporate offices, architects, planners, and state officials on both sides of the Atlantic lauded the benefits of international-style architecture as efficient and representative of a new official outlook. From the 1950s onward the affordable and quickly built structures of the disciples of Mies van der Rohe, Philip Johnson, and others helped provide the spaces required for government and industrial bureaucracies to flourish. Banks proliferated, adopting the functional style to symbolize their power and influence. Urban in-fill apartment blocks, such as Mies's Lake Shore

Drive in Chicago, celebrated the individual's ability to live in luxury in the city—the antithesis of the tenement. Hotels, banks, department stores, homes for broadcasting and media networks all used modernist architecture to expand their claim on the growing urban world of white-collar employment, leisure, and commerce.

The International Style Comes to Ireland

Ireland, and Dublin's Ballymun, did not stand apart from this international story. But their relationship to the grand narrative of metropolitan modernism, which entailed the search for a literature, art, and architecture capable of representing the rhythms of modern life, remains distinctive, defined by Ireland's unique history. Just as modernism in Ireland throughout the nineteenth and early twentieth centuries had been mediated by postcolonialism, so, too, in the aftermath of World War II did Ireland find itself in an unusual position regarding the modernizing trends of the welfare state. The discourse of postwar urban modernization arrived later in Ireland than it had in Europe. Ireland had sat out the war on account of its own particular postcolonial legacy; having just gained independence from Britain, the country's leaders and citizens were loath to align themselves with their former master. Irish towns experienced little of the destruction that had leveled large areas of European cities, and, hence, there was no immediate and urgent need to rebuild. And, while the Irish had suffered some hardships during the war, such as rationing, air raids, and the deaths of thousands of volunteers, when the war was over, there was no compelling national motivation to renew or re-fashion society through large-scale social reforms. Irish industry did not benefit greatly from the war; there was no mass production of arms, no factories working to full capacity, no mobilization of the workforce, and no centralized planning—forces that helped launch and sustain the postwar reconstruction effort elsewhere.

Ireland, however, was certainly not immune to the postwar changes in Europe. Although it did not have a large economy, it was geographically and politically strategic in the developing Cold War environment. As part of the conditions of receipt of Marshall Plan money, the Irish government was required to open its markets: in 1948 it created the Industrial Development Authority (IDA) to attract foreign industry to Ireland. Import restrictions were removed, exports were encouraged, and Ireland joined the UN (though, interestingly, it opted out of NATO so long as the British military presence in Ireland continued). While the full effects of the new international order would not be made tangible until Ireland's own version of the "great rebuild" in the 1960s, incipient elements were clearly laid down in the preceding years.

The 1950s were a time of recession in Ireland. A series of coalition governments ended the stability of seventeen years of Fianna Fáil rule. Fianna Fáil had largely been Michael Scott's sponsor during the 1930s and 1940s, and the government had commissioned much of the main architectural work of that era. The political atmosphere of the 1950s was very different from the relatively stable postrevolutionary era. The 1930s were noted for de Valera's populism and his attempts to win hegemony through civic largesse. The instability of the frequently changing governments made for an era not conducive to awarding political and architectural patronage. The decade was a time of transition, as culture and politics were about to emerge into a full-blown commitment to economic internationalism. Against the backdrop of mass emigration, political instability, and the movement of international capital to the more promising markets of Europe and America, writers, planners, and historians began to question previous economic policy and lay the groundwork for the upcoming changes of the 1960s. In 1957 an editorial in the journal *Architectural Survey* argued for future change based on past neglect: "This country must come into line with today's techniques in industry and agriculture. We are one of the least developed countries in Europe and for that reason have the greatest potential for development."

The changes of the 1960s were prefigured in architecture at the beginning of the 1950s. Michael Scott's Busáras (1944–53), his largest Fianna Fáil commission, was an emphatic, loud, bold, and deliberate statement. Out of place in the 1950s, but commonplace by the mid-1960s, its sheets of glass, concrete, and steel lorded over the adjacent eighteenth-century Custom House. Scott himself was proud of his local adaptation of the international style's rejection of tradition and ornament. "It caused," he asserted, "terrific controversy. There were a lot of people who thought it was wrong at the time. And you had all these goody-goodies who only loved the past, and they couldn't bear the idea of a modern building going up on that site so close to the Custom House" (Scott 1995, 158).

The transformations in Europe and America in the 1950s and 1960s were most visible in the changing urban landscapes, as new suburbs, highways, tower blocks, and housing projects were built. In Ireland, it was only in the 1960s and early 1970s that the "brave new world" of modern architecture, promised by its leading proponents to produce orderly and efficient cities, came to play a central role in the future vision of Dublin. By then, critical modernism had turned fully into state-sanctioned modernization. The wide-scale use of flat, cubic, cost-efficient architecture in Dublin was motivated by two mutually reinforcing impulses. The first was a recognition by a new generation of leaders that much about the nationalist project had failed (self-sufficiency, the return of the Irish language, creation of wealth), and that nationalism, correspondingly, would have to be redefined less in cultural (Gaelic) or ideological (republican socialist) terms and more as an economic endeavor, one tied to export-driven industrial development. The second, a corollary of the first, was an acknowledgment that Ireland needed to engage more with the international community and to integrate with its financial and political structures. Rather than identifying with the decolonizing world, Ireland's task was to align itself with the hegemonic Western powers, with whom, especially Britain, it had always had an ambiguous relationship.

Ballymun was a crucial example of an answer to the complicated question of how to negotiate between these two mutually reinforcing impulses. Ballymun's aesthetic was clearly borrowed from numerous other government-sponsored modernist blocks that had sprung up across Europe and Britain (for example, in London's Bethnal Green, in Sheffield's Le Corbusier–inspired Park Hill, and the Gorbals in Glasgow). Ballymun's form rejected both ornamentation and tradition. Its style engaged the desire to move beyond the rhetoric of cultural nationalism to create an ideologically objective and progressive urban space, one that was uniform, egalitarian, and ahistorical in design. Its location—a flat, greenfield site on the outskirts of the city and at the base of the Dublin mountains—spoke to the larger planning and development needs of a modernizing government, intent on attracting foreign capital into the previously protectionist economy. The site's peripheral location enabled a long-promised slum clearance program in the city. Ballymun's projected population of sixteen thousand people was to be moved out of centrally located, working-class areas of the city. This would leave sections of the city open to Dublin's version of urban renewal—the destruction of older, Georgian buildings, and their replacement with office blocks. These new commercial structures, it was hoped, would house an internationally subsidized, white-collar workforce. Ballymun's location was also central to the latest planning vision of the state (Myles Wright's 1967 plan for the city), one that still influences development: the construction of a new motorway around the city, along which an outer ring of suburbs nestles. Ballymun formed part of the government's 1960s regional planning strategy, which sought to create a series of new towns to the west of the capital around which industrial parks would be built. Ballymun, like many other architectural and planning developments during the 1960s, illustrated a dramatic shift in how the nation was being defined: from an Ireland marked by a history of anticolonialism to one proud of its easy embrace of internationally led economic development.

Ballymun was just one of many major architectural and planning developments in Dublin that drew a firm line between the past and the present. Lemass, who became Taoiseach in 1959, believed that the historical task of his generation was "to consolidate the economic foundations of our political independence."[13] To accomplish this, he prepared Ireland to enter "a unified Europe." He redefined self-reliance to mean "an economy sufficiently viable to enable all Irish to live in their own country" (Lee 1989, 399), and launched society on an export-led industrialization drive. He initiated three economic expansion programs, all of which included tax relief for foreign companies, tariff cuts, research subsidies, tourism encouragement, and marketing aid to companies.[14] T. K. Whitaker, Lemass's finance minister, pondered that "after thirty-five years of native government people are asking whether we can achieve an acceptable degree of economic progress" (Walsh 1979, 29). He recognized that "reliance on a shrinking home market offered no prospect of satisfying Ireland's employment aspirations, and that protectionism would have to give way to active competitive participation in a free-trading world" (Keogh 1995, 244). Others agreed and welcomed a more competitive and capitalist future: "American and West German industrialists," wrote Denis Meehan, a professor at Ireland's leading Catholic college, "will be attracted in by the cheapness and geographical convenience of Ireland as a distribution center" (Brown 1985, 186). David Thornley suggested that the new era of economic vitality was the beginning of "delayed peaceful social revolution" (1964, 16). The implication was that the earlier, more militant revolution had brought little in the way of social change, and might have hindered economic and cultural improvement.

The language of planning paralleled this modernization discourse, expounding the virtues of "development planning" for its ability to move Ireland away from unproductive old tensions. Planner Loraine Donaldson defined development planning as the manipulation of economies "to achieve established objectives," and specifically "to shake the Irish loose from the lethargy of the past and move them boldly into the formulation of long-range plans for the nation's future" (1966, 2). Most admirable, for Donaldson, in the Irish adoption of this bold discourse was "the determination to place the conflicts of the past behind" (13). After decades of conflict, consensus became the primary goal for these new professionals, and planning was the means to achieve it: much of Ireland's history they reduced to simple disruptive behavior, which then created a useful and pragmatic approach in the 1960s, "a positive reaction against the divisive effects of ideological commitments of any kind" (Fitzgerald 1968, 198). Geoffrey Copcutt, a planning adviser to the Irish government, as part of the UN Special Fund, further promoted the connection between the need for "physical planning in Ireland" and the amelioration of Irish history. Fifty years after the Rising (which was being commemorated at the time Copcutt was writing), the nation remained divided, he argued: "its cornerstone is laid on dynamite" (Copcutt 1967, 17). Only planning would move Ireland away from this explosive foundation and onto firm and peaceful ground.

Revisionism, which is now a debate within historiography, was, in the 1960s, suffused in professional conversations about architecture, as well. Just as Busáras and Dublin airport prefigured the mass of work completed in the 1960s, so some architectural journals in the 1950s constructed nationalism as the enemy of progress. In 1954 the *Architectural Survey* drew the connection between the rewriting of the national narrative and the quest for a new kind of physical space. International style was lauded, as were technological advances in building and engineering, such as systems building and prefabrication. The editors stated, "The first bogey is the danger of an 'international style' as opposed to the merit of a 'national style.' The whole idea of an architectural 'style' is dangerous.... [S]tyle is ... irrelevant to the appreciation of architecture." By 1958, eager to mimic the "'post-war reconstruction'" in Europe, the *Survey*'s editors called on the building industry to focus less on housing and "to concentrate a higher proportion of our building potential ... in the industrial field." A 1959 editorial picked up on the iconoclastic atmosphere that was stirring in the country. In architecture, it claimed, "the 'battle of the styles' [is] virtually at an end. The demands for a rigorous economy on the one hand, and of an increasingly educated public taste on the other, have led to a situation where, with few exceptions, the architect is free to devise solutions to his clients' problems in truly contemporary terms, untrammelled by any preconceptions." Within this modern project, the *Survey* imagined a somewhat heroic role for the architect: "No longer thought of as a long-haired luxury, but accepted as a skilled technologist catering for certain complex social needs, his role demands high courage and integrity as well as skill and inspiration." The following year, when Lemass's first economic program was up and running, the *Survey*'s editors reached beyond architecture to argue the necessity for free trade: "The day is long past when the hick industrialist, safe behind his tariff wall, could turn out shoddy goods in rusty iron shacks and survive to make his fortune.... Ireland's industry has accepted her place in the markets of the world." By 1962 the journal was championing "the magic formulae of twentieth century man—'mechanisation, organisation and method, automation.'" In 1966, on the anniversary of the Rising, the journal's editorial notably referenced Le Corbusier, signaling what had been obvious for many years: the appropriation of international style had become the official aesthetic of the new Dublin. Hand in hand with the promotion of technological innovations, the commemoration of the Rising allowed planners and architects to reflect openly on the legacy of independence. As would occur more vigorously within historiography, this reflection became an opportunity to attack the ideological underpinnings of the Irish state. A bright international future appears all the brighter when measured against the apparent failures of fifty long years of self-rule. The *Irish Builder and Engineer,* in one of its editorials during the jubilee year, blamed the poor quality of urban life on a caricature of nationalism and the state's achievements since 1922. The editorial expressed hope that the carnival atmosphere "might muffle forever more the explosive utterances of a provocative and bleak nationalism that denies the equal splendour of cultures other than the Gaelic."[15] Likewise, *Build* magazine, in the same year, warned that the coming decade would "form a baseline for the future: a baseline of real progress onwards, or an effective terminal point to the extremely modest hopes and inordinately unambitious aspirations of the Irish nation in this century. 1916 began and finished nothing."[16] Throughout the 1960s two strands of thought slowly merged in architectural thinking. The first, that Ireland needed to embrace outside influences, became dependent on the second: that such changes were more than just surface improvements; they were necessary to move the country away from old sectarianisms and prejudices, which themselves had held the country back economically. The contours of revisionism were becoming clear. Nationalism had been to blame all along for the country's lack of development and prosperity. If "1916 began and finished nothing," the 1960s would rectify the problem and the narrative. Revisionism would come to juxtapose, in later historiography, scientific interpretations with mythological, nationalist readings of the past. This method found its spatial counterpart in Dublin during the 1960s as a cubic, rational, and concrete architecture made its appearance. Scientific and technological approaches to urban design signified an upbeat quest for ideologically neutral public spaces and the outward trappings of economic modernization.

Architects who had emigrated during the 1950s would return to Ireland during these years and contribute to the creation of the new kind of national space that was then emerging. They had all received modernist training. Robin Walker, for example, who had graduated from University College, Dublin, in 1947, returned to Ireland in 1958, where he became a partner in Michael Scott's firm. In the intervening years, he studied in Paris at the École des Beaux-Arts. In Paris he worked with Le Corbusier, after which he migrated to Chicago to apprentice with Mies van der Rohe. Several of Walker's buildings in

Ireland were notably influenced by his architectural studies abroad: for example, the Bord Fáilte Building on Baggot Street and UCD's glass-clad Restaurant Building. Peter Doyle and Cathal O'Neill studied with Mies at the Illinois Institute of Technology before returning to Ireland. As chairman of Ireland's largest architectural school for over twenty years, O'Neill helped perpetuate the modernist message. Doyle's principal works were industrial in nature, a series of factories, health centers, electrical plants, and waterworks.[17]

In 1960, Dublin had only one large modern office block—Michael Scott's Busáras. By the mid-1970s, there were over three hundred, providing over ten million square feet of bureaucratic space to a still shabby and quite provincial city, a city still in the process of constructing its own middle class (McDonald 1985, 4). To make way for Miesian structures of glass and steel, many of the city's inhabitants were displaced to western suburbs and "new towns," which the government was enthusiastically building in line with Myles Wright's development plan for the city, commissioned in 1964 by Neil Blaney, the minister for local government. As suburbanization proceeded apace, and office blocks took over ever more of the city's skyline, central Dublin increasingly became a "downtown," a place to and from which commuters plowed their way, leaving the streets quiet and deserted after six o'clock in the evening.

In the official drive for progress and prosperity, the interventionist, modernizing state would lead the way in the city's rebuilding and restructuring. Perhaps the first significant spatial shift occurred in 1960, when Radio Telifís Éireann (RTE), the state broadcasting company, moved its headquarters from the General Post Office in O'Connell Street to a twenty-three-acre suburban site at Montrose, south of the city proper. The site itself, the former playing fields of St. Andrew's College, was purchased for an inflated sum, so eager was the government at this time to promote urban development.[18] The first RTE structure, the Television Building, was designed by Ronald Tallon in 1961 and was an act of homage to Le Corbusier and Mies: standing on concrete pillars, evocative of Le Corbusier's beloved *pilotis,* the long, three-story building reflects light from its horizontal expanse of window walls; its open floor plan and lack of ornamentation signify a functional, bureaucratic space. Other buildings were added to the campus through the 1960s, connected by linear, concrete walkways that highlighted the right angles and objectivity of the structure. The rational design of the RTE complex sought to reconcile the contradiction of modernizing nationalism in Ireland. On the one hand, the building reflected economic intervention in nationalist terms—the need for economic sovereignty. RTE, after all, was a monopoly; commercials for foreign firms were not allowed, Irish-produced programs were emphasized, and Irish-language shows were promoted. Like its model, the British Broadcasting Company, RTE had a nationalist mission. Both were "one-nation" projects, aimed at the ritualistic invocation and reproduction of a somewhat illusory community. The ideology of sovereignty, however, soon clashed with the reality of Ireland's insertion into the new internationalizing economy. Ireland's modernizing ethos, which Lemass was so keen to peddle, sought to obscure this contradiction by presenting the country's integration into the expanded economic arena as a national task—the coming of age of a sovereign state in the modern world. In other words, internationalism was necessary to save the nation. The building of RTE reflects this tension: the concept nationalist, the design internationalist.

Another important state institution that fled the city for a greenfield site in 1964 was University College, Dublin. Michael Tierney, who became president of UCD in 1947, masterminded the move based in large part on his disdain for Trinity College, Dublin's influential and traditionally Protestant university. Throughout the 1940s and 1950s Tierney had purchased parcels of property and houses in Belfield, in the heart of Dublin's expanding and prosperous southern suburbs. Tierney, in alliance with Dublin's hard-line Catholic archbishop, John McQuaid, had long pushed to move UCD out of its original home at Earlsfort Terrace, adjacent to Dublin's central St. Stephen's Green. During the 1950s the government had hinted at merging the two institutions, a move that sent these defenders of traditional Catholic Ireland on a mission to remove UCD from Trinity's august sphere of influence. Only UCD, McQuaid and Tierney argued, could provide a proper Catholic education, against Trinity's "origin in the Tudor conquest of Ireland [and its ideology that] still remained true to that origin" (McCartney 1999, 197). UCD's modern architecture and greenfield site brought together the reality of a national

Catholic university with the confidence and innovation that was being touted by economists and politicians. McQuaid also had plans of his own when it came to pushing for UCD's migration to Belfield. He wanted to move St. Vincent's Hospital, the state's largest Catholic teaching hospital, from St. Stephen's Green to Elm Park, a site just down the road from the university's new home. This, he felt, would help create a Catholic presence that would balance Protestant hegemony in the city center (Cooney 2000, 339).[19] The horizontal, concrete, and streamlined architecture of UCD suggests a shift in the ideological needs of state-run education in Ireland, from the humanities to technical subjects, which in turn is illustrative of broader social changes.

As Ireland sought to improve its economy during the 1960s, the state attempted to overhaul education also. Sponsored by the Organization for Economic Cooperation and Development (OECD), the Department of Education launched a series of reforms aimed at creating a more modern education program. For secondary schools, the leaving age was raised to fifteen, fees were abolished, and state-supported, nondenominational comprehensive schools (which stressed technical subjects, such as metalwork, engineering, and carpentry) were instituted. Nine new regional technical colleges were built, illustrating the state's commitment to the creation of a technically skilled population, ready to play its part in the new society. UCD was at the forefront of this educational effort, having the largest student body as well as the largest technical (engineering, architecture, urban planning) and business departments in the country. The new, peripherally located campus, with its corporate-style buildings and overwhelming scale, reinforces the formal and professional atmosphere. Gone are the traditional aesthetics of academic buildings—a clustered group of classical-style buildings organized around a public space.

"The Factory," as UCD was nicknamed, stands as a monument to a different intellectual purpose: functional, bureaucratic, and technocratic. The international architectural competition held for UCD's design was won in 1964 by A. & D. Wejchert, from Warsaw. Science was the first of the faculties to be moved into the new complex. The first building erected, Wejchert's Administration Building, set the tone for those that followed: standing in the corner of an exposed plaza, a series of cement pillars holds up four glass-curtained stories, each separated from the levels above and below by large slabs of white-washed concrete. Futuristic concrete walkways originating in other parts of the campus enter the upper sides of the building. One approaches the structure by climbing a series of wide concrete steps, which visually reinforce the strength and bulk of the building. Other buildings reflect this highly modernist style: horizontal lines, sharp angles, glass walls, and intimidating scale. The Restaurant Building (1967–70), designed by Robin Walker, is in the same vein as Mies's New National Gallery in Berlin and the Illinois Institute of Technology (Figure 13). Three continuous concrete balconies support three floors of glazing, set in black steel frames. As economic and educational change quickened in Britain and Europe during the postwar period, Lemass's government, keen to sign Ireland up to the EEC and partake in Western industrial expansion, pushed for a more pragmatic and functional approach to education. The results are clearly visible in Ireland's largest university.

The arrival of modernist architecture in Ireland during the 1960s critiqued the achievements of nationalism since independence, in particular its failure to create an industrial economy and a prosperous bourgeoisie. But the shiny new structures that were rapidly appearing on the urban landscape were equally dismissive of the city's Georgian architecture, the most obvious physical legacy of colonialism in Dublin. Preservation had never been much of an issue in the city. The Local Government Planning and Development Act (1963), "an act to make provision in the interests of the common good, for the proper planning and development of cities ... (including the preservation and improvement of the amenities thereof)," did not offer any explicit preservation or heritage guidelines.[20] The demolition of Georgian Dublin in the 1960s—the houses themselves with their ornate, interior plasterwork and their elegant doorways, the wide, elongated streets laid out to display vistas of the surrounding mountains—created a conservation movement. At the same time, organizations such as the Irish Georgian Society laid the groundwork for today's commodification of all things Georgian: the popular "Doors of Dublin" posters and cards, the classical façade of the corporate office, the pastiche arches, columns, and brickwork of a suburban home. Belatedly, in 1976, the 1963 Planning Act was amended to allow for

Figure 13. Restaurant Building at University College Dublin. Photograph courtesy of the Irish Architectural Archive.

the preservation of specific areas and structures. Even then, the only part of Dublin carved out for protection was the wealthy southern section around Merrion and Fitzwilliam Squares. The message was clear: the rest of the city was fair game. A common view at the time, expressed most succinctly by Neil Blaney, minister for local government, was that Georgian buildings were representative of British conquest on the island. "I was glad to see them go," he said. "They stood for everything I hate" (Kearns 1983, 70). Frank McDonald details this "destruction of Dublin," tracing its origins, ironically, to the Office of Public Works decision to demolish two Georgian houses in Kildare Street, beside the National Museum, in August 1957. These developments paralleled the shift in other arenas that I have already discussed, such as economics, planning, and nationalist discourse.

The modernization drive in Ireland during the 1960s was initiated by the state; as with today's globalization, the national government acted as the catalyst for foreign investment. Lemass's government brought about the reduction of tariffs, lowered corporate tax rates, provided subsidies to foreign businesses, and guaranteed a healthy purchase price for property under development for the housing of the civil service.[21] Likewise, the planning of a more modern city to serve as the incubator for development was initiated by the public sector, as semi-state companies led the way in constructing the buildings that came to define and symbolize Irish urban modernization. The nation-state was a political and economic actor, a promoter of internationalization, not its victim. It functioned as an intermediary between early postcolonialism and its contemporary successor, an exemplary neoliberal European economy. In 1961, Córas Iompair Éireann (CIE), Ireland's public transport company, knocked down two Victorian façades on O'Connell Street to make room for a glass-and-concrete infill structure. Glaring in its contrast to its neighbors, the new CIE public information office reflected light via its curtain-walled glass front, which was surrounded by concrete. Inscribed on its façade in stained glass are the four provincial shields. But these nods to Irish national tradition are no cover for the structure's dominant symbolic references: corporate power and white-collar efficiency.

Another state company that joined in this urban renaissance was the Comhlucht Siúicre Éireann, the state sugar company. When UCD moved out to its new site at Belfield, the area it had controlled in the city was primed for construction. In 1960 the sugar company initiated the building of its new headquarters at the corner of Earlsford Terrace and Leeson Street. The finished building, designed by Liam Boyle and Seamus Delaney, was mammoth in comparison to the low-lying buildings nearby. Visually, it seems to swallow the surrounding landscape; symbolically, it represented the end of one era and the beginning of another. By sheer design, a local sugar company suddenly took on the weight of a world-scale corporate player.

The 1960s were a time when Irish firms and politics sought to "catch up" with the corporate model of development already laid out elsewhere. The erection of dozens of new office blocks did not occur in a vacuum. Architecture was the most hotly debated and visible display of the debate between a putatively modernizing nationalism and its colonial legacies. The construction of the Electrical Supply Board (ESB) building in 1963 and its attendant controversy are a microcosm of many of the tensions that arose out of Ireland's quest for development during these years, as conservationists butted heads with speculators. A debated version of Irish tradition clashed with an idea of progress that, too, carried its own complexities within it. Most revealing, Irish history itself became embroiled once again in architecture and displayed its inescapable connections to international modernism.

For many years, the headquarters of Ireland's electricity industry had been located in a run-down Georgian house at the corner of Merrion Square and Fitzwilliam Street. (Interestingly, Ireland's pride in the 1920s and 1930s in being one of the first countries to provide electricity to everyone in the nation ended up tarnished, after forty years, with the heart of the national grid crowded into a building behind the original property.) A growing population, expanding suburbs, and a hoped-for thriving industry requires energy, and it was not long before the ESB was looking to build a progressive, worldly new administrative headquarters. The company purchased fifteen Georgian homes on Fitzwilliam Street, opened an architectural competition to design the new building, and in so doing, inaugurated a fierce cultural fracas. Both sides rallied their troops. The Irish Georgian Society, led by respected Anglo-Irish personalities such as Desmond Fitzgerald (the Knight of Glin) and Lord Talbot of Malahide, recruited Sir Albert Richardson, an elderly, renowned scholar on British Georgian architecture, to defend the integrity of the street. At a crowded meeting in Dublin's Mansion House, Sir Albert suggested that behind the original, intact row of Georgian houses, the electricity company should build an "'electricity palace'... in the form of a skyscraper surmounted by a revolving guilded statue of Mercury" (McDonald 1985, 21). In spite of this particularly eccentric proposal, many citizens supported the preservationist campaign.

On the other side were government ministers determined to impose the new aesthetics on a reluctant populace. Kevin Boland, minister for local government, liked to refer to the leaders of the conservation movement as "a consortium of belted earls," deriding them and "their ladies and left wing intellectuals" as malingerers "who can afford the time to stand and contemplate in ecstasy the unparalleled manmade beauty" of these downtrodden eighteenth-century structures, while dismissing "the unskilled amateurish efforts of Mother Nature in the Wicklow Mountains."[22] They, too, had their international supporters. Walter Gropius sent them an encouraging telegram, while Sir John Summerson, another English expert, denounced the buildings as "architectural rubbish...just one damned house after another" (Kearns 1983, 59). Despite the public outcry, Dublin Corporation in 1963 granted planning permission for the ESB's new building, designed by Sam Stephenson, the winner of the competition and the latest promoter of the severe "brutalist" international style. The four-story building was clad in brown, precast concrete panels, with vertical brick fins between the windows. Its development required the destruction of the longest complete Georgian streetscape in Europe.

In a prerestoration era, when professional interests lay in constructing large, original, and profitable buildings, several principal architectural journals supported the wave of new construction. An article in *Building,* an English magazine, described the efforts of the preservationists to "preserve any rebuilding" in Dublin's Georgian arteries "as a policy equivalent to hiding one's head in the sand in view of the physical condition of the buildings and the requirements of a modern economically healthy city."[23] Irish newspaper critics, too, celebrated Stephenson's modernist creation. An editorial in the *Irish Independent* argued that the ESB had settled on "a modern building of intrinsic architectural worth designed to harmonise with its noble neighbors yet having the integrity of belonging to its own day. It is better to have this than the meaningless shell that retentionists would ask us to preserve. Architectural ability and artistic inspiration...did not stop dead in the eighteenth century."[24] Even the traditionally Protestant *Irish Times* wrote that the "winning scheme is honest, straightforward and very free from gimmicks.... Any fool can design a complicated and involved building to fulfill certain requirements. It takes talent and genius to devise a simple answer to the same needs."[25] In the ESB episode, certain questions were spatialized: is it a nationalist endeavor to knock down the remnants of colonial architecture? In the shadows of colonialism, is international style a step forward, a form gesturing to a time beyond sectarianism? Modernizing agents in Ireland—state officials, architects, and foreign investors—did not only seek to escape the claims of nationalist history. In their desire to clear the vista, to develop a brand-new economy, they needed to be free of history's unfinished business. When the ESB built its headquarters on Fitzwilliam Street, it erased material vestiges of eighteenth-century Ireland, the high point of colonial conquest. Ironically, in doing so, it unearthed the powerful psychological remains of an unresolved historical conflict.

The financial strength of modern cities is clearly represented in their high-rise buildings. Monuments to corporate power (from the Chicago Tribune building to Rockefeller Center to Trump Tower), skyscrapers of American cities have symbolized class hierarchies, new wealth, and Western prosperity: the events of September 11, 2001, underscore this complicated truth. In London, as in other European cities, after World War II, "the high rise building became a status symbol of 'modernity'" (Mumford 1961, 430). The American skyscraper, in all its bravado, was quickly imitated throughout Europe and then in Ireland. The high-rise building that combined "expansion and congestion, horizontal and vertical, produced the maximum opportunities for profit: that was in fact the principal motivating force" (ibid.). In Dublin during the 1960s, with an influx of foreign capital and a government eager to subsidize the property market, this powerful symbol found a home on the changing skyline. But the arrival of these buildings on the world scene was hardly greeted with unmixed enthusiasm. In one of the foremost antimodernist tracts, *The Death and Life of Great American Cities,* Jane Jacobs rails against the high-rise for perpetuating "dullness and regimentation," for smothering the "buoyancy and vitality of urban life," and imposing uniformity on urban space (1961, 4). These critiques were almost beside the point, however, in a Dublin keen to regard itself, and to be regarded, as equal to other thriving capitals.

The shift from a postcolonial to a modern capital necessitated more than just the creation of manufacturing and industrial jobs, a primary aim under Lemass. Along with an industrial base, the government was intent on creating a services and retail workforce. Indeed, at a conference on "Office Location and Regional Development," Michael Lawless, secretary for local government, asserted that the state was fully committed to developing "shopping, tourism, and other types of service employment" (Foras Forbartha [FF] 1973, 7). "Tourism," noted Kevin Boland at the time, "is now our greatest earner of foreign currency" (1968, 174). In 1966 Lemass ceremonially opened Stillorgan Shopping Centre—"an ambitious and exciting concept entirely new to this country, and the most modern of its counterparts in Europe."[26] Stillorgan was built to cater to the new and expanding southern suburbs, with their inhabitants increasingly reliant on automobiles, an inevitability that comes with "economic and social advance."[27] Beyond increased consumerism, Lawless asserted that the government's aim to increase the number of white-collar workers was "clearly reflected in the construction of a large number of modern office blocks" (FF 1973, 7).

Michael Bannon, Ireland's leading urban planner at the time, helped to implement this government policy—the reinvention of the city center as a predominantly commercial, rather than residential, district—by arguing for increased functional and spatial separation between a factory and its office headquarters: "As production increases and as the desire for prestige becomes important," he argued, "the trend is to move the office staff into a specially designed office building" (FF 1973, 12). He cited growing companies, such as the Irish Sugar Company, the ESB, and Ford of Ireland, as examples of the need to concentrate industrial offices in the heart of Dublin. "Today," he said, "the number and importance of vertical linkages between the office and the plant are minimal: rather the location of the company office is increasingly governed by the need for 'horizontal' linkages with other office and service establishments, which assist in the management of the factory, the conducting of research, the marketing and sale of the product, and the innovation of new development" (ibid.). The effect of subsidizing the creation of new commercial premises with the lure of "financial, infrastructural, and advisory" assistance, along with state departments promising to pay top dollar in rent, led to a commercial real estate boom in Dublin during the 1960s (ibid., 18). The policy of centralizing office space in a small area fed the property bubble, which found architectural expression in the high-rise block, that most profitable of buildings.

Ireland's first skyscraper was Liberty Hall, a seventeen-story tower, 197 feet tall. In the context of low-lying Dublin, its height was impressive (Figure 14). Built as office headquarters for the Irish Trans-

Figure 14. Liberty Hall. Photograph by author.

port and General Workers' Union (ITGWU), located along the Liffey Quay, it dominates the river view, overshadowing its nearest neighbor, Gandon's Custom House. Liberty Hall stands atop a radical past. The original building, dating back to the 1820s (when it contained a hotel), had been the union's headquarters since the turn of the twentieth century and the turbulent days of the 1913 Lockout. The building suffered a bomb blast during the Easter Rising, was partially restored, but was ultimately declared unsafe in 1958. The rebuilding of Liberty Hall as a high-rise began in 1961, and when it was completed in 1965, its rooftop terrace was a major attraction. The Troubles broke out in Northern Ireland in 1969; in 1972 a Loyalist bomb destroyed all of Liberty Hall's clear glass windows. They were replaced with the current reflective glass curtain. The union did not need such grand quarters, but the symbolic potential of a skyscraper was not lost on the labor leadership, which was keen to announce the organization's newfound influence on the city's skyline.

In 1963 the ITGWU, whose largest constituency was public workers, entered into partnership with the government, helping to form the National Industrial and Economic Council—an alliance of government, employers, and trade unions (the "social partners") that negotiated yearly salary increases and productivity quotas in exchange for the union's legally binding promise not to initiate strike action.[28] In the case of Liberty Hall, the modernist advance in architecture reflected similar progress being made in the area of class relations: the arrival of labor as a neocorporate player willing to compromise with the free-trade tendencies of the state. Liberty Hall also included a ground floor of shops and a large conference center. The same year that Liberty Hall was unveiled, the government made a short film, *Ireland: The New Convention Country,* promoting the country as a prime location for international business meetings and executive tourism.[29] The brief film marketed the country's mix of technology (audio and translation equipment), traditionalism (hospitality, folk parks, and ancient architecture), centrality of location (between Europe and America), and "aloofness" (for remote recreation).

Private companies and banks also created new corporate headquarters in Ireland during the 1960s. *Build* magazine described the new Bank of Ireland headquarters as "one of the most advanced building complexes in Europe, giving the occupiers a standard of environmental comfort far above the present norm for similar office development in these islands" (Figure 15).[30] The 1958 Office Premises Act—"an act to provide for the protection of the health, welfare and safety of persons employed in offices"—furthered the creation of new office blocks like the Bank of Ireland's.[31] The law mandated standards for offices on everything from temperature and cleanliness to overcrowding and lighting. Developers and executives soon learned that it was more profitable to build newer and bigger structures than to attempt the expensive restoration and remodeling of Dublin's creaky old Georgian homes for commercial use. Michael Scott's firm cashed in on the demand for functional, modern office space during

Figure 15. Bank of Ireland, Baggot Street. Photograph courtesy of the Irish Architectural Archive.

the 1960s. The Bank of Ireland awarded its lucrative contract to one of Scott's partners, Ronald Tallon, a devout follower of Mies. The three slab blocks, arranged around a corporate plaza (complete with a steel sculpture), the glass cladding and bronze stanchions, do far more for Dublin, reported *Build* in 1972, "than the Seagram Company did for New York."[32] The theme of "giving space back to the city" (in the form of a courtyard) is strengthened, the editors of *Build* suggest, by the use of the ground floor, which admits more "light than any comparable building in the city... as a public area for art."

Architect's Journal declared the modernist style of the bank "the ideal idiom for Georgian renewal, but there are some who disagree with this, favouring always a 'mock Georgian' style. Those who advocate the latter for all renewal projects are living in a dream world from which creativity can never escape."[33]

These high-rises, dramatic in the context of Dublin, were but a few of the numerous commercial and government buildings erected in Dublin during the 1960s in the style of international modernism, though in a stripped-down version. That decade also saw the state actively promote free trade, pursue membership in the European Union, and engage in the politics of reconciliation with the unionist administration in Northern Ireland.[34] It was a time when leading sociologists, observing the trends toward greater urbanization and industrialization, argued that the "national question had been relegated to the margin of Irish politics" (Moran and Purdie 1980, 160). Nationalism, it seemed, was becoming obsolete in the new international order, thus clearing the way, in the words of Luke Gibbons, "for a realignment in politics along class lines, or on a left/right division, as in other advanced European countries" (Gibbons 1996, 83). International-style architecture and modernist planning were the spatialization of these ideological shifts. They both symbolized a new kind of lifestyle, an erasure of the past in favor of a clean, orderly, sophisticated urbanism, one concerned with the quotidian, functional details of commerce and capital, rather than the messy complexities of memory and history, the textures and layers of local politics and geographies. In many ways, this marked an attempt to transcend the divisions left over from the Civil War: parochialism, sectarianism, underdevelopment, and stagnation. These buildings were meant to represent and create prosperity.

Going West: Urban Planning and the Pursuit of Progress

Architecture's companion in spatializing Ireland's revisionism was urban planning. The minister for local government, Kevin Boland, argued that the government's five-year plans could only be implemented in conjunction with strict planning guidelines: "economic and physical planning operate hand in hand" (Boland 1968, 173). Bally-mun's construction functioned as part of a new regional plan for Dublin, one that sought to direct future economic and population growth in the city. "An outward movement from Central Dublin of both employment and population is desirable.... If in the next 20 years, 75 per cent of all new jobs are sited on the periphery and numbers employed in the Canal [Central] Ring drop by 10 per cent, we will have done well" (Wright 1967, 7). This influential planning report, conducted by Myles Wright, was the first nationally commis-sioned plan to cast Dublin in a regional context.[35] (In addition to Dublin, it covered the adjacent counties of Meath, Wicklow, and Kildare.) Wright, a British planner (the postcolonial reliance on for-eign intellectuals remained high in Ireland), based his proposals on an increase in the metropolitan population of 275,000 over twenty years, based on estimates taken between 1961 and 1966, years of considerable growth. (The population of the capital and its environs grew considerably during the 1950s as rural areas depopulated. In 1951 the population of the city was 575,988. By 1971 the census re-vealed that Dublin and its environs held over 1 million inhabitants, almost one-third of the state's population.) Such rapid expansion, his influential report suggested, required 175,000 new dwellings, 140,000 jobs, and because he refused to consider investing in public trans-port, forty square miles of new roads and motorways (ibid., 17).

As restrictions for urban expansion existed to the south ("the scenically attractive mountain area," as he referred to it, which also, not coincidentally, contained most of the wealthier suburbs) and to the north (airport noise), Wright suggested creating four "new towns" to the immediate west of the main city, in an area that twenty-five years earlier Patrick Abercrombie had proposed as part of a green-belt. Each of the new centers was to house one hundred thousand people.[36] (Around the same time, this process was echoed in the north of Ireland with the foundation of the suburban "city" at Craigavon, thirty miles from Belfast.) Three of these new towns, at Condalkin, Tallaght, and Blanchardstown, expanded both rapidly and haphaz-ardly, although not in the Le Corbusier–inspired version of high-rise dispersal then popular in Britain, as seen in Highgate and Peckham in London. Rather, the late 1960s and early 1970s saw a series of sprawling housing estates grow up on the western periphery of Dublin. Within two decades, Tallaght consisted of twenty-seven main estates, twenty of them built by the local authority. Straight, wide streets facilitated traffic flow, while grass verges and pavements of standard width reinforced their uniformity (MacLaran 1993, 199). Built at a density of twenty-five units per hectare, each house with its own front and back garden, the estates lacked any historical reference points. Often older farm or manor houses were knocked down to accommodate the linear layout. There was no provision for local shops, civic centers, or sports halls, and, hence, no physical or psychological center to many of the new estates. The required percentage of public space was broken up into small allotments, resulting in fragmented corners of open space and marginally located playing areas. Architectural design was homogeneous, while row after row of identical houses fronted onto the street, making the thoroughfare the dominant feature of the landscape. Private developments in Tallaght ended in the late 1970s when recession came once more. Some held, until recently, empty shells of houses the builder had decided not to finish because of a fall in demand.

By the early 1980s Tallaght had a population of over eighty thousand, making it, after Dublin and Cork, the third largest city in the republic. Of Tallaght's population, 87 percent was under the age of forty, and eleven thousand children were under the age of four in 1985; the family unit size in Ireland was at the time considerably higher than elsewhere in Europe. Its residents, a mixture of inner-city Dubliners, often in the public development, and rural transplants, often in the private estate, existed at times alongside each other as class antagonists, separated by high walls, cul-de-sacs, or narrow strips of parkland. Until recently Tallaght had only a single post office, one library, one swimming pool, no hospital, no cinema; many of the estates were too poor to support such amenities. The mobile shop, a traditional image in rural Ireland, became a regular sight, with vans selling eggs, bread, milk, and other essentials replacing the corner shop in an area with only two supermarkets for over eighty thousand people. And there were only ten pubs since the area, originally zoned as a rural district, could not have two pubs within a mile of each other. Dublin Corporation had no office there to answer any queries. Locals had to make the trip downtown on the region's only bus route. Each estate was mandated by the local authority to provide a minimum of 10 percent open space, but these plots were most often narrow strips of land adjacent to the bigger roads or pieces tucked away in odd corners of the development, unsuitable for safe play and far from the original requirements of communal, green space. It was a landscape of contrasts, as urban fringes often are: to the west, the Dublin mountains; at their base vast, flat housing estates, some totally uncultivated, others unfinished, their waste ground adding to the emptiness of the scene. All of which is to say that the people whose lives took shape there (no doubt people of great resourcefulness) had to struggle constantly against environmentally reinforced middle-class stereotypes that perceived the poor as unable to look after themselves and unwilling, metaphorically, to cultivate their own gardens.[37]

In encouraging unhindered expansion westward, Wright's 1966 regional plan proposed opening the door to the prime symbol of Western consumerism, prosperity, and urbanization—the automobile. "Throughout the free world," he writes, "urban populations are 'voting with their wheels,' and there is every sign that as prosperity grows Dubliners will do likewise.... Dublin's circumstances do not call for the introduction of costly and complex public transport systems" (Wright 1967, 17). Establishing the American connection between the automobile and liberty, and its concomitant dismissal of public bus and rail, Wright called for bigger and wider roads. Killinarden, a 1972 housing estate in Tallaght, for example, is typified by long terraces of housing served by broad, straight roads, designed with speed and parking in mind. Ballymun, taking its cue from the British Department of Environment's 1966 "Roads for Urban Areas Manual," had 25 percent of its land area zoned for roadways and junctions (McGrath 1992, 36). The suburban developments called for by Wright, which provided the basis for the long-term development of the Dublin region, were based on the idea that each household would have its own car. This was reinforced by the regional nature of Wright's plan: as smaller, rural towns were rezoned for exurban housing and roads to them widened, car reliance was further encouraged. That this did not happen (due to the oil crisis and recession)

merely added to the social isolation felt by certain groups, in particular women, the elderly, and the unemployed, whose lack of mobility
contributed to their alienation from a society and economy apparently "on the move." The sprawling nature of development made
these areas even harder to serve with public transport.

A prime objective of Wright's report was to provide a new road
framework for Dublin, dispersing traffic by pushing jobs to the
periphery. In this, Wright showed great enthusiasm for the grid pattern, which he believed was the best layout for distributing traffic
across a wider area, and encouraging it to bypass the cluttered, historic core of the city, upon which all previous roads converged (Figure 16). The grid system, although dating back to Greek times, is
often associated with colonial settlements, especially since the seventeenth century. Most efficient at parceling out property, it was deployed in early American cities, for example, to facilitate the sale of
real estate to distant speculators.[38] Updated for Dublin in the 1960s,
the grid had not changed much in its objective. Wright envisaged the
geometrical design as another means to sell Dublin to the international investor and the American company.

The depopulation of the inner city and the subsequent decay of its
housing stock left many older roads and neighborhoods ripe for road-
widening schemes to accommodate newly suburbanized motorists. To
facilitate road widening, the corporation bought up older properties
and let them deteriorate, thereby hastening their demolition.[39] In
1968 the state hired a German traffic planner, Karl Schaechterle, to
devise a solution to the city's traffic problem. He proposed paving
over the historic Royal and Grand Canals, creating an inner ring road
(Schaechterle 1976). Only a major citizens' initiative halted the idea.
The western new towns were also constructed with large swathes of
open land between houses to allow for road expansion and motorway construction.

Wright's proposed grid plan for Dublin's traffic, and its ample provisions for new roads, was designed for efficiency of movement and
increased mobility of labor; its aim was also to provide the semiotics
of open, visible, modern space. His plan would bring Dublin into line
with the automobile-centered infrastructure required if international
industrial firms were to locate in Ireland. Spatial barriers would have
to be overcome.

Figure 16. Proposed road framework for Dublin. Existing and new roads form a grid of routes that distribute traffic and link the new western towns with Central Dublin and Dun Laoghaire. The reservation for a future national route is shown to the west. From Wright, *The Dublin Region* (1967), 23.

Legitimating the Present: Historiography and Revisionism

International-style architecture and modernist planning had as their ideological goal Ireland's disengagement from its entrenched and petty historic grievances: to be over and done with the past, and to turn the future into ambitious, far-reaching prosperity. We see these ideological oppositions clearly mirrored in the field of historiography, where in the 1960s and 1970s academic and popular attacks on the contemporary meaning and relevance of Irish nationalism intensified.[40] The task of forging a new set of cultural values—objectivity, cosmopolitanism, urbanism—for a liberal, modernizing society is easier if one demonizes the opposition; to argue in favor of the new cultural values, one portrays the old ideology as provincial, irrational, and repressive. These historical arguments about nationalism reared up in the 1960s, gaining energy and urgency against the backdrop of the fiftieth anniversary of the Easter Rising, the initial successes of Lemass's modernizing project, and the outbreak of the Troubles in the North. Scholars began to revise inherited understandings of the past and to reevaluate popular memory about key dates, events, and figures ("myths," as the new historians, intent on promoting their own objectivity and academic rigor, would label them). Many of the previously cherished beliefs about the struggle for independence—the heroism of its leaders, the motivations of "the people," the cruelty of the landlords, and the oppression of British colonialism—came under sustained intellectual and public pressure as historical revisionism gained momentum and popularity.

There has always been revisionism in Irish history, of course. The task of reinterpretation is the basis of any academic project. Within Irish intellectual circles, critics on both ends of the political spectrum have long debated the historical shape and significance of nationalism—its beginnings, its class interests, its leaders, rhetoric, and objectives. Luke Gibbons points out that revisionism had to wait until the late 1960s and 1970s to make a popular impact on Irish life (1992, 561). It was in the production of urban space, I argue, that revisionism made its most concrete mark. Gibbons and others trace the origins of Ireland's revisionist controversy to the founding of the journal *Irish Historical Studies* in 1938. This journal was formed by two Oxford-educated Irish historians, T. W. Moody and R. D. Edwards, whose goal was to update history-writing with a modern emphasis on objectivity, documentation, research, and the confrontation of national bias both "in the interests of academic probity and as a means of alerting teachers and general readers to the deficiencies inherent in the texts they had come to treat as authoritative" (Brady 1994, 4–5). *Irish Historical Studies,* its creators stated, was a deliberate attempt to imitate in an Irish context historiographical journals such as *Historiche Zeitschrift,* the *English Historical Review,* and the *American Historical Review,* there being no "counterpart" to these for the Irish scholar (Moody and Edwards 1994, 35).

In the preface to the first volume of their new journal, Moody and Edwards consistently stress the word *scientific* with regard to the study of history, elaborating on historical "research methods ... [and] annual lists of writings on Irish history" (Moody and Edwards

1994, 36–37). Theirs was not to be a political or polemical criticism that engaged in grievance or blame. Ireland, they argued, had no academic venue for the propagation of such research-oriented history, and their aim was to inculcate their work into school curricula. Up until the 1960s, when revisionism landed on fertile public ground, it remained a rather academic and lofty pursuit for professional historians; not a single anthology about this highly contentious and widespread historiographical project includes *Irish Historical Studies* articles from the 1940s or 1950s. When the national question exploded in the late 1960s, enflamed by the potent cocktail of modernization and the violence of the Troubles, the idea of reevaluating Irish history, especially its republican, socialist, and radical roots, took hold.

In the 1930s, in the shadow of independence, professional historians, keen to develop a "neutral" methodology, were not the only critics of nationalism. In the opposing ideological camp were a host of left-wing writers and cultural critics who were disenfranchised by what they saw as the collapse of the revolution into a mediocre, pandering state. Among these were figures such as Peadar O'Donnell, Liam O'Flaherty, and Sean O'Faolain, all of whom had fought against the treaty during the Civil War, and in the aftermath of partition became spokesmen for and symbols of those for whom the promise of independence had not been fulfilled. In his novels, Peadar O'Donnell charted the difficulties experienced by the Irish peasantry, fishermen, and small farmers in the wake of independence, when conservative land reforms pushed many people off the land and into the cities, or out of the country entirely, in search of work. O'Donnell's own life reads like a résumé of twentieth-century left-wing activism: he was a schoolteacher turned union organizer, an anti-treaty IRA soldier, the editor of *An Phoblacht (The Republic),* a founder of a Marxist splinter group called the Republican Congress, organizer of support against Franco, and, along with O'Faolain, editor of *The Bell.* It was around this last-named magazine, formed by O'Faolain in 1941, that the antiestablishment, revisionist left in the 1940s and 1950s congealed.

In contemporary criticism, the *Bell* receives accolades for being the "only counterweight to the ideological monolith of independent Ireland" (Brown 1985, 91). "Liberal in outlook and defiant in tone," O'Faolain's *Bell* editorials attacked clericism, puritanism, censorship, and, perhaps most devastatingly, what he depicted as Ireland's history of chauvinistic Gaelic nationalism, an ideology "that preserved a mythical past isolating Ireland from the realities of the present and prospects for the future" (Ruckenstein 2003, 33). Against his depiction of Irish nationalism as a backward ideology and authoritarian movement, O'Faolain lamented not only the "dismal social reality of Ireland," but the country's historical lack of industrialization and popular democracy, which he blamed not on the history of colonialism, but on the stubborn, ignorant mind of the Irish peasant. Over the centuries leaders and poets, writes O'Faolain, conned the people, the peasant majority, with visions of a traditional order restored and a land populated by "poets, nobles, friars, clerics, learned folk, heroes, seers, bards" (1980, 25). Romantic Ireland, he continues, had all the "trappings [of] an effete aristocratic order" (ibid., 29). Only one Irish politician, Daniel O'Connell, had the courage and vision to say, "Start afresh. Modernize ... [T]hrow overboard every scrap of the past that ha[s] not already, like the Wild Geese, abandoned the sinking ship [of nativism]" (O'Faolain 1992, 570). In 1944, he wrote that the "cult of the Gael" was "the opponent of all modernizations and improvisations—being by nature, in its constant reference of the middle ages—terrified of the modern world, afraid of modern life, inbred in thought, and, so, utterly narrow in outlook" (1992, 573).

In O'Faolain's writing was a classic revisionist move, one recognized by Gibbons, Kiberd, and Deane, the original analysts of revisionism: he expertly shifts the blame from colonizer to victim. O'Faolain's Marxism takes its place in a long intellectual history of radicalism that has refused to embrace nationalism on the grounds that the ideology, along with its purveyors, is racist and exclusionary, and disingenuously claims to speak for the "people."[41] In "The Gaelic Cult," O'Faolain set out to undermine the idea of cultural continuity in Ireland, arguing that the notion of Gaelic traditions is of quite recent origin: "We have, in recent times, created a very wonderful delusion," he writes. "It is variously called the Gaelic Tradition, or the Gaelic Nation, or simply The Gael. It is a mystique that ... has tried to discover in the old Gaelic world a model, or master-type—rather like the National Socialist mythology of the Pure Aryan—to which we all must conform" (1992, 569). All this despite the obvious ideological complexity of Irish nationalism.

In the context of the Troubles, and the way they came to dominate national and political life, along with Lemass's economic revolution, the historical project initiated by Moody and Edwards in the
1930s moved to the forefront of public conversation. What had before been a relatively obscure and independent pursuit increasingly
overlapped with the economically expansionist objectives of the state.
In reviewing thirty years of *Irish Historical Studies* in 1968, Moody
sums up the condition of Irish history writing, in the years before
and after his journal's appearance: "At every level, from that of the
school text-book to that of the popular survey for the general reader,
the available modern publications on the general history of Ireland
are still, with a few shining examples [his own, presumably], meagre
in scope, narrow in sympathy, amateur in treatment, uninformed by
new research and often unreadable" (Moody 1994b, 38). But the
good news, he maintains, is that as the Irish economic expansion advances, and as Irishmen become more forward-looking and outward-
looking, they become more, not less, interested in history, and they
follow "the lead of historians in breaking away from servitude to
national myths and instead to studying them" (ibid., 46).

In 1966 the building of Ballymun coincided with the fiftieth anniversary of the 1916 Rising. The two events are not unrelated. Both
sought to redefine the relationship of a reputedly "modernizing" society to the legacy of the past. Ballymun's architecture aimed to repress any traces of national style or iconography, to clear a space in
which a new kind of industrial, urban, and internationally oriented
community could prosper, free from the myths and historical spaces
of the past. Likewise, the anniversary of the Rising raised a chorus
of discussion over the meaning of nationalism in contemporary Ireland and the accomplishments of the postcolonial state. In this context, revisionist historiography prospered. In 1966 Father Francis
Shaw wrote one of the most damning and influential historiographical revisionist texts, "The Canon of Irish History—A Challenge,"
which iconoclastically attacks Patrick Pearse, writer of the Proclamation of Independence and inspiration behind the 1916 uprising
(Shaw 1972). Shaw's article was to set the tone for many of the intellectual debates that would dominate the next decades. Perhaps
naturally for a cleric, Shaw focused his critique on Pearse's messianic
cult of nationalism, a patriotism in which holiness combined with

the discourse of blood sacrifice, redemption, and national resurrection. Pearse's rhetoric of national predestination, along with the "cult" of the Easter Rising, perpetuated by overly nationalist pedagogy in the state's schools, merely fed, according to Shaw, a cycle of violence that was encouraging a new generation to take up arms for unattainable and false ideals. "It is time," Shaw writes, "that we as a Christian people should forget the past. There can surely be no more criminal disservice to Ireland than the determination to keep the fire of hatred burning" (153).

Shaw discredits Pearse's motivations, beliefs, hopes, personality, and knowledge of history. Pearse, along with a half-dozen other men, took it upon himself to decide what the nation should want, when he and his followers seized control of central Dublin in 1916. In doing so, they proved their elitism and disdain for the "common Irishman." Pearse, we learn, was "cold" and "withdrawn," a "mystic" and a "dreamer," a hypocrite, and, perhaps worst of all in a priest's eyes, a socialist, who advocated the "idea that the land and soil of a country were the property of the State" (Shaw 1972, 120). Shaw accuses Pearse of conjuring up ancient myths, those of Cúchulainn and Colm Cille, about whose history and production we know little, to further his own aims—the portrayal of a pristine Gaelic past, destroyed by the Saxon invader. Nationalist history, in effect, is taken to task for being sacrilegious and mythological. All of this is stated with no reference to the larger context in which Pearse wrote, a time when the major European powers were fighting the Great War, and creating their own myths of sacrifice and service.

Shaw, in a now familiar theoretical move, critiqued the binary oppositions, which, he felt, lay at the heart of Ireland's inability to escape its own past. The opening lines of "The Canon of Irish History" point to the boredom and inertia felt by many historians toward the inherited and official narrative of the nationalist struggle: "In the right corner virgin Éire, virtuous and oppressed, in the left the bloody Saxon, the unique source of every Irish ill and malaise; round eight, the duration of each round a hundred years" (1972, 117).

Adding complexity to the interpretation of history is, of course, all for the good, but in attempting to distinguish between the rhetorical uses made of history by nationalists like Pearse and the skeptical, rational search for complexity and objectivity conducted by "revisionists" like themselves, the new historians refused to submit their own language and prejudices to ideological self-examination or questioning. They presented their arguments as social science opposed to mythology. True history was the opposite of literature, while fiery nationalism, which down through the years has had its share fair of writers and poets, has manipulated the hearts of even the strongest men. Modern history, like the rational architecture that was its spatial contemporary, was not supposed to be passionate or to flirt rhetorically with tradition and emotion.

How accurately the term *colonialism* describes Anglo-Irish relations remains one of the more disputed notions raised by the revisionists. In the final paragraph of "The Canon of Irish History," Shaw writes, "Ireland and Britain are two islands placed by God's creation beside one another. The paths of their respective histories have of necessity constantly crossed: in a sense they have always got in each other's way, and their relationship throughout the centuries has not been happy" (Shaw 1972, 153). Shaw's rhetoric works to convert what had previously been taught as the conquest of a smaller, less powerful country by a much larger and industrial one into a history of two "islands" (not, noticeably, two nations), whose paths have merely crossed, as if it were a serendipitous encounter between equals.

By the 1970s revisionists claimed that these myths still pervaded Irish history, and they set out to question them. The famine, Moody suggests in "Irish History and Irish Mythology," had little to do with British policy in Ireland, and more to do with bad weather, falling prices, and unemployment (Moody 1994a, 82). The government, he asserts, prevented an even worse catastrophe through the provision of massive food relief. Likewise, arguing against popular memory, he maintains that landlords in the post-Famine era were not "characteristically predatory nor tenants victimized" (83). Another mythology that Moody sets out to falsify is that which he calls the "predestinate nation," the myth that "identifies the democratic Irish nation of the nineteenth century with pre-conquest Ireland" and "incorporates the concept of an eight centuries' struggle with England as the central theme of Irish history" (84). This tale, for Moody, celebrates the achievement of independence in 1922 as the partial fulfillment of a destiny that requires the extinction of British authority in Northern

Ireland to complete itself. (Here one sees a particular bent to revisionism: the promotion of partition and a continued British presence in Northern Ireland.) Moody's thesis, both in the essay "Irish History and Irish Mythology" and throughout his work, critiques the accuracy of the colonial model for studying Irish history.

Revisionism, at first glance, has an almost radical appeal. Not unlike moves within postcolonial theory subsequent to it, revisionism can appear to critique bourgeois nationalism: the cultural nationalism of the Catholic middle class who had inherited the state structure after 1922. Subaltern studies, for example, emerged in Southeast Asia and emphasized the need to rewrite the history of the nation from a "bottom up" perspective, one that sought to tell the stories and lives of those whom more traditional historiography—conservative, liberal, Marxist—had ignored. The narrative of the nation that subaltern studies seeks to dispel is one that portrays nationalism as a united and an emancipatory movement, whose journey is developmental, moving from precolonial society through the violence and upheaval of the colonial moment and up to the postcolonial moment, that is, the formation of a national state, in which everything is finished. The educated elite, according to this idealistic narrative, has mobilized, organized, disciplined, and led the disparate social groupings and political ideologies that made up the anticolonial struggle, shaping them into a coherent nationalist movement. This has never been precisely the case, of course, and the linearity of this nationalist plot belies the fact that much of what was embedded in the original desire that was anticolonialism remained unfulfilled after the creation of an independent state.

In Ireland the anticolonial struggle consisted of a constellation of competing forces and ideologies (feminist, peasant, worker, and nationalist), all of which, as Lloyd stresses, had their own "temporalities" and were "defined by a different rhythm because they [had] different ends," such as the elimination of the oppression of workers or women, or the redistribution of land.[42] Subaltern studies, then, addresses the "historic failure of the nation to come into its own" (Guha 1982, 7). Like revisionism, it stands in opposition to the political and social structure of the postindependence state and disavows what its purveyors see as the ideological structure and cultural essentialism that emerged at the state level as a result of anticolonialism. Subaltern studies and revisionism differ, however, in their motivations and their politics. Subaltern studies moves to recover the various struggles of resistance that have been occluded by the nationalist endeavor to attain and hold the reins of state.[43] Revisionism's agenda is not radical, not an exploration of history from below; it merely points to and debunks nationalist myths. Revisionism sets out to deradicalize the past for the purposes of creating a deradicalized present, whose physical manifestation is the arrival en masse of international-style architecture and planning.

As the rest of Europe began to critique the kind of architecture and urban planning associated with international-style buildings, standardized housing schemes, and ahistorical new towns, Ireland was embracing them. Ballymun was as much a product of urban planning as it was a result of a new take on history and modernization. Likewise, the new towns on Dublin's western fringe, and the new regional plan for the city, instantiated a pervasive ideology of global progress made concrete. The high-rise offices and cubic slabs that appeared on the skyline of Dublin from the early 1960s onward encouraged a new urban population of white-collar commuters. Architecture in Ireland during the 1960s, as in other periods of ideological realignment, demonstrated these changes physically and, in so doing, helped to entrench them. The rewriting of history that was required to naturalize the economic and cultural transition of the 1960s found its spatial manifestation in the flat, rational, and concrete structures of international modernism.

4 | Memory and the City: Globalization and Urban Renewal in Dublin

Catching Up: Ireland in the 1990s and the Myth of Prosperity

Contemporary Dublin is bursting at the seams. Simultaneously crowded and sprawling, the city tosses up new upscale apartments as fast as the suburbs can absorb more countryside. Industrial cranes are everywhere. The city's streets are jammed with tourists and consumers. Something new has been happening to the city, to the nation—but what, exactly? There has been a wave of unprecedented economic growth, immigrants from many different foreign countries are arriving, the Irish diaspora is returning, multinational companies are setting up factories, and Irish popular culture, whether on the big screen, in theater, or in music, has struck a chord worldwide. Suddenly, after years of urban blight, Dublin is the fourth most expensive city in Europe, after Milan, Copenhagen, and London.[1] To make sense of Ireland's putative success, politicians and cultural commentators have enthusiastically adopted the language and policies of economic globalization—privatization, free trade, and cuts in public spending—along with the attendant cultural vocabulary of cosmopolitanism and postmodernism: upscale worldliness, mobility, urbanism, and cultural hybridity.[2] Ireland, it would appear, is now part of the wider European project of national fragmentation and continental

172

consolidation, its economy no longer mired in the so-called dead-end of nationalism. Ireland, led by Dublin's growth, has at last, it is said, made it into the first world. The country, according to optimistic critics, is finally free from the troublesome and distorted myths of the past: the history of British colonialism and its corollary, chauvinistic nationalism. Only now is Ireland free to stand on its own two feet, independent and confident.

Financiers of all sorts have jumped on the neoliberal bandwagon, promoting Ireland's success story as the best example of a European economy gone global. In 1994, in an obvious reference to the "miracle" economies of the Far East, an American investment bank, Morgan Stanley, labeled Ireland a "Celtic Tiger"—a country with low inflation, few tariffs, rapid export growth, a commitment to privatization, and a willingness to do almost anything to attract transnational corporations (O'Hearn 2000, 67).

The nickname "Celtic Tiger" has become a cliché, a resonant discourse, at once superficial and powerful, and capable of simultaneously arousing praise and drawing criticism. In the popular press, the acclaim emerges from a cursory reading of the recent consumer habits of Ireland's middle and upper class. As a lead article in *Fortune* magazine reported recently: "Striding through the streets of Dublin these days is an entirely new species of Irishman and Irishwoman: educated, optimistic, and affluent—unaffected by the twin demons of poverty and despair that hounded their ancestors for the last several hundred years."[3] At last, the implication seems to be, history has righted itself; after all the fake starts and U-turns, the nation is fulfilling its destiny and promise. As *Fortune* put it: "Ireland has caught up with the rest of Western civilization." The Celtic Tiger, then, is a myth behind which lies a reservoir of upbeat associations: Europeanization, youth, sophistication, newness, confidence, happiness, and faith in the market.

The current forces of multinational capital are enacting changes on the physical landscape of Dublin, too. What do those changes tell us about the shifting needs and priorities of nationalism in Ireland? How are memory and the past invoked in contemporary space and urban planning in order to help make sense of, and make excuses for, the present? I argue that, unlike the modernization of the 1960s, which sought to repress historical references and indigenous styles, contemporary globalization embraces tradition, seeing it as both a commodity (to produce profit) and a means to gain control over history (the representation of the past in commodified form—tourism, movies, festivals, and heritage). Ireland now has a government minister and agency responsible for "heritage." Globalization must also work within and through the past, so as not to appear hostile to local traditions. It is not a coincidence, therefore, that the temporal structure underlying much of the discourse of prosperity in Ireland today combines references to the very old and the very new. History is required to bestow depth on the fleetingness of the present; multinationals do not, after all, have deep attachments to where they locate.[4]

If history, simply put, is the collective, public understanding of the past, then memory is a more personal, individual affair, less reliable perhaps, but essential to the construction of our identities: we remember our families, our childhoods, our emotions, the better to know our present selves. Memory and history can never truly be separated—personal memories bear all the traces of public events, just as public events ultimately register with the personal self. But memory and history can often be at odds, as accounts of historic or public events are remembered differently, or as personal memories fade and official history takes over. One manifestation of Ireland's participation in the marketplace of global culture has been the rise of literary memoirs and their attendant international popularity. What might this mean ideologically, one wonders: why memoir now? The genre of memoir draws our attention to the struggle over the production of memory. Memoirs, particularly the Dublin kind, are often read as exercises in nostalgia. However, nostalgia is not to be dismissed merely as compensation for the alienating effects of the present, as it is often portrayed. Rather, we need to ask what it is in these memoirs that appeals to people. The answer, I argue, rests with seeing in nostalgia and memory not just a concern with the past, but, as Keya Ganguly writes, "a desire for what is not yet possible" (2001, 89). Memories bear the trace of what we would like to be. Nostalgia, then, whether in the memoir or in the "heritage industry," can serve as a critique of the present as much as it can be a lamentation about the past.

I aim to tease out the equation between memory and the city. But first, I shall return to the discourse of the Celtic Tiger and highlight some of the ways in which critics theorize the relationship between economics and culture and how the idea of globalization is deployed in Ireland, both as the cause of current prosperity and as the legitimating discourse behind the Europeanizing, market-driven narrative of official nationalism.

What do commentators identify as the economic indicators contributing to the stellar performance of the Irish economy? The "magnificent" growth in the GDP throughout the 1990s—approximately 10 percent for 1995, 1997, and 1998, reports one booster—coupled with the "handsome" 5.2 percent average growth for the thirteen years between 1986 and 1999, adds up to a "superb" performance, "when a growth rate of 3 per cent is considered good for most economies" (Sweeney 1999, 1). The list of high-tech companies that have established assembly plants in the country during the last decade is impressive: Apple, Gateway, Dell, Hewlett-Packard, Microsoft, and Seagate. Situated mostly on the fringes of the city or in more rural locations, these transnational companies were, according to the *Economist,* positioned to avail themselves of a 10 percent corporate tax, massive state subsidies, and a cheap, educated, English-speaking workforce.[5] Intel, a defiantly nonunion employer, has steadily increased its Irish workforce to over four thousand employees, expanding substantially in Leixlip, just beyond Dublin's sprawling suburbs.[6] These companies perpetuate an image of industrialization without a working class;[7] science-based pharmaceutical and computer companies do not conjure up images of smokestacks and unions. Ironically, this situation places Ireland in the European tradition of modernization, but having skipped over the two-hundred-year process of industrial development, the country now sits at the core of Europe's present drive of postindustrialism and deregulation. According to the U.S. Bureau of Labor Statistics, in 1993, at the birth of the Celtic Tiger, Irish companies compensated their employees in the manufacturing sector at an average rate of $12.18 per hour, while those in Germany paid $25.71, and French companies, $16.23.[8] Today, although labor costs in Ireland have risen, the cost of employing workers remains significantly below that of other Western European countries.[9] For promoters of the new economy, Ireland is a shining example of a deregulated, free-market economy finally crawling out from under the rock of statist interventions and social welfare.

The Celtic Tiger, though lauded by much of the media, Irish and otherwise, has been recognized as having a negative impact on older forms of employment. Dozens of industries have disappeared in Dublin since Ireland's entry into the European Union: Guinness, once the city's premier employer, has all but halted production at its famous St. James's Gate brewery, shifting much of its production to Kenya and Ghana; the local fishing fleet has been greatly diminished; and bakeries, flour mills, and textile companies have all closed. Outside the city, the number of farmers and agricultural workers has fallen dramatically, as intensive production, driven by European policies, reduces even further the number of smallholdings. As critics, among them economic commentator Denis O'Hearn, have pointed out, much of the job growth has been in the lower-paying services sector. Half the new positions are for clerical workers, shop assistants, and hotel, restaurant, and kitchen staff, along with other personnel associated with the spending spree of the new wealthy minority (O'Hearn 2000, 79). Beneath the myth of the Celtic Tiger, then, lies a range of economic effects associated with globalization: displacement of rural workers, diminished job security, longer hours, more low-paying service jobs, weakened unions, and rising disparity between rich and poor. Furthermore, as the EU expands eastward, liberal critics argue that the country now faces competition from new, low-cost European locations. With unions closely allied to government through a series of national pay agreements and, until recently, a relatively unspoiled environment, Ireland has become a good place to set up a subsidiary from which profits can be transferred, exaggerated, and readily repatriated. According to O'Hearn, "U.S. companies overall have profit rates of about 30 percent in the south of Ireland, while Irish companies average 3 to 5 percent" (76). The profits of American multinationals in Ireland are five times greater than those they receive elsewhere around the world. All of this, according to O'Hearn, is attributable to dubious corporate accounting practices. To make the state still more competitive and to reassure foreign investors about the safety of their assets, a series of Irish administrations over the last ten years have made dramatic cuts in welfare and challenged public monopolies (the national airline, telephone, road, and rail services have all seen total or partial privatization).

Another critic makes the connection between the rhetoric of the Celtic Tiger and its reality. According to James Wickham, the Celtic Tiger perpetuates the illusion that everyone in the country is well educated and technologically literate. Mainstream articles regularly cite the well-trained workforce as the key to all the economic success. "Throughout history," suggests one such writer, "Ireland has been known as the land of saints and scholars.... It has always been very focused on education" (Barron 1995, 16). The repetition of the high-tech mantra, combined with flattering educational rhetoric, creates another myth of the Celtic Tiger, that of an "intelligent island" (Wickham 1998, 81). I contend that just as the phrase "Celtic Tiger" combines a reference to the premodern with an allusion to the post-industrial, so too the use of the phrase "saints and scholars" helps to legitimate the process of globalization by displaying neoliberalism's attentiveness to and knowledge of history. Globalization—its languages and images—appropriates the past to anchor itself more thoroughly and to present itself as the logical outcome of history.

The economic transformations in Ireland during the Celtic Tiger have their cultural corollary in the changing image of the nation. Both metamorphoses can only come about with an attendant reconfiguration of certain basic expressions of Irish history and identity: emigration, the Constitution, and popular culture. Unlike the repression of history associated with the modernization project of the 1960s, quite literally through the physical destruction of historic sites, the opposite has happened during this recent phase of globalization. History, often reimagined as "heritage," or downsized to the more generic "past," has been embraced. Tradition is no longer seen as retarding economic growth; rather, it may hasten it, especially with regard to tourism, which is now Ireland's leading industry.[10] While European tourism on the whole did not grow during the 1990s, Irish tourism increased from 2.2 million visitors to 5.5 million (Sweeney 1999, 66). This is remarkable for a country whose history has been largely defined by poverty and embattlement, a land that has been a point of departure, not a destination. Ironically, Ireland's deserted and scarred western landscape lends it an air of exoticism and historical depth; its literature and music have proven marketable to an English-speaking clientele. Ireland is cleverly situated as a rural "other" to the excessive industrialization and dense population of Europe. At the same time, it is not meant to be too different or challenging; it is presented as a safe, friendly, hospitable environment. A significant percentage of Structural Funds (30 billion euros in total) granted to Ireland between 1989 and 1999 by the European Union were to be spent on developing a tourist infrastructure. In the 1990s over 150 heritage and interpretive centers sprang up around the country (Sheerin 1998, 40). Many of these drew on aspects of Irish culture that could be funneled into a tourist experience: Joyce's Tower, the Irish Writers' Museum, the Famine Museum, and Temple Bar, a revitalized urban leisure district.

Emigration, the traditional symptom of Ireland's dependent position in the world economy, has also been naturalized to promote the possibilities afforded by contemporary commerce. Until very recently, emigration was discussed in Ireland as a tragedy that had its roots in trauma—specifically, the Famine. Before the recent economic upturn, the Famine was taught in schools as the defining moment in Irish history, the primeval event from which all ills emerged—the most long-lasting being large-scale emigration. Emigration was a uniquely Irish sorrow, and it permeated the culture. But in much the same way that the pursuit of tourism has molded certain aspects of Irish history and tradition, those who wish to see Ireland's new prosperity as a permanent upswing have reshaped the narrative of emigration as well. In 1987, just before Ireland's economic take-off, Brian Lenihan, a leading politician, declared in a *Newsweek* interview, "We should not be defeatist or pessimistic about [emigration]. We should be proud about it. After all, we can't all live on a small island."[11] A second politician remarked that "the way forward is to invest in children and give them the skills to compete anywhere in the world."[12] In addition, students who could not find work after graduation were suddenly academic victors. As Senator Joe O'Toole reported, "There is nothing wrong with the fact that 10,000 students [had] to go to Britain to study. Let them out there to do the business."[13]

Emigration had once been akin to exile. In the changed climate, Irish emigration was no longer something to be ashamed of, but a factor that would ultimately help sustain the new economy. Revisionist rewritings of recent (1980s) emigration celebrate those who left as part of what Lenihan calls "our global generation.... What we have now is a very literate emigrant who thinks nothing of going to the United States and going back to Ireland and maybe on to Germany and back to Ireland again."[14] This idea of the Irish as a mobile, entrepreneurial, and global workforce reinforces mainstream globalization theory, which argues that our concepts of home, permanence, sovereignty, and identity are constantly in flux. The Celtic Tiger has turned tragedy into entrepreneurialism, trauma into celebration, providing an elite, indigenous defense of emigration.

Even the Irish Constitution has been rewritten, boldly redefining what it means to be Irish to fit the contours of the new economic and cultural circumstances. In May 1998, as if prefiguring that age-old cosmopolitan dream in which notions of territorial authority are undone, the Irish people voted overwhelmingly to give up part of their national territory. In order to have better relations with their Unionist neighbors in Northern Ireland, they renounced the 1937 constitutional claim to the six counties of the North as being part of the nation of Ireland; in other words, people in the North could "opt out" of the nation.[15] In the words of Declan Kiberd, "If constitutions are written in the language of the nineteenth century, revolving around concepts of sovereignty and boundaries, this was a gesture of the twenty-first century, a recognition that identities are overlapping and dialogic and that it is now possible to be British or Irish or both" (Kiberd 2000, 154).

Article Two of the Constitution once defined the nation confidently in territorial terms as "the whole island, its islands, and its territorial seas."[16] The newly adopted version defines the nation of Ireland more vaguely, and less in terms of a physical place than in terms of its people: "It is the entitlement and birthright of every person born in the island of Ireland, which includes its islands and seas, to be part of the Irish nation.... Furthermore, the Irish nation cherishes its special affinity with people of Irish ancestry living abroad who share its cultural identity and heritage."[17] The constitutional reference to the descendants of Irish emigrants around the world is also an interesting legal development, addressing, as it does, the many subjects of other nations who may be unaware that the Irish state "cherishes" them. The only internationally recognized claim over the North is now the British one. Article Three of the Constitution, which had aspired to "the reintegration of the national territory," has also been revised as part of the Belfast Agreement, dropping the assured nationalist language. It now "recognizes that a united Ireland shall be brought about by only peaceful means with the consent of the majority of the people, democratically expressed, in both jurisdictions in the island."[18] Partition has now been codified, as unionists in the North, through this consent clause, have effectively been given a veto over any future incorporation of the North into a united Ireland.

For the mainstream press, the constitutional alterations, the Belfast Agreement, and, indeed, the IRA ceasefire itself are a result, in part, of the economic policies of globalization, which are seen as bringing about the irrelevancy of the nation-state. Nobel Peace Prize winner and leader of the Social Democratic and Labour Party (SDLP), John Hume, holds that concepts of nationality based on the definition of territory are "old fashioned."[19] Denis Coghlan, chief political correspondent of the *Irish Times,* explains, with regard to the constitutional changes, that the Celtic Tiger allowed for the "dismantling of outdated, arthritic concepts and perceptions in favor of open-ended dual citizenship and closer relations within and between these islands in an EU context."[20] In Ireland, economic progress and neoliberalism have accompanied constitutional change in bringing about the literal redefinition of the nation.

Meanwhile, the popularity of Ireland's mass culture continues to grow. *Riverdance,* a postmodern pastiche of Irish folk forms, sells out night after night to metropolitan audiences. It has been celebrated in the press as another example of Ireland having shrugged off its postcolonial inferiority and taken its place confidently on the world stage. In the cinematic novels of Roddy Doyle—*The Commitments, The Snapper,* and *The Van*—representations of working-class deprivation in cheaply constructed, postcolonial, gray housing estates are transformed into quaint tales of local color, upbeat yarns of personal survival during times of economic restructuring. Brothers Frank and Malachy McCourt in their books marketed their own regional mixture of poverty, Catholicism, and cute proletarianism. The aim of *Riverdance* is to create spectacle. The show replaces the forms, aesthetics, and spaces of the older, more rigid style of Irish dancing, asso-

ciated with the project of cultural nationalism, with a broadly appealing, sexier style designed to meet the demands of a global market.
(*Riverdance* for a moment became *Eurodance* when it was performed
at the launch of the European Central Bank in Frankfurt.)

Current neoliberal trends in Ireland appropriate the signs and
images of Irish history in order to lend themselves an air of permanency. The nickname "Celtic Tiger" celebrates the power of the free
market to liberate both individuals and nations from the chains of
tradition. It suggests that the Irish should give up their age-old sense
of victimhood and compete with the rest of the world in a game
whose rules are already prescribed. The rhetoric of globalization directly affects the production of culture. If capitalism in America and
elsewhere is touted as having killed off socialism, then in Ireland it is
claimed to have defeated nationalism—not by denouncing it but,
ironically, by appealing to it. I turn next to a discussion of how the
discourse of neoliberalism assimilates the language of history and
nationalism, approaching the question primarily through a reading
of urban space in Dublin.

Urban Renewal and Globalization in Dublin

It is, perhaps, in the current wave of urban growth and rebuilding,
especially in Ireland's capital, that the effects of the country's newfound wealth appear most vivid and stark. Dublin's planners and
architects have, with a new intensity, been busy preparing the kind
of urban space required to maintain Dublin's role as an up-and-
coming Euro-city. New motorways, laid down with money from the
European Community, ring the city, bypassing congested neighborhoods, facilitating travel, and encouraging an ever greater number of
car users. The new M50 corridor, circling the western fringes of the
city, is creating American-style "edge cities," where hotels, shopping
centers (such as the Liffey Valley Center, Ireland's largest mall), and
industrial estates occupy the major intersections. Low-density housing estates hug the length of the corridor. Dormitory communities
are springing up relentlessly in every direction from Dublin, fifty and
sixty miles outside the capital. But despite recent investment in public transport, traffic congestion is still the norm, and the speed of

travel in the city now averages around nine miles an hour, slower than ten years ago and slower even than when the horse and buggy was the primary method of transportation.[21]

Between 1998 and 2000 the number of hotels increased from 80 to 115, with 20 under construction.[22] As the power of consumption in Dublin strengthens, the city witnesses a greater emphasis on the creation of spaces of distinction that accommodate differentiated tastes.[23] Shopping "gallerias," such as the upscale Powerscourt Town Center or the Westbury Mall, house fashionable boutiques, imported-food markets, and art galleries instead of chain stores. Exclusive new golf courses, installed in the grounds of refurbished Anglo-Irish estates on the outskirts of Dublin, cater to an international business class.[24] Health clubs and fitness centers offer new leisure choices. The population of the republic increased at a rate of around a thousand people per week during the 1990s, the majority of them settling in the Dublin region. This population growth, along with the speculative property market, has led to a surge in house prices.[25] Houses, both in the city proper and in some of the older suburbs, now regularly go for over 1 million pounds, leaving the less well-off having to travel farther out to the hinterlands to find cheaper housing. This results in more housing estates colonizing the countryside, and ribbon development stretching for miles along the edges of rural roads. Many rural towns have become suburbs of Dublin.

With banks eager to lend and the state, in deregulatory fashion, getting out of the house-building business, many young people find themselves heavily mortgaged, working to maintain a house that they rarely have time to enjoy. The fear exists, too, that Dublin is repeating the cycle of boom and bust that London experienced under Thatcher and that the rules and regulations drawn up for quieter times no longer fit. With planners and engineers fleeing previously cherished state jobs for the private sector, there are fewer officials left to enforce the already lax planning laws. Nor does Ireland follow the British planning model of taking into public ownership the tracts of land that are going to be developed. In Ireland, therefore, individual developments can go through several planning and appeal stages, each one increasing the risk of bribery and corruption, which, as is now coming to light, has dominated proceedings and politics for decades. The overall result, then, is a rather chaotic, unplanned, sprawling, yet bustling city. Those who can, reap the benefits, while those who cannot get left behind, often in pockets of the city where unemployment, illiteracy, and crime are met with increasingly hostile responses.

At the heart of Ireland's integration into the world of global finance is the recently constructed International Financial Services Centre, a glistening office park occupying the city's abandoned docks (Figure 17). Completed in 1991, it now houses several hundred companies from around the world, dealing in everything from corporate financing to aircraft and bloodstock insurance (O'Brien 1993, 10–14). Constructed on the old Custom House Docks, it is, like the Custom House of two hundred years ago, a self-conscious symbol, the physical proof of commercial faith in a future linked with the wider world. The IFSC is the new symbol of the Celtic Tiger, generating around 500 million dollars per year for the Exchequer (Sweeney 1999, 51). A regional variant of Canary Wharf, the IFSC has gained a reputation as Europe's back office, dealing in pushing around the dreary bits of paperwork that it would cost twice as much to process in Frankfurt or London. Around it, hundreds of luxury condominiums, invisible to the passerby, provide the latest styles of urban living: gated (moated) communities sealed off from the ghettos just beyond, continental bistros, private security, and public spaces designed with only the salaried and childless in mind. (Signs read, "No Playing Allowed.") The IFSC's glass transparency is disingenuous, a bank of windows that implies welcome but enforces exclusion. Safe from outside intruders, yet at the center of things, the docklands is Dublin's homage to its new entrepreneurial class. The IFSC has drawn the most attention to the process of gentrification in Dublin because of its construction in the heart of Sheriff Street, a deprived street at the core of Dublin's working-class community. Sheriff Street was seen by commercial interests as threatening the success of the IFSC. The civic planners had to retroactively erect a giant net around the building to keep the regular volleys of stones and bricks out.[26]

Beginning in 1986, as Dublin courted international capital, the state followed British and American precedent and inaugurated a series of tax-driven urban renewal schemes in specified areas of

Figure 17. International Financial Services Centre. Photograph by author.

Dublin's inner city. The intended effect of the tax-relief schemes was "to promote urban renewal and redevelopment by promoting investment and reconstruction of buildings in designated areas."[27] These run-down areas tended to be geographically and historically central. The original neighborhoods marked for renewal were the Quays along the River Liffey, Gardiner Street, and Henrietta Street. Each of these areas was tied to the history of the city: the Quays dated back to the 1700s; Gardiner Street was once the heart of ascendancy Dublin; Henrietta Street held Gandon's King's Inn. The Custom House Docks also benefited from particular incentives aimed directly at attracting financial service activity (leading to the creation of the IFSC). Following the successes of these original projects, the government has continued to demarcate older areas, relying on their history to market their rejuvenation and gentrification. In the last several years, the government has earmarked the area around O'Connell Street for renewal, deeming the region the "Historic Area Rejuvenation Project" (HARP).[28]

Smithfield, too, one of Dublin's last urban villages, and the working-class Docklands have seen their downmarket status altered for tax investment purposes. The idea was to rejuvenate older neighborhoods that had seen little or no private investment for many years and to attract new residents and investors to the city. The first schemes were launched in 1986, and by 1994 almost thirteen thousand new apartments either had been built or were in the works.[29] The first survey that recorded these dramatic changes showed a substantial increase in population in parts of the city that had long been in decline.[30] But the demographic makeup of this population was revealing: the majority were childless, single, well educated, and in their twenties. These were the people celebrated in laudatory discussions of the Celtic Tiger, the new economy, and the nation's new cultural confidence. A stroll through any Dublin street that contains one of the new apartment blocks vividly illustrates the nature of this change: the houses are small ("shoeboxes," they were colloquially called), they were hastily built, and now, only a few years later, they already show signs of wear and tear in their peeling paint and rising damp. These one-bedroom apartments were made to look bigger and more ornate than they really are: early showrooms sported furniture that was smaller than normal in order to create the illusion of more space; the units include nonfunctioning, metal balconies screwed to the outside walls. The housing is also, not surprisingly, faux exclusive, with its fortress architecture, apartment buildings overlooking private courtyards, roof gardens for residents only, and high-security electronic gates, all of which feed into the logic of a pioneering entrepreneurial class.

Within a few years, it became impossible to ignore the poor quality of this housing. The government, under the leadership of Liz McManus, a practicing architect and minister of the environment, ordered a review of the urban renewal schemes that had led to both great prosperity and obvious profiteering. The international firm that oversaw the government review drew public attention to the usual

flaws associated with gentrification.[31] The government, caught between the reality of these findings and its own commitment to becoming one of the most open economies in Europe, was loath to intervene
in the property market. As the 1990s closed, urban renewal schemes,
bar minor reforms, continued to be created in older neighborhoods
where the rhetoric of history and preservation could be successfully
used to promote the property speculation that was feeding and housing the new economy. As Prime Minister Bertie Ahern said upon the
launch of the Smithfield development, "This change must cherish
the history and traditions of the area, while embracing the culture of
modern city life. Rejuvenating Smithfield will also hold a place in the
heart of future generations of Dubliners."[32]

That there is little resistance to the ever growing process of renewal also speaks to the city's enormous dependence on foreign capital and to the desire to support trends that are seen as putting money
into the urban core (renewal equals jobs) after years of decline. Gentrification, so visible and apparently laudable, has most often been
viewed as the long-awaited answer to the city's most intractable problems: poverty, population decline, and destruction. An EU report
lauds the arrival of urban renewal methods in Ireland. Temple Bar
had been "dying the slow death of an inner-city district that had
outlived its usefulness" until "in 1991 its redemption became official
when the Irish Parliament passed an act for its renewal and development."[33] Frank McDonald, principal architecture critic for the *Irish
Times* and an influential commentator on urban issues, sees the development of vibrant communities in the city as vitally important.
He finishes his book about Dublin's dereliction in the 1980s with a
call to "lure back the middle classes" in order to achieve "a balanced social mix" (1985, 335). Others, including Neil Smith, David
Harvey, and Jane Jacobs, whose longstanding critique targets urban
property speculation, have seen dangerous pitfalls in this approach.
Discussing gentrification in the American context, twenty years before
the debate began in Ireland, Jacobs writes: "City officials today prate
about 'bringing back the middle class,' as if nobody were in the middle
class until he had left the city and acquired a ranch house and a bar-
becue and thereby become precious. . . . However, cities need not
'bring back' a middle class, and carefully protect it like artificial
growth. Cities grow the middle class" (Jacobs 1961, 282). In contrast

to McDonald, Jacobs has long believed that inner-city communities are vulnerable to being trampled on in a speculative gold rush of renewal.

The faith that people have in gentrification in Dublin, therefore, is much the same as they have in the myth of the Celtic Tiger: a rising tide will lift all boats. But rising property prices might well be counterproductive, displacing young professionals and middle-class families as often as low-income families. From the beginning, urban renewal in Dublin has been the terrain of both public and private energies. In the three initial areas designated for renewal, the state provided the tax incentives for private developers to do their work. The Custom House Dock Authority (CHDA) was significant in that it established a private company to oversee the creation of the International Financial Services Centre and its attached residences. Following from that success, in 1997 the development of 1,300 acres of former docklands was handed over to another private conglomerate, the Dublin Docklands Development Authority (DDDA), which took over the operations of the CHDA. This ambitious scheme, which planned to bring twenty-five thousand new residents to the inner city and to provide eleven thousand new jobs, was the largest development proposal ever submitted to a local authority. Because of problems with earlier gentrification, the DDDA was given approval to proceed only if 20 percent of its new residences were put aside for social and affordable housing.

Developers reacted strongly to this mandate. They successfully campaigned to have the law changed. Instead of mixing social housing with market-determined property, they lobbied to provide the required 20 percent in an alternative location, often a less desirable one. The answer to gentrification's inequities would have appeared to lie in the state's providing affordable housing, but, as a government minister recently said, "Dublin is closer to Boston than Berlin." Spoken in the context of Ireland's 2000 vote on the Maastricht Treaty, which paved the way for greater integration among the economies, judiciaries, and policies of those countries in the European Union, the minister, Mary Harney, highlighted what were, for her, Ireland's stronger economic and cultural links with individualistic North America than with social welfare–oriented continental Europe.[34] Despite an actual increase in the building of local authority housing over the past ten years, the number of people in need of state-subsidized housing and on waiting lists for it has outpaced the ability and willingness of the state to keep up.[35]

In the heart of the city, gentrification is the urban face of privatization. Frank McDonald is fond of saying how contemporary Dublin is being recast in concrete, and that actions of the present will structure the city for many generations to come, just as over two hundred years ago the Wide Streets commissioners laid down the foundations of the modern city. Yet to compare Dublin's current potential with the mighty schemes of the commissioners in the 1700s is to ignore the scale of upheaval and displacement caused by those early modernizers and the political aristocracy whose authority they were reinforcing. It is, moreover, unclear whether urban renewal can sustain a vibrant, living city over the long run. There is a rapid turnover in Dublin's gentrified enclaves, and the pace of sprawl outside the city has only intensified.[36] A back-to-the-city movement may only exist as a temporary phenomenon for a small cadre of high-earners, the appearance of urban renewal amid growing inequality.

The International Financial Services Centre was an early seed planted by the Irish state to grow the new economy and to attract transnational companies to Dublin as it tried to become a global city.[37] The initiation of urban renewal schemes and the construction of thousands of new apartments helped attract more speculative capital to an already hot economy (in the form of tax relief schemes for developers and mortgage write-offs for buyers). This quest for new urbanism—the creation of a sense of place, higher-density living, mixed-use areas—would also appeal to the aesthetics of young people who were earning a great deal of money. This group, according to urban sociologist Saskia Sassen, makes up 20 percent of the population of global cities. The latest and largest of Dublin's new housing developers, the DDDA, plans to construct twelve thousand new units of housing adjacent to Ireland's financial citadel, further evidence of the tight correspondence among urban regeneration, the high-paying jobs of a globalizing economy, and the need to house this rising class of professionals.

The lifestyle of this internationally oriented group also inscribes the urban environment, creating spaces in its own image. For this reason, the example of renewal that is most cited as a sign of Ireland's cultural maturation and approximation to modern, European standards of urban living is the Dublin neighborhood of Temple Bar. For contemporary standards, read: a diverse mix of architectural styles, ranging from the historically renovated to the eclectic postmodern; an emphasis on intimate, bohemian shopping; and a more compact, premodern sense of scale, achieved through the creation of public squares, walkable streets, and multifunctional buildings that emphasize sustainability. Over the last fifteen years, Temple Bar has gone from being a shabby, run-down, forgotten part of Dublin to an area packed with restaurants, art galleries, boutiques, cinemas, nightclubs, and crowds. The narrow streets of the area have been recobbled, and reproduction Victorian lamps erected. The pubs that used to be shabby, dark, and all too typical of Temple Bar's former marginal status are now bright and prospering. Their interiors have been renovated and re-themed, and the pubs are now in line with Temple Bar's new image as a mandatory tourist spot. (Ironically, they are engaged in the successful business of marketing their former authenticity.) Restaurants in the area display the usual eclectic combination—from French haute cuisine at Pierre's to American burgers at the Bad Ass Cafe to the unimaginable at Luigi Malone's—associated with other such constructed urban glamour zones, ranging from Boston's Faneuil Hall to London's Covent Garden.

Supporting Sassen's thesis that a new, globally integrated workforce informs the city and requires expensive leisure opportunities, *Fortune* magazine in 1997 named Dublin its number-one city "to do business in," ahead of Amsterdam, Barcelona, and London. It cited the "cosmopolitanism of Temple Bar" and the "young, educated workforce" who frequent it.[38] Commerce and culture are inextricable. Temple Bar Properties, the state company set up to oversee Temple Bar's overhaul, received massive subsidies from the European Union. This money has helped to transform Temple Bar into a heretofore implausible area of the city: Dublin's left bank.

On the one hand, Temple Bar represents, according to Mary Corcoran, "the artistic and architectural aspirations" of a new European-oriented Irish population (1998, 10). A newly constructed square (Paul Keogh Architects) is home to the National Gallery of Photography and the Irish Film Center, which, apart from airing the latest European releases, projects movies onto its exterior wall on summer nights. (Significantly, the movie chosen for the square's opening was Fritz Lang's *Metropolis,* that ultimate cinematic warning about the evils of the industrial city.) The new semipublic space (locked much of the time), writes the architect, is "essentially an outdoor room, intended as an open-air performance space [for] celebrating all forms of contemporary culture" (Temple Bar Properties [TBP] 1996, 103). Overlooking the Meeting House Square is another older building, the Printworks (Derek Tynan Architects). This structure's early twentieth-century international-style façade—whitewashed planar walls and large rectangular windows—and factory-like sawtooth roof have been preserved and recycled to hold a mixed-use development (Figure 18). The raised, private interior courtyard, which allows shop units to exist at the lower level, marks, Tynan argues, a return to the "prototypical urban type" (181). A Mediterranean-style roof garden tops the Printworks. The Green Building (Murray O'Laoire Associates), too, has European aspirations, attempting to tap into the continent's growing ecological awareness, as well as its EU funding (in this case, the "Thermie" conservation fund). The structure was partly built with recycled material (terracotta tiles and pine), while solar panels and wind turbines provide electricity. The Green Building's eclectic exterior—combining art nouveau metal railings and projecting bay windows-cum-turrets—is, write the building's creators, "archetypal" of the "historic European centre" (TBP 1996, 187) (Figure 19).

On the other hand, Temple Bar is an altogether more mundane affair, symbolic of the more lowbrow attempts to foster European harmony, such as MTV Europe and Sky TV. Temple Bar survives as a mini–theme park, with pastiche neo-Georgian and "Tudor-bethan" architecture (McDonald 2000, 294). A medieval Gothic church was converted into Dublin Viking Adventure (subsequently closed), which, among other things, displayed the archaeological remains of the area that was dug up as Temple Bar's development proceeded. Most nights, the area plays host to "stag parties, lost tourists, gangs of teenagers, out-of-tune buskers" from various countries, and mildly bemused older Dubliners.[39] In 1996, five years after the scheme was initiated, there were thirty-nine restaurants, eight pubs, nine clubs and hotels, and forty-three shops. This neighborhood has now become Ireland's prime example of urban renewal; it is at once "a geographically

Figure 18. The Printworks. From Temple Bar Properties, *Temple Bar* (1996), 182. Photograph courtesy of Temple Bar Properties Ltd.

demarcated entity, a tax designated area, an archaeological site, a center for the culture and arts, a tourist attraction, and a building site" (Corcoran 1998, 9). Understanding how it came to be this way helps clarify the uses made of history in a city eager to market its culture and past while at the same time striving, in the words of one supporter, to be "a modern, forward-looking European city" (McDonald 2000, 285).

A recent EU report describes Temple Bar as "one of the last fragments of central Dublin which gives a picture of the city before the Wide Streets Commissioners replaced its medieval street pattern with the spacious formality of Georgian design" (Bennett 1991, 214). Temple Bar acquired its name from William Temple, the provost of Trinity College in the late 1600s, whose mansion and gardens were located there. His grounds backed onto the banks of the Liffey. A "bar" was a river walkway. During the eighteenth century, when Dublin

Figure 19. The Green Building. From Temple Bar Properties, *Temple Bar* (1996), 187. Photograph courtesy of Temple Bar Properties Ltd.

housed its ascendancy Parliament, the area attracted a blend of craftsmen—tailors, watchmakers, and bookbinders—stockbrokers, and general traders. Their traces live on in the locale's street names: Merchant's Arch, Exchange Street, Copper Alley, Fishamble Street, and Crow Street.[40] The nineteenth century saw a sharp drop in the demand for these specialized trades, and the area fell into decline. In Abercrombie's *Dublin of the Future,* the region was slated to become a new traffic terminal. In 1921 members of the Free State government prepared to implement aspects of Abercrombie's scheme, and plans were made to tear Temple Bar down and replace it with a central bus station. But there were delays in getting planning permission. During that time, the state transport company, CIE, rented the derelict properties to those willing to live with a short lease. The area accordingly became an artists' district. Studios, galleries, flea markets, and alternative pubs sprang up. What was meant to be only a temporary stay of execution ended up saving the neighborhood.

In 1991, when Dublin was "European City of Culture," the state granted Temple Bar a special package of incentives and deemed the refurbishment of the neighborhood its cultural flagship program. Temple Bar Properties managed to secure 200 million pounds, around 7 million pounds per acre, for the district's improvement, with half coming from the European Union. One of the principal arguments against this process of urban renewal is apparent from these numbers: the allocation of significant financial resources to downtown projects siphons funds that might otherwise go to more pressing urban needs, such as public housing, improved public transport, and so on. While this company (again, a state business overseeing the process of globalization) administered grants to businesses, it also commissioned a consortium of eight Dublin architectural firms, collectively called Group 91, to develop an overall framework for the site.[41] The plans of this group included creating spaces for ten new cultural centers, including the Irish Film Center, the National Photography Archive, Arthouse (a visual arts center, developed to bridge art and technology), Ark (the national children's theater), the Designyard (an upscale arts and crafts store), and the Dublin Viking Adventure. The resulting buildings, for the most part, seek an aura of authenticity by emphasizing the history that underscores the consumerist project.

The Designyard in Temple Bar, for example, is an up-to-date emporium of expensive jewelry, custom furniture, textiles, glass, and ceramics, which hides behind its original eighteenth-century warehouse façade. The Irish Film Center acquired the 1692 Quaker meeting house. Over the centuries the society had accumulated a disparate collection of buildings and had added extra rooms. The renovation sought, in the words of the *Architectural Review,* to achieve "a symbiosis between the old and the new.... [T]he new interventions continue the historical pattern of organic evolution on the site, reflecting a process of gradual growth and change."[42] The newly outfitted structure connected the various sections of the older complex with a series of narrow passageways. The dense, remodeled building is centered on an enlarged courtyard. The weathered brick façades of the old walls combine with modern raw materials—brick, limestone, and steel—to suggest an urban character of history and artisanship. The Film Center itself forms one side of the new public plaza, Meeting House Square, carved out of the haphazard structure of Temple Bar. Another side of this square is the wall of the Ark children's theater, which opens up to reveal a stage on which actors, as if in a medieval fair, can perform for the public. This modern reinterpretation of supposedly "indigenous" traditions speaks to the generic appropriation of premodern notions of city life that are at the center of Ireland's attempt to market itself as a European nation, as part of that "organic evolution" of bourgeois history.

The influence of European architects and urban theorists, such as Aldo Rossi and Leon Krier, is at the center of the Temple Bar plan. The architects of Group 91 make no secret of their admiration for Krier and Rossi's small-scale, local, and antitechnocratic attitude to the creation of place. Both of these architects offer alternatives to the impersonal designs of modernism. Rossi is considered the principal advocate of "neorationalism" or "new regionalism," an architectural and urban movement that emphasizes the lived experiences of urban space and the importance of diversity in the city's fabric. Rossi's theories, as spelled out in his *Architecture of the City,* are based on the rehabilitation rather than the redevelopment of older buildings. Here, as so often in architecture, it helps to think about what Rossi was reacting against. The targets of his theory were Walter Gropius and other high modernists, whose style rejected historical architecture. Rossi, like the writer Jane Jacobs in the United States, disavowed impersonal high-rises and advocated vernacular styles of building. Rossi argued for a set of urban "types," a word he uses interchangeably to mean structures such as houses, temples, or gardens that are "associated with a [particular] form and way of life," along with the smaller elements of architecture, such as corridors, rooms, foundations, and walls (Rossi 1982, 40). This search for a deep historical spatial structure is driven by the quest for the elemental, universal institutions of life that existed before the chaos of industrialization. His aim was to transcend functionalism. Paul Keogh, Niall McCullough, and other younger Irish architects organized an exhibition of Rossi's work in Ireland in the 1980s. Many of these same figures came together later as part of Group 91.

Krier advocates a small, walkable, multifunctional city, one whose spaces have overlapping uses. Krier's city would include dwellings above shops, places that remain vibrant both day and evening, areas hospitable to different generations at once. Krier's philosophical language opposes modernism: modernist architecture, he argues, wreaked havoc on the traditional cores of historic European towns and imposed artificial, functional zoning on areas that historically had supported multiple uses. Krier's aim, though with all the benefits and possibilities of modern technology, is for planners and architects to return to the basic suppositions of preindustrial urban living. "The principal modern building types and planning models such as the Skyscraper, the Groundscraper, the Central Business District, the Residential Suburb, etc. are invariably horizontal or vertical overconcentrations of single uses in one urban zone, in one building programme, or under one roof" (1987, 42). Opposed to the modernist urban quest for uniformity and control, Krier visualizes "cities within cities," neighborhoods that support "the totality of urban functions," and where daily life can be lived pleasantly, on foot (41–42). Residents of this "good city" have a greater ecological awareness and no longer require the speedy, efficient channeling of populations between districts. Temple Bar's rehabilitation of older structures and its self-contained culture are, its Irish creators imagine, a worthy illustration of Krier's philosophy.

Temple Bar has tried to capture this postmodern spirit of community and urban design through the creation of new public spaces of moderate scale and the construction of buildings that combine working, residential, and leisure environments. Three public squares and a new street, Curved Street, have been carved out from the dense fabric. Curved Street embodies the nostalgic tone of Temple Bar, adding to the labyrinthine network of narrow streets in the attempt to restore a lost sense of place (Figure 20). Like all the other streets, it is a pedestrian thoroughfare, encouraging the stroller and the consumer, enhancing a vague atmosphere of eighteenth-century European tradition. In Temple Bar, a particular urban mood—at once nostalgic and technological, premodern and cosmopolitan—has been placed at the center of national life in the hopes that it can perform a particular cultural task: to further integrate Ireland's economic fortunes with the trends of European and global capital, bringing architecture around to build a playful zoo for the Celtic Tiger. The architects responsible for the refurbishment of the area loudly proclaim their worldly influences, referencing other European capitals every chance they get, in the hopes not only of procuring European government funding but also of capturing the layered, textured pasts and bohemian present of these capital cities.

Simon Walker, head of UCD's School of Architecture, writes in "Dublin Masque" that Dublin has seen "an emerging Euroconsciousness" (TBP 1996, 46). An air of confident individualism pervades much of the conversation about Temple Bar, and it is presented as a superior ethos to the worn-out nationalism that held Ireland down in previous decades. As Walker suggests, "at the end of a century which has known traumatic changes for Dublin and the island as a whole...[n]ow we have an opportunity to stabilise the future of the city. Instead of herd-like behaviour...we should by now be able to hold our ground and let services and businesses adapt themselves to work around us" (ibid.). Temple Bar's architecture adapts, rehabilitates, and molds older spatial forms; it is the built equivalent of Ireland's rising, flexible economy. Temple Bar represents, in short, "a sign of growing maturity" (49). As the area plays its part in transitioning Dublin's industrial economy to one based on tourism and the marketing of culture, a demand grows for "heritage, art, entertainment and cultural consumption" (68). As Sergio Arzeni, a cultural commentator and leading European economist, wrote in the marketing literature for Temple Bar, the selling of culture has

Figure 20. Curved street. From Temple Bar Properties, *Temple Bar* (1996), 101.
Photograph courtesy of Temple Bar Properties Ltd.

"reshap[ed] the function of cities and urban areas alike" (ibid.). It is no wonder, then, that Arzeni references Francis Fukuyama, for whom "the end of history" was equated with the collapse of communism; for Ireland, Temple Bar has come to represent the collapse of nationalism.

For these commentators, Temple Bar is the thriving sign that Ireland has grown up and the symbol that the country's heavy ties to an unwieldy history have finally been severed. Furthermore, the transition that Temple Bar represents is wrapped up in revolutionary rhetoric. As Walker again puts it, "if building is a political act, then the modern architect is involved in the politics of revolution" (TBP 1996, 48). Temple Bar is celebrated as creating "subversion, self-reference, and autonomy of form," establishing "new identities," which have always been "the underlying cause of revolution" (ibid.). The idea that Temple Bar makes and reflects a revolutionary spirit is both creative and crass. The architecture is conservative, looking back to a medieval bourgeois urban milieu that never quite took root in Ireland. (Ireland's bourgeois public sphere got stymied and repressed by the weight of colonialism, while European political environments evolved without such imposed contradictions.) And the bohemian air of Temple Bar may seem thrilling to consumers, but the money-making heart of Temple Bar that beats beneath its shiny surface is far from revolutionary.

Temple Bar holds another important place in the Irish imagination. It signifies a profound twist to Ireland's long, sad emigration story. As Frank McDonald recently put it, "What we are witnessing is the reclamation of the city by a new generation of Irish people who have traveled widely and worked in European cities, shed their *cultural baggage,* and now returned home to demand the same sort of lifestyle they experienced elsewhere. They see no reason why the Hibernian metropolis should be less *civilized* or interesting to live in than, say, Amsterdam, Paris or Barcelona" (McDonald 2000, 26; my emphasis). To be developed, then, is to be European; to seek culture is to look elsewhere.

The gentrified and speculative architecture of contemporary Dublin serves as the visual key in unlocking the semiotics as well as the material exclusivity of the Celtic Tiger. The postmodernism of the IFSC and the eclectic cosmopolitanism of Temple Bar, along with

Dublin's urban renewal schemes, are the clear links to the Celtic Tiger's cultural marketing and to its hopeful, but tenuous, economy.

Architecture and History in Contemporary Dublin

Temple Bar is an Irish version of a common urban phenomenon. From Baltimore's Inner Harbor to London's Docklands, tourist-friendly shopping districts have sprung from the ashes of older industrial urban areas, usually as a competitive response to the growth of suburbs. At the center of discussions about these transitions are the issues of history and memory. In a time of increased competition between cities for a limited share of global investment dollars, civic leaders have sought to create spaces around which to build the idea of the city as a community and, in a time of greater internationalism, as a site that welcomes cultural, although not class and racial, diversity. Spaces like Temple Bar seek to make the urban respectable again, after a long period of economic and demographic decline. Given that the areas of gentrification cater to international audiences, it is only natural that they have produced an architecture with a sense of glitter and surface display signaled by the historical façade.

Why the new capitalism requires a glamour zone in the heart of downtown is a harder question to answer. According to Saskia Sassen, it is, in part, because the new urban elite "are not owners. They could be out of their jobs tomorrow and discover that all they have are their fancy clothes. Elites need places for their representation to themselves, with their fancy boutiques and cafés. That becomes a mechanism that produces loyalty to the system."[43] While each city creates images of its own unique history and identity (in the case of Dublin: Georgian, colonial, literary, and so forth), the cities cannot appear radically different from other cities, for that would make them exceptional, uncomfortable, unplaceable in the narrative of modernization. Global travelers seek moments of comfort in the exotic; indigenous residents benefit from these same accoutrements of broadly familiar mass appeal.

The architecture of Dublin in the 1960s was strictly functionalist and austere, a reflection of the internationalist and revisionist tendencies of those years. The architecture that emerged in the city during the 1990s was, however, quite different. It sought to preserve the faces of historic buildings, was respectful of Dublin's modest skyline, unlike Liberty Hall and other 1960s high-rises, and adopted no over-arching style. The buildings in Temple Bar, for example, display a mix of genres, from renovated Georgian and Victorian structures, through formally modernist constructions, to postmodernist experimentation and the neo-industrial. In this eclecticism, we can observe a tempo-ral contradiction that sits at the heart of the process of globalization, a tension like that found at the core of modernism: on the one hand, globalization must reference the past, while on the other, it is driven by the dictates of new technology, information, and communications. Globalization must exist *in* history, while remaining flexible enough to move away from the deeper demands that local or national his-tory may make on it.

In the 1960s, architecture in Ireland, along with other aspects of culture, such as the media, historiography, and politics, tried to re-press the history of nationalism and ignore the systemic problem of partition. When traumatic historical events are repressed, however, they are more likely to return in some thwarted form to trouble the health of the present. The 1970s in Ireland, for example, exploded in violence, in a confrontation between the long-festering forces of na-tionalism and socialism on the one hand, and the official military, political, and cultural institutions of the British state on the other. The more the southern establishment tried to ignore the militant pro-ceedings in the North, and to function as if Ireland were a "normal" European state (without a civil war raging in its territory), the more the unresolved "national question" made itself felt in various un-comfortable ways: repressive legislation, censorship, and the stigma-tizing of traditional Irish culture (including speaking the indigenous language, performing political ballads, or promoting economic self-reliance).

By the 1990s, however, architecture, music, literature, and other aspects of Irish culture no longer shied away from making historical or patriotic, though rarely nationalist, statements; *Riverdance* became a phenomenon, Irish folk music grew in popularity, and historically resonant memoirs sold in great numbers. Likewise, in today's archi-tecture, the past is invoked, not overlooked. But the inevitable de-struction of memory that accompanies gentrification (indeed, that attends the demise of all architecture) is replaced with a materialized form of nostalgia for a sense of history itself, for identification with tradition and continuity with the past. Preservation, therefore, stands in opposition to a ruin; a ruin signifies our break with the past, a restoration our continuity. Techniques devised to evoke this urban nostalgia are numerous; they include the sandblasting of façades, the unmasking of brick walls and the exposure of old timber (asceticism becomes public display), and the use of wrought-iron railings and ornamental pillars, along with imitation plasterwork and reproduction light fixtures.

An important point needs to be made here about the historical gestures created by contemporary planning and architecture. The idea is not to critique these new developments for displacing a true and genuine working class and replacing them with a somehow false urban middle class. To level that criticism would be to fall into the phenomenological trap of claiming that there is an essential meaning to space, a natural bond between a people and their place, to which others may not gain access. New inhabitants, of whatever class or race, have a right to call these older spaces home, too. I am not interested here in determining the history of Dublin's working class or in establishing who was there first and has originary rights to place, although there is, of course, an imperative to ensure that the less well-off not be driven from an area by those with more collateral. Rather, I wish to draw attention to how the past is glorified in architecture, literature, and tourism so long as that history can be safely brought into the present. What cannot be carried comfortably into the present is represented as traditional, backward, or atavistic—for example, cultural forms of nationalism; Dublin's large population of travelers, who refuse to be settled in one place; and, increasingly, Catholicism, as opposed to the new secularism.

The pasts that urban renewal copies—Georgian, or late medieval in the case of Temple Bar—are, of course, largely dependent on what was there before. This is not to say, however, that historical spaces could not be leveled and built over as if they were a tabula rasa. That is, after all, what happened in Dublin during the 1960s. The time periods chosen for renewal, I suggest, have less to do with the specifics of those eras than with the ability of contemporary capitalism to profit from the nostalgic impulses of modernity and postcoloniality. The Georgian period, for example, which was the "high point" of colonial Dublin, a time of great wealth, monumental architecture, and, indeed, of gentrification, was also the zenith of British repression of Irish Catholics—not a time, one would think, that would lend itself to Irish glorification. Historical preservation, then, is less a longing for what was than a rejection of what is—complexity, distance, alienation.

Each of the spatial examples that I have discussed so far with regard to globalization and spatial change in contemporary Dublin has engaged the politics of memory. The ways in which we remember particular places and events, as well as the reasons we do so, have been altered by planners and architects with a modernizing vision that is driving the country deeper into European and transnational modernity. Temple Bar, for example, ostensibly re-creates the design, architecture, and mood of a generic, early modern market town in the hopes that this may propel the present and future city toward a more central position in the European marketplace. Urban renewal takes over the semiotics of Georgian Dublin to gain an aura of urban authenticity and distinction. In doing so, the meaning of the original Georgian moment—the consolidation of Ireland within the empire—is recast with the ethos of the contemporary economy: financial security, symbolic capital, and urban individualism.

Another example of this use of national history is the International Financial Services Centre's deployment of the Great Famine. In the heart of Dublin's Docklands, a commissioned statue commemorating the event adorns the main entranceway to Dublin's home to international commerce (Figure 21). Presented to Dublin Corporation in 1997 on the hundred-fiftieth anniversary of the Famine by one of Ireland's wealthiest families, Rowan Gillespie's bronze sculpture displays gaunt, wraith-like victims carrying their few possessions toward an unseen coffin ship. About to embark for the New World, they are destitute and hopeless. With their backs turned to the city, they stand in telling juxtaposition to the power-dressed office blocks and corporate glass of the IFSC. Perhaps, as Dean MacCannell argues, "the best indication of the final victory of modernity over other sociocultural arrangements is not the disappearance of the nonmodern and its traces, but their preservation and reconstruction in modern society" (MacCannell 1989, 8). The statue, by bringing the Famine and globalization together, suggests that, despite the elapsed time,

Figure 21. Famine sculpture. Photograph courtesy of Philip Greenspun, http://
philip.greenspun.com.

the two histories are directly connected. The IFSC's symbolic gesture to Ireland's traumatic and impoverished past suggests that we are now over all that; the time of poverty, mass emigration, and foreign landlordism is past. The time is ripe, the sculpture suggests, both to separate that time from ours—that was then, this is now—and, for the corporate community that commissioned the statue, to claim that they are the custodians and heirs of that tragedy. This may be the case, but the implication is that their coupling is a good thing, that the original event is somehow righted by the ability of the present to make amends for the past by bringing emigrants home (to work in offices and call centers) and by creating wealth the likes of which those earlier victims could never have imagined. And yet the statue is unaware of the irony of globalization memorializing the Famine, for it was laissez-faire economics that caused the colonial catastrophe in Ireland 150 years ago.

Modernity, the City, and the Crisis of Memory

The purveyors of globalism, therefore, in looking forward to a post-nationalist future, are forced to look back and re-create, even if superficially, the historical spaces of the past in order to make the present appear more like an actualized version of it—the fruit that has matured from history's seed. At the same time that Dublin has undergone widespread urban renewal, the literary field has seen the publication of many new Irish urban memoirs. Elaine Crowley's *Dublin Girl: Growing up in the 1930s,* Peter Sheridan's (brother of filmmaker Jim Sheridan) *Dublin Made Me,* and Nuala O'Faolain's *Are You Somebody?* to name a few. Memoirs are particularly interesting because they locate themselves in urban terrain, a landscape that is now undergoing rapid change. Furthermore, this last decade has been represented as a moment of self-proclaimed modernization by the Irish state—the moment when the country was at last able to vie with its global competitors. Memoirs can be both critical and reaffirming of the present. Inasmuch as they remember a city of an earlier time, particularly in a nostalgic way, they may lodge a protest about the current wave of "creative destruction" taking place in the capital. In contrast, as Fintan O'Toole put it, the Irish, or at least many of them in the South, are now supposedly standard European citizens.[44] It is, then, appropriate that memoir, *the* coming-of-age genre, is prevalent in a country that wants to believe that it has grown up. Memoirs help draw that age-old line that modernity always etches between the modern and the traditional. Demonstrating just how bad things were in the old days (a particular Irish fascination with miserable childhoods), these memoirs may help convince us of how far we have traveled in the few short years since the gloom and poverty depicted in many of these works. The emergence of new memoirs, therefore, allows us to further explore the relation between memory and the city in a rapidly globalizing Dublin.

Debates about memory and the city have a long history. All the major theorists of modernity placed urbanism and memory together at the center of their theories of modern life. For Freud, consciousness represses potentially dangerous and destabilizing memories. The violence of modern life exposes consciousness to greater levels of shock and trauma and, hence, repression. But the key to recovery and mental stability lies in memory as well: making the latent manifest, and the invisible visible. Like psychotherapy, memoir relies on this ability to retrieve and organize images and events from the personal past, turning those that are threatening and fear-inducing into surmountable and daily challenges. For Freud, the modern city best exemplifies, though in an ultimately flawed way, his model of the psyche. In *Civilization and Its Discontents,* he draws on the archaeology of Rome to clarify his discussion on the nature of memory, forgetting, and the timelessness of the unconscious. "Now let us make the fantastic supposition," he writes "that Rome were not a human-dwelling place, but a mental entity with just as long and varied a past history; that is, in which nothing once constructed had perished and all the earlier stages of development had survived along with the latest" (Freud 2001, 70). The history of Rome, of course—its physical memory— is fragmented, and what is visible to the viewer are "scanty remains" and ruins of ruins. In the mind, however, memory preserves entireties, "and the observer would perhaps only have to change the direction of his glance or his position in order to call up the one view or the other" (ibid.).

For Freud, the contours of memory are fundamentally spatial and best described architecturally: the structure of consciousness, built out of the half-known, partially fictional remembrances of our lives, sits atop the unconscious, which lies remote and threatening deep beneath the surface, like the ancient foundations of a restored house. It is there, in the bric-a-brac–laden basements of our psyche, that truth lies—in our dreams, in our verbal slips, and in our nervous laughter. It is there, too, that we are at our most universal, all humankind motivated by the same drives, instincts, and fears. It is the hard-to-confront memories of our past—trauma, loss, grief—that find their way into our everyday lives, causing all sorts of mishaps and mental disorders, from parapraxis to depression. Repressed material is to be excavated and remembered so that it may be controlled and channeled into a normalized quotidian narrative. Memoir writing is one way of addressing this psychic need.

The material space of Vienna further linked the rise of psychoanalysis as a discipline to the changing urban conditions of Austria's capital. At the time of Freud's arrival in Vienna, the city was rapidly expanding. The flat, open area that had been kept clear around the city during medieval and early modern times was increasingly being encroached on by the new, expensive suburbs of the city's cultured elite. The space of the city's former fortifications gave way to the monumental Ringstrasse.[45] Adjacent to this grand new European boulevard, Freud set up his practice. He did this, in part, to attract his clientele, who lived not in the center of the city, where the wealthy had once dwelled, but on the periphery. His neurotic patients would be able to visit Dr. Freud's office without having to enter the crowded and congested inner city. Urbanism in all its facets—the flight of the new middle class, the neuroses and anxieties that the speed and tension of the modern city produced—was part and parcel of the complicated origins, development, and structure of psychoanalysis. The city and the crisis of memory—the simultaneous modern need to remember and forget—were symbiotic.

If Freud's project was, in part, to bring untold stories to light, and the city mirrored his own image of the psyche, then the city, as the material carrier of history, has the ability to bring untold history to light, to function as the sociological unconscious. Brick walls and remodeled townhouses of gentrification meet still impoverished public housing. Medieval streets now dressed up for tourists and the anticipated new elite crumble and buckle under the weight of too much traffic. Polluted streets and bustling neighborhoods with no visible reminder of their ancient Gaelic pasts still retain their ancient Irish names. Dublin's districts keep their original monikers: sprawling, populous Clontarf (meadow of the bull); teeming, urban Kilmainham (a seventh-century monastery). The equivalent of Freud's Roman ruins, these are urban memories that refuse to be entirely repressed.

Freud's individual model of the unconscious is countered by Marx's more materialist analysis of collective experience and forgetting under nineteenth-century capitalism. Workers who fled into the towns and industrial centers had to unlearn many of their rural traditions and habits and adapt to the new realities of city living. In Marx's schema, the new urban workers became alienated, not only from each other but from their own labor, which the market transformed into capital, wages, and commodities. The commodity is about forgetting. The hidden heart of capitalism is its ability to erase the traces, the exploitative and alienating work, from the final object, its glistening presentation, and its gratified reception. Moreover, cities themselves are part commodity, bought and sold in the midst of battles over memory, gentrification, and speculative building. Neighborhoods are destroyed and rebuilt, street names are altered and translated, buildings are torn down or renovated in the name of preservation.

But urban space, for Marx, would always also be revolutionary space. The boulevards and architecture of Europe's capital cities became the stage where accumulated energies could potentially explode with beneficial effects. The city was the flashpoint of memory, where capital was most concentrated and, hence, where the proletariat and bourgeoisie had the most at stake.

By the end of the nineteenth century the semiotics and geography of the modern city had become key discourses in the regulation of everyday life. Modern town planning arose to monitor the urban crowd and control industrial space. Paris is but the best known example. Haussmann's assistants—urban geometers, he called them—bulldozed linear streets through the heart of the old city, separating and dividing communities of the poor with boulevards of traffic, interrupting the continuity of long inhabited neighborhoods. Wide roads were opened up to the periphery and the emerging suburbs. Speed and circulation became the dominant metaphors in that discipline. As Engels wrote in "The Great Towns," "hundreds of thousands of all classes and ranks of society crowding past each other...

as though they had nothing in common, nothing to do with one another" (Legates and Stout 1999, 48). For Marx, the city could be either the progressive site of collective action or the passive arena of social fragmentation, in which inhabitants are cut off from each other and possess no communal memory.

Walter Benjamin, too, was aware of the potential for shared amnesia associated with the process of commodification. Commodities, especially those connected with the rise of mass communications—the photograph, the cinema, the radio, and the newspaper—had begun to play the role of memory keepers for us, stockpiling and saving our experiences: consciousness relying on prosthesis. "The techniques based on the use of the camera and of subsequent analogous mechanical devices extend the range of the *mémoire volontaire*" (Benjamin 1968, 186). But there was another side to the commodity for Benjamin, a potentially liberating aspect of emerging consumerism, one that forced him to split memory in two, as Freud had done with repressed and conscious memory. Just as we looked to commodities to perform our remembering for us, so we also looked to mass culture to do our collective dreaming. In mass culture one could locate the desires of the collective unconscious projected onto the commodity. In the modernist architecture of the Parisian Arcades, some of the first buildings to come of age under international capitalism, Benjamin inferred the unconscious of the dreaming collective. In those forerunners to the modern mall one was able to see utopian longings and age-old aspirations at work—unlimited wealth, fashion, gambling, and leisure. In today's mall, we witness similar yearnings: the mall has become a substitute for vanishing neighborhood, with aisles named as streets, new areas to be discovered, ethnic foods harmoniously arranged, and a canopy, not of stars, but of corporate logos, sheltering us against the weather outside. For Benjamin, then, the role of the commodity, and the department stores that housed it, could not be dismissed out of hand. While the commodity collected our memories for us, it was also in the object that one could find society's deepest wishes: health, well-being, and above all community.

For Benjamin, writing on Baudelaire, there are two kinds of memory in the modern era: real and false, just as there is real and false experience. Benjamin splits modern life in two—the false that we increasingly live, and the potentially authentic that is hard to achieve.

False memory is voluntary memory, the past that can be conjured up through technology. Voluntary memory "reduces the scope for the play of the imagination" (1968, 186). It provides us with information without experience or depth. Involuntary memory, in contrast, consists of "frequently unconscious data" (157), which accumulates and converges in memory. But because of its deep and murky nature, we can only rarely call it forth. Involuntary memory had once been accessible via rituals and festivals in rural Europe, blending individual memory with the collective past, but as modern society has erupted in its succession of jolts and dislocations, involuntary memory has become less and less available.

The city is involved in this modern problem about the meaning and possibility of living a "real" life, one that is guided by natural, layered recall based on sensory perception. Living amid metropolitan energy "involves the individual in a series of shocks and collisions" (Benjamin 1968, 175). Walking on city streets, in other words, means jostling with a crowd and contending with traffic lights, homeless people, and all manner of urban upheaval and disturbance. The response, therefore, of the individual psyche, according to Benjamin's reading of Georg Simmel, is that the individual erects a shell around himself to protect his consciousness from assault. For Benjamin, the city inevitably becomes a struggle between the forces that seek to control memory—advertising, monumental architecture, controlled movement—and the possibilities of surprise, moments when the alternative, repressed histories or pasts can be glimpsed, even if only momentarily. The city is a battleground where involuntary memory is under siege. "The true picture of the past flits by. The past can be seized only as an image which flashes up at the instant when it can be recognized and is never seen again" (255).

Each of these theorists wrote against the backdrop of rapidly changing cities. During Freud's life, Vienna was producing influential urban designers, such as Otto Wagner, Camillo Sitte, and Adolf Loos. And Benjamin's theory of modernity, as it engaged Paris, the capital of the nineteenth century, was also predicated on a host of urban advances, from street lighting to the steel-frame constructions of the arcades. Benjamin wrote about Haussmann that "the true goal of [his] works was the securing of the city against civil war. . . . The width of the avenues was to prevent street barricades and the new streets were to provide the shortest routes between barracks and the working class sections." All over Europe, as Benjamin witnessed, capital cities were undergoing massive reconstruction, their old quarters being razed by people like Le Corbusier or Albert Speer. During the time that Benjamin was writing, urban design was being increasingly driven by totalitarian aesthetics. Benjamin's writings on cities, especially in *One Way Street,* are often sad and melancholy, describing towns "in ruins, social rituals empty and objects morbidly cold" (Buck-Morss 1989, 18). But there are moments of contentment. In his memories of Berlin he writes of his trips to the Tiergarten with his mother and of his early wonder with reading: "For a week you were wholly given up to the soft drift of the text that surrounded you as secretly, densely, and unceasingly as snowflakes." It is in memory that he finds fleeting moments of happiness in a life increasingly lived under the threat of fascism.

For all of these thinkers, the role of memory, both personal and collective, is central to any theorization of modern life. Modernity—the experience of modern life—is constituted by a memory crisis. On the one hand, we desire to be free of the past, to create our world anew. In the cities of North America the newness of the emerging nation was reflected in its place names—New York, New England, New Amsterdam. The French Republic declared that 1792 would be Year One of a new calendar. On the other hand, we struggle ceaselessly with our obligations to previous generations, with fulfilling some of those ambitions that we have inherited from our nation, our class, our family. For Marx and Freud, this crisis can have two outcomes: libratory results, or dangerous ones. In Marx's paradigm, memories can recall alternative modes of production and other social systems; in a Freudian context, we can use the past to reveal the obstacles that block current understanding. For both, the message is the same: memory has the ability to tell us how the past became the present. Yet modernity tries to erase all traces of the past—nations mold and modify subaltern histories into their own sanctioned narratives; planners, architects, and engineers raze medieval sections of emerging European capitals, erect monuments and museums, channeling unmanageable events and peoples into stories with beginnings, middles, and ends.

The Memoir and the City

Modernity is a memory crisis. Freud, Marx, and Benjamin draw our attention to the ways in which, during the nineteenth century, the past increasingly evaded memory. Throughout that era, sociological upheavals were represented most emphatically for these writers by urbanization and industrialization. Of course, these debates about memory and the city are still with us. At every stage when the city undergoes a major spatial reconfiguration, especially one conducted in the name of modernization, a struggle over memory also ensues. From memory, therefore, present-day Irish writers are constructing this generation's burgeoning genre of memoir and writing about the personal lives of those growing up in urban terrain. That urban experience now features at the center of contemporary Irish literature is, despite the obvious example of *Ulysses,* a significant shift in the nation's self-representation from a rural, Catholic, nationalist identity to a more cosmopolitan and European one. Rapidly transforming cities lend themselves to reflection on what is being lost and how identities are being reshaped. In an Ireland that posits itself as a country finally reaching maturity, the unapologetically individualistic genre of memoir has attained a new level of popularity. *Are You Somebody?* (O'Faolain 1996), *44 Dublin Made Me* (Sheridan 1999), and *A Dublin Girl: Growing Up in the 1930s* (Crowley 1996) all cast the city in different lights, drawing on personal memories to display the various ways in which collective and individual identities are being reshaped to meet the needs of a globalizing economy.[46]

Memoir is typically understood to exist in counterpoint to the more upstanding and canonical tradition of autobiography. Memory, unlike official narratives, is multiple, ephemeral, and fragmented. As its literary equivalent, the memoir, claims, each of us has a story to tell and the potential to introduce complexity, the individual voice, into the supposedly shared narrative of history. One of the genre's latest defenders, Patricia Hampl, conjuring up images of those airbrushed photographs of Stalin's depleted politburo, writes: "If we refuse to do the work of creating this personal version of the past, someone else will do it for us" (1999, 32). Hampl, with her liberal, humanist approach, suggests that memoir is the route toward "ethical development" (36), a concept particularly apt in relation to Ireland, where memoir writing mirrors the country's coming-of-age story, of awakening to a broader, postnational consciousness. Nancy Miller, another theorist of the genre, also offers us a useful rubric for understanding the popularity of memoir in Ireland: "memoir reading, like memoir writing, participates in an important form of collective memorialization, providing building blocks to a more fully shared national narrative" (2000, 422). The country is currently seeing increased economic mobility and insecurity, as well as societal confusion brought about by a crisis in the Church, one of the traditional social anchors. As Miller puts it, "memoir is the record of an experience in search of a community, of a collective framework in which to protect the fragility of singularity in a postmodern world" (432).

Contemporary Dublin memoirs demonstrate two ideological uses of memory, two different ways of remembering the city that produce contrasting interpretations of the present and, by implication, of the direction of the future. One way of remembering the past highlights the poverty and struggle of everyday life in Dublin, a city that until recently offered few possibilities for economic upward mobility or financial comfort. Despite an interest in the city's history, as manifested through familial stories and personal urban exploration, and an affection for the community's hospitality, many of these memoirs share familiar features: privation, overbearing fathers, resourceful yet burdened mothers, abuse, and repression. The bleaker they are, the more we like them. In a time when Ireland is simultaneously arrogant and unsure of itself, these memoirs serve to remind us of how much better off we are today than we were in the bad old days of postcolonial reconstruction—meaning economic and cultural isolation, rigid ideological boundaries, a dogmatic valorization of historical clichés, and limited opportunities for employment. These memoirs are, one might say, the literary version of historical revisionism, and while they find moments in the past to savor—familial loyalty, childhood friendships, and intimate geographies—their general thrust is one that sides uncritically with modernization. They regard today's economic progress as the social equivalent of the child's own growing up: an inevitable process that leads from naïveté and vulnerability to self-confidence and maturity.

The second way of remembering that is evoked in these memoirs draws our attention to the dark side of progress, to those older forms of community that had to be expunged to make room for the forces of modernization. Crowley's *Dublin Girl*, for example, begins with the line: "A motorway is to be built on the street where I lived" (1996, 1). Set in a tightly knit, working-class community during the first decades of independence, Crowley's book describes how her family and hundreds like it were transferred from their inner-city communities to the edges of Dublin (Cabra, Coolock, and later Ballymun) so that more space in the city center could be made available for renewal and modernization. Crowley's memoir forces us to reflect on how the objective, powerful forces of history become personalized, causing immense economic and social loss to individuals, families, classes, communities, and traditions. Crowley's recollections set up a contrast between the past and present, in which the present is seen as no better, if not worse, than what existed before. These memoirs use memory to question the notion of progress and to force us to acknowledge that so-called modernization proceeds at immense social cost. Written during the latest round of urban upheaval (the 1990s) about an earlier period of renewal (the 1930s), Crowley's memoir argues that history is cyclical and destructive, rather than linear and progressive.

No book is pure in its theory; no tale presents a monolithic, utterly coherent worldview in its pages. Every work of literature includes moments of contradiction and tension, sending out different ideological messages. Within the memoirs currently coming out of Ireland, we find elements of both the approaches described here. While Peter Sheridan, whose memoir I will discuss below, celebrates, for the most part, the arrival of the 1960s and the benign effects of modernization, he also expresses fondness for the warm, communal surroundings of a compact geography. Crowley admits that the same modernizing forces that disrupted her fondly recalled inner-city childhood also provided her family with a house and a garden, two of her mother's deepest desires. My focus, however, is on the predominant thrust of each of the memoirs—that is, one ideology that reinforces the line between an undeveloped and limiting past and a bright and less nationalist present, and the other that nostalgically remembers a premodernized history of communalism and affection bred from intimate geography.

Sheridan's *44 Dublin Made Me* (1999) and O'Faolain's *Are You Somebody?* (1996) are two examples of the kind of memoir that sees progress in urban development. Sheridan's memoir of growing up in Dublin begins on New Year's Eve 1959, in the kitchen of the family home at 44 Seville Place, a road off Sheriff Street (now dominated by the shiny new structure of the IFSC), the area that Sean O'Casey, Brendan Behan, and others immortalized as the rough-and-tumble center of working-class Dublin. Sheridan himself came to prominence in the late 1970s as a theater director who, along with his brother Jim, producer of the films *My Left Foot* and *In the Name of the Father,* helped popularize the contradictions of contemporary Irish life. Sheridan's memoir tells the story of his working-class family: a patriarchal father whom he idolized, a long-suffering mother, his brother's tragic death, his own coming-of-age as a bohemian and, eventually, as an artist.

A leading liberal journalist for the *Irish Times,* Nuala O'Faolain tells a different sort of story, with similar underpinnings. Born in poverty, she grew up in Dublin during the same era as Sheridan and rose to prominence in the 1980s. *Are You Somebody?* begins even before O'Faolain does, detailing her parents' courtship, her father's army days, and his journalistic career—one that served as her own inspiration but also created a complicated, largely absentee father. She tells, too, of her school years and of the particular kind of emerging sexuality that happens in an all-girls' school. Later, as a talented but undisciplined student at University College, O'Faolain enters Dublin's loose-living intellectual scene, drinking regularly and sleeping around even more often, eventually moving to London and pioneering the Open University there. *Are You Somebody?* showcases O'Faolain's successes as she makes her way as a radio commentator, first emerging as an eloquent analyst of "lost Dublin," later establishing herself as a journalist, feminist, and anti-Irish-Republican. The memoir confronts and attempts to make sense of the author's failures and losses as well—her loneliness, her struggle with alcoholism, her childlessness. In the book's afterword, letters from readers describe hundreds of experiences similar to O'Faolain's, exposing a generation of women's suffering in a Catholic, patriarchal society.

The first line of Sheridan's book establishes the author's inner-city, working-class credentials. An advertisement aimed at displaced rural workers who come to Dublin in search of work reads: "Lodgings available. Center city location. Adjacent to RC church. All modern conveniences" (1999, 2). Sent by his "da" (a word that appears thirty times in the first five pages) to deliver this message to the newspaper, the author quickly re-creates his childish sense of Dublin in the 1960s as an intimate and knowable community and as a place of history, folklore, and local personalities: "I loved going on messages uptown. I loved the adventure. I loved discovering places and finding short-cuts. I loved the oul' wans and the oul' fellas. I loved the statues and the buildings and the shops. I loved Dublin. I loved everything about Dublin. I wouldn't let anyone say a bad word about Dublin, espe-cially country people. If Dublin were a woman, I'd marry her" (6–7). Sheridan's narrative traces the events of his family through the 1960s, a time when the city's future was being recast as a car-friendly, consumer-oriented, internationalized space. Against the backdrop of these changes, Sheridan writes about his family life—his father's job selling tickets at the train station; his mother's housekeeping; the countrified, and occasionally pedophilic, ways of the family's rural tenants; his own school days; the death of a younger brother—and Dublin's slow emergence from its postindependence stupor.

The forces of progress are represented through the now canonical symbols and events of 1960s modernization: the arrival of television and domestic consumerism; the downplaying of Ireland's nationalist past, through the author's verbal attacks on his Catholic teachers; and his own and his brothers' unfolding interest in modern theater (Beckett), film, and music (the Beatles). An early scene of father and son raising a TV antenna on the roof of their Georgian home re-inforces the sense of a new, outward-looking Ireland about to come out of the shadows: " 'Reach up your hand and turn the aerial toward England . . .' 'Where's England, Da?' " (1999, 17). "Half an hour into 1960 we all sat staring at the television. It felt very different from 1959" (19). "I couldn't wait for the rest of the sixties to begin" (20). And what were the first images to enter into this Dublin home? Pictures of the British royal family. "[T]here it was. . . . Lots of snow, but a definite picture. We all clapped. It was a woman on a horse. She looked majestic and regal. A big silver sword in her hand" (19). Sheridan's nationalist-leaning mother protests the sudden appearance of the British monarch in the corner of her sitting room: "What do we need that woman for. . . . She's not the queen of this country" (19). The rest of the family successfully shushes her. Da throws his hands up to heaven, complaining in another imported dialect: "Dames" (19). Fifty years after the Easter 1916 Rising, "We stayed glued to the television. The music blared out, and the queen inspected the guard. Da and Paddy stood behind us. Their father had fought in 1916, and here they were, stealing pictures from London" (19). If the symbolism was not obvious enough about Ireland's fealty to older institutions, the father shouts to his son on the roof: "The church is blocking your signal. The church stands between you and a perfect picture" (18). A later scene shows the author and his brother wandering through a music store. As they enter a room of drum kits and microphones, Sheridan writes, "we'd left the land of accordions and diddle-de-di and stepped from the past into the present" (102). This incident reinforces the distinction between the old and the new, with folk music (now, ironically, one of the strongest symbols of Ireland's global popularity) being associated with a dying social order—"Dead people. Dead Music. Dead Culture" (102).

Throughout Sheridan's memoir, a bland process of modernization is acknowledged and celebrated. Sheridan's own memories serve to denigrate nationalism, a movement that might challenge the oncoming tide of modernization with its own recollections about the quest for cultural sovereignty, economic independence, and linguistic purity. Sheridan's Catholic teacher, "the Mongrel," "hated Lloyd George because he tricked Michael Collins into signing the Treaty. He hated de Valera for signing the Oath of Allegiance. He hated Hitler for losing World War II. He hated America for joining up with Britain against Germany. He hated all foreign games except soccer. He loved Gaelic football, the Irish language, the Gaelic League, anything with the word Gaelic in it, Connemara, Mayo, the Ring of Kerry, Sinn Féin, the IRA, and most of all he loved 'nancy boys'" (1999, 42). Sheridan falls for the easy revisionist move of equating nationalism with Catholicism, nationalists with Nazis. But in a story written from a child's perspective the author can get away more easily with simplifications and generalizations in the guise of naive memory. The sparse, childish tone of *44 Dublin Made Me* minimizes description and internal reflection, and the plot progresses in an imagistic, abbreviated style. Remembering a trip to the local sweet shop, Sheridan writes: "I looked in Mattie's window. There they were, staring back at me. Bull's-eyes. I'd forgotten about them. They looked delicious. I loved the way your whole mouth went black eating them. ... Lucky Lumps were a sweet and a surprise" (7). The simple language and truncated syntax presents the supposed unmediated impressions of a child, but the narrator is an adult, selective in what he culls from his vast, but always partially recollected, memories.

In *44 Dublin Made Me,* the past operates as a foil for the present. Like the trauma experienced in one's own personal past, the neuroses of previous historical moments are to be confronted, overcome, and transcended. The present is the location of clarity, the site where insight and health are obtained, while the act of narration is the means through which the past is to be arranged and made understandable. Narration, however, has its own stylistic traditions, its own set of national tropes and metaphors. And in Ireland (for the modern-day liberal) nothing serves to construct the past as nationalist, insular, and underdeveloped better than the image of the narrow-minded priest: "Denehy's prematch talk was passionate. He reminded us of our duty to our school, to our parish and to our country. He reminded us of Fionn MacCumhaill, Cuchulainn, and the brave Fianna warriors; of Michael Davitt, Micheal Cusack, and Bishop Croke; of Parnell, Casement and Padraig Pearse; and of the proud tradition of Mayo football (his county) and the West's awake; ... he reminded us most of all of our duty to ourselves. We had a debt to the past but we owed it to the future to excel ourselves; what would we want our children and our grandchildren to say of us?" (86). Then, too, when Sheridan is a young teen, the Troubles re-erupt in the North, and his mother begins sheltering Catholic refugees from the conflict and even attempting to import arms. Sheridan was sorry about "the tribal hatreds of Belfast ... but [he] wanted [his] bed back" (267). Catholicism and nationalism act as weights on the maturing process. While slightly quaint, they are fundamentally outdated doctrines.

For Sheridan, then, memory serves to re-create the past so that we can see how bad it was, and, by implication, how far we have progressed. The contemporary globalizing city in which Sheridan lives and writes is no longer dominated by outdated notions like nationalism (especially its militant kind) or essentialist symbols of culture. Likewise, the subject of memoir—the mature individual—has the

confidence to confront the Church's history of abuse and authoritarianism, thereby reinforcing the postnationalist, cosmopolitan ideology of the liberalizing present.

If Sheridan describes a home ruled by a strong, argumentative
father and a city where the only public roles appear to be for men,
then O'Faolain maps the city from the position of women and children who suffered silently—by necessity, hers is a tale more grounded
in history and one that has the potential to expose the sexist ideologies of the 1960s. The book's opening line establishes the gulf of
separation that exists between the past and the present: "I was born
in a Dublin that was much more like something from an earlier century than like the present day" (1996, 3). O'Faolain uses memory to
excavate her own past, taking the city as her text, and architecture
as the background. The built environment demonstrates new freedom
for women today, as opposed to her own somewhat stifled past as a
young student: "Today's apartment-block Dublin," she writes, offers
single women greater autonomy (62). In her mother's generation,
women could not maintain independent identities away from their
families.

Despite an overall bleakness, the urban context allows O'Faolain
to use memories of the city to highlight her happiest days, when she
was free to wander and develop an organic sense of the place: "I
could not get enough of looking at Dublin," she writes, "which was
Joyce's Dublin still, then, brown and dusty and dense with street
life." Later her father passed down the details and history of Dublin
to her (19). For O'Faolain, space triggers memory: remembering her
days as a lecturer at University College, Dublin, she is moved by
"every room and corridor"; she recalls her mother's emotional distance by evoking "a rented bungalow meant for a farm laborer, on a
gentry estate in north County Dublin...surrounded by fields...
in...an isolated landscape" (14). These may be memoiristic tropes,
but they are also Freudian methods. Peeling back the spaces of our
past, layer by layer, exposes the wounds and joys of both the psyche
and the urban landscape.

For O'Faolain, however, images of Dublin serve, for the most
part, to highlight the repression of Irish society in the days before
1960s modernization. She draws on the notion of suburbia as a

prison for women. When she tells her mother of her plans to go to college, she is met with scorn: "'I don't really care if you get a degree or not.... I'd far rather see you with a husband and a few kids.' This—when ... she felt as trapped as a slave, kept out in a suburb with children!" (1996, 82). As a student in the late 1950s, O'Faolain sees the city as "little and dark," the claustrophobic atmosphere reinforcing the sexual repression of a generation groping toward the outside world: "City people lived alone in cold bed-sitters, with stained curtains and dripping bathrooms down linoleum covered walls.... Couples went into musty beds in the afternoons by silent agreement, she in her jumper and skirt and suspender belt, he pushing down his trousers under the blankets. The fumbles to this and—ugh! ouch—that; Buddy Holly serenading Peggy Sue on the Dansette record player so that the fellows playing cards next door wouldn't hear" (50). The male-dominated literary scene in the early 1960s—one thinks of Patrick Kavanagh, Flann O'Brien, and John McGahern—humiliated women who dared take on a public role: "If you were a young female, no one asked you what you did ... or what you wanted to do.... Outside the home, in circles where academics and journalism and literature met, women either had to make no demands, and be liked, or be much larger than life, and feared" (70). This hard-drinking environment, O'Faolain writes, "could not be survived, only abandoned" (76).

Like Sheridan, O'Faolain identifies the 1960s with a paradigm shift—"An old Ireland was ending, in the 1960s"—one that usefully paralleled her own formative personal developments (1996, 81). For Sheridan, it was the discovery of Beckett that signaled his break with Irish provincialism. For O'Faolain, it was modernist poetry: "The English Department in UCD was just coming into the modern world then. Denis Donoghue introduced us to modern American poetry.... He showed us Pound.... He showed us Wallace Stevens.... He showed us Robert Frost" (1996, 48–49). "Everything I was learning was new to me" (50). "Nevertheless, it was a feature of the intellectual life ... of the Dublin I knew then that it wasn't interested in the condition of Ireland.... Northern Ireland was a far-off place" (57–58). Despite the intellectual shifts taking place, feminism made few inroads. The rules of patriarchy remained. It was in the 1980s, after a long stint of working with the BBC, that O'Faolain returned to Ireland and, working for the national broadcasting company, produced pieces on "incest, prostitution, abortion, women's pay, and employment, contemplative nuns, health issues and Unionist women" (149). Her slow assimilation into the elite world of Irish media has mirrored the cause of women in general. In her view, the dark, somber days of an earlier, isolationist Ireland have made way for a more confident, articulate, tolerant society. The afterword to her book consists of snippets from dozens of letters she received from other women—potential "somebodies"—who, thanks to her book, are finding the courage to speak up and tell their own tales. The world of bedsits, musty basements, and repressive families of *Are You Somebody?* is a world now coming to an end, one best forgotten. Its opposite clearly suggests contemporary Dublin, an urban cosmopolitanism viewed as more confident, tolerant, and egalitarian, consisting of bright new buildings, modern apartment living, and bustling suburbs. O'Faolain's critique of the dark, limiting past brings to mind a vibrant Temple Bar, for example, where young women are relatively free to exercise newly won social freedoms and commercial gains. It confirms the opportunities now afforded for young, college-educated, middle-class women in the shiny corporate offices of the IFSC.

Memoirs propose that an author has passed through time, has surmounted obstacles, and has emerged on the other side, more melancholy, perhaps, but wiser. O'Faolain's own personal development is deeply grounded in the rise of feminism in Ireland, the coming into history of a previously marginalized majority: "The women's movement had happened. Women had emerged from the silence of the past and had begun to make their marks." "[Their emerging histories] complicate Ireland enormously" (1996, 104). As a woman who found success in Ireland through the last several decades, navigating the city on her own, living in cheap flats, working in the city's stalwart, sexist institutions (RTE and UCD), her enlightenment is bittersweet. She is the voice of European liberalism in Ireland, but she recognizes the price that still must be paid—she is regretfully single, ruefully childless. But while the present is complicated and imperfect, it is a vast improvement over life in Ireland in the 1950s.

What these two tales—Sheridan's *44 Dublin Made Me* and O'Faolain's *Are You Somebody?*—reveal is an attempt to stake a claim within the hotly debated territory of Irish history using the medium of personal memory. Whether or not Ireland has successfully overcome its difficult past of partition, economic dependence, and rigid ideological hierarchies, these memoirists make use of an unapologetically individualistic genre to spin their own answers to the question. Economic rhetoric suggests that Ireland is now postnational, postcolonial, and postmodern. O'Faolain's deliberate lack of nostalgia and her praise for a liberal present and an improving future are the continuation of revisionism's attempts to draw a clean line between the present and the past. The coming-of-age genre is appropriate to a country that wants to believe it is coming of age itself.

Elaine Crowley's memoir, *A Dublin Girl: Growing up in the 1930s* (1996), performs a different mnemonic function from either Sheridan's or O'Faolain's. While it also recalls the author's impoverished— but far from grim—childhood in the years before World War II, the inflection of memory is toward nostalgia, a form of longing driven by the urge to record a disappearing urban environment whose dissolution was threatened by the modernizing forces of the state. Crowley's recollections of her early years growing up in a lively, familiar neighborhood, which offered a sense of security, adventure, community, and entertainment, are contrasted with the family's later move to a new suburb on the outskirts of the city. There, despite the dream of finally owning their own home, her parents are never able "to get used to the place" (130). Out "here," her mother says, "you might as well be dead. Every house alike, every road the same" (ibid.). The narrative charts this progression from a poor, yet sustainable, inner-city neighborhood to life in a gray, postcolonial housing estate. Throughout, memory serves to remind us of the damage done to communities in the name of progress and forces us to complicate the question of whether the city, for many of its residents, is ultimately a fairer, more equitable place than it was during the reputedly failed early years of postindependence.

The book begins with destruction: "The house in which I lived is knocked down to the ground floor. The windows of the shop over which we had our accommodation are covered with sheets of corrugated iron. There are gaps where they meet. I can see it. See the piles of rubble, shards of planks that was the floor on which I played, plaster and layers of wallpaper, stained, faded, rotting, clinging to the bricks" (1996, 1). Their house had been destroyed to make way for a new motorway; we see the exposed layers of personal history laid bare to public inspection. Crowley's mother reared her children in a one-room apartment. Her ambition was to own "a private house ... [S]he put her name down for a Corporation place. But as she often said, 'There's families of ten and twelve children all over the city. . . . And if it wasn't for the hall door always open and anyone from the street free to use the lavatory, I'd stay where I am. Corporation schemes would never be my first choice'" (3). The street on which Crowley played becomes the symbol of communal life, a public sphere that offers safety and intimacy, the qualities of life that are most valued and whose loss will later be rued by a transplanted generation of inner-city residents. "'You can go down and play but don't go away from the door,' my mother instructed me the first time I was allowed into the street on my own. 'And don't go near the road,' she called after me. The road was the only danger she could envisage, for the road wasn't the street. The street was the people who lived there. She knew every one of them and they knew I was her little girl" (10). The city pervades the memoir. Throughout the book, urban geography is imbued with wonder, multiple detail, and infinite complexity. A tour reveals a city bursting with life and deep with history:

> On Sunday mornings my father took me with him to stable his horses. Dressed in my best and holding his hand we'd set off for the undertaker's yard in Denzille Street. Through William's Place passed the back entrance of the Meath Hospital, though York Street where women sat on the steps of the tenement houses breastfeeding their babies, talking, laughing and shouting to their barefooted children playing in the road. Then out of the poverty-ridden street and onto the Green where all was sunshine and the women were pretty and wore beautiful clothes and from the gratings of the Shelbourne rose smells of delicious food. On through other streets where no women sat on the steps and the letter-boxes and knockers gleamed. . . . If the weather was fine we went to the zoo. . . . On other Sundays we went to the Botanical Gardens. . . . I liked the National Art Gallery but not as much as the Natural History Museum. All the stuffed animals and the enormous Irish elk. (1996, 8–9)

As Crowley's memoir progresses, we learn of her father's affair, how he contracts tuberculosis, and how Crowley is forced to quit school to support her family. By this time, on account of her father's illness, her family was offered a council house many miles from their original home, a move that never compensates for the loss of family, friends, and more affordable urban living. While her mother likes the new house, she never enjoys it: " 'God knows I tried hard enough, but I miss the city. There was always something going on in the street. Fifty times a day you could look out of the window and see something or someone to interest you. But here... it's enough to send you out of your mind.... Between [bus] fares and paying... for everything locally I'm robbed. I'm telling you if I could put the house up on a cart I'd be back in the street tomorrow' " (1996, 130). As for Crowley, when she gets a job in a downtown Dublin textile factory, she is "constantly occupied—rediscovering the city" (159). "Between the factory and the Liffey," she writes, "I wove in and out of narrow streets: old cobbled streets with intriguing names, Crown Alley, Merchant's Arch, Temple Bar, Fishamble Street" (158).

In Crowley's memoir, therefore, nostalgia is turned against modernization, which is seen, in part, as threatening and destructive. Nostalgia becomes a reasonable reaction in the face of rapid and consequential change, and memory becomes a method of critique with which to confront the normalization of development carried out in the name of progress. In a memoir that appeared from the context of contemporary globalizing Dublin, nostalgia for a grounded past can be seen as the lodging of a protest against the most recent wave of urban renewal.

Since the early 1990s Ireland has witnessed unprecedented economic growth. After a century of underdevelopment, mass emigration, and violent conflict, the country has seemed to be entering a new phase of history. There has been a degree of peace in Northern Ireland. Thousands of young Irish emigrants have returned home, and American multinationals—principally computer and pharmaceutical companies—have invested in the country, bringing unemployment to an all-time low. The rate of economic growth earned the country its nickname Celtic Tiger, which has become part of a discourse used to construct Ireland as postnational, *post*-postcolonial, even postmodern. Globalization has been most visible in the rapid pace of change that has occurred recently in Dublin. Suburbanization, gentrification, and inner-city renewal in Ireland created and destroyed the kinds of spaces that produce memoir writing. The memoir is the literary bridge to the Celtic Tiger. While some memoirists vilify the past through their own personal experiences of it, thereby legitimating the present, others mourn the loss of valuable social codes and communal practices of pre-1960s Ireland. What is clear is that an altered and altering landscape necessitates its own literary form, the urban memoir—a genre as individualistic as the personal coming-of-age story and as rooted in the physical environment as theories of geographical and psychological change.

Conclusion

Dublin is no ordinary city. Its culture and history have been at the center of debates over the meanings of modernism, modernity, colonialism, and globalization. The clash between colonizer and colonized, unusual in the proximity of its antagonists, has defined much of Irish society, from the economy and government to the psychology, language, and, as I have attempted to prove in this book, the physical urban shape of Ireland's capital city. The collision between England and Ireland that unfolded over many centuries resulted in contradictions: control and resistance, suffering and creativity, tradition and modernization. An experimental literature arose, a literature written in the English language and bearing the traces of a deeply rooted Irish one. Emigration was also born from these tensions: a global Irish community emerged from a national trauma. The material landscape of Ireland, too, carries the history of the colonial encounter. From the growth of market towns in the seventeenth century, through the building of wide streets in the eighteenth and railroads in the nineteenth, to the creation of modernist high-rise office blocks and gentrified tourist districts in the twentieth century, controlling the urban environment has been one of the key strategies through which political leaders, both colonial and nationalist, have attempted to gain, consolidate, and maintain their power. In this book I have attempted to show how the politics of Irish independence—the winning and holding of public consent—was made manifest in the built environment. If the construction of space is fundamentally about the production of new subjectivities, then it is not surprising that at key moments in Ireland's history, architects and planners have sought to transform the physical core of the city. In the decade before independence, leading campaigners within the garden city and city beautiful movements argued that their spatial practices could help ease the rising discontent. In the postindependence decades, government officials and architects employed the policies of inner-city renewal and suburbanization to alleviate social problems that otherwise might have had the potential to undermine the fledgling state. During the 1960s and 1990s another round of economic restructuring was both expressed and facilitated by urban remodeling: 1960s internationalization and modernization was embodied by international style, while 1990s globalization saw its physical counterpart in postmodern eclecticism and historical preservation. While much has been written about the role of literature in giving voice to the postcolonial Irish experience, there are fewer accounts of the role the urban environment played in helping to implement the constantly shifting values and prejudices of the independent Irish state. In this book, I have explored how the process of urbanization in twentieth-century Dublin offers us a fruitful and alternative avenue of investigation into many of the central concerns of modern Ireland: the legacy of colonialism, the relevance of nationalism, the meaning of modernization, the function of history.

Many contemporary critics have collapsed the binary opposition between center and periphery, demonstrating how material wealth and cultural accomplishment depended on colonization. Edward Said, for example, famously argues in *Culture and Imperialism* that, from Defoe to Austen to Kipling, literature is marked by the easy movement of a new class of men across different geographies in order to amass fortune. But the colony is not just a passive site where wealth waits to be extracted. Many of the social practices that came to define modernity in Europe took shape in the colonies. In Ireland, for example, the police force was centralized early in the nineteenth century. Years before a national curriculum was developed for primary schools in England and Wales, the chief secretary of Ireland, Edward Stanley, established a national school system in Ireland. Rather than thinking of the colony as a peripheral space, I have, in this book, worked in the spirit of Marx's notion that it is, instead, a "crucible of modernity." I have paid attention to the ways in which colonial urban planners used planning in Ireland as a means to control space and regulate the population.

In chapter 1, I argued that the origins of the modern town planning movement were firmly fixed within the context of a colonial emergency. Patrick Abercrombie's 1914 plan, *Dublin of the Future*, emphasized order out of chaos, a new birth for the city, and a plan to industrialize a provincial imperial center. The plan stressed mobility, transparency, and efficiency—hallmarks of modernity. Also in chapter 1, I showed that town planning, while it began as a colonial discipline and was used to flout republican and nationalist aspirations, was soon appropriated by nationalists both in their efforts to combat colonialism and in their various attempts to define what an independent Dublin would look like. Moreover, contrary to popular representations of Irish nationalism and culture as intractably rural, I have maintained that debates over urbanization and development were at the forefront of the unfolding ideologies of nationalism. I have argued in this book that nationalism was a site of struggle. Town planning and the discourses it spawned have been central tools in the attempts to define such key nationalist concepts as the nation, progress, prosperity, and modernity.

Contemporary portrayals of the postindependence years in Ireland, whether drawn by an older breed of empirical historians or by younger critics trained in postcolonial theory, have tended to emphasize the bleakness and one-dimensionality of Irish society. The 1930s and 1940s still call up images of state repression, censorship, and darkness. Critics suggest that these years were a period when essentialist notions of identity and oppressive political policies were strictly enforced in an insecure attempt to consolidate the state and to police the national image. The common view is that the 1960s began the process of liberating the culture from parochialism and claustrophobia. In this paradigm, the internationalizing of the economy in the 1960s culminates in the cosmopolitanism of today's global Ireland. I have suggested, on the contrary, that this depiction of the 1930s and 1940s is a stereotype and a cliché, which, when examined more closely and with a fresh eye, does not stand up. For example, in chapter 2

I reread the discourses of architecture and urban planning during the early years of the Irish postcolonial state. I have argued that contemporary portrayals of the grim, dark days after the British left have more to do with consolidating the present neoliberal regime than with understanding the unfolding context of postcolonial Ireland.

I also believe that the image of a censorious and deeply Catholic nation is the view one sees when looking at this period of Irish culture through a literary lens. Several of the big modernists—Joyce, Beckett, O'Casey—left the country and blamed the new society for driving them out, and incorporated that bitterness into their work. When one turns to architecture and urban design, however, one sees in Dublin a city whose architects and developers were engaging the latest technologies and ideas about the future of cities that were emerging from Amsterdam, the United States, and elsewhere. Moreover, far from ignoring the interests of their urban population, leading state figures actively sought solutions to the city's housing crisis, experimented with both suburbanization and inner-city urban renewal, and employed a variety of architectural styles, such as art deco, modernism, and neoclassicism, to reflect different interests. I have also argued, against traditional wisdom, that the postcolonial state sought to win the consent of its citizens by actually building for them, rather than by imposing its will on them in an authoritarian fashion. I maintain, therefore, that postcolonial nationalism was itself a modernizing force, inherently internationalist, and not merely a reactionary, isolationist, and autarkic regime, as has been traditionally suggested.

Throughout this book, I have tried to pay close attention to the ways in which urban design, architecture, and planning are forms of history writing, as much as any text is. The location of a building, along with its style and the public debates that surround its construction, reflects the prejudices and ideologies of a culture. Any attempt to alter the built environment will also change the way the past and the future are perceived. Geography is history. The physical landscape bears the traces of the past, and all alterations to the built environment are a direct means of rethinking and determining which memories survive and which are thwarted or suppressed. Each of my chapters engages the politics of memory. In chapter 3, for example, I theorize the discourse of modernization as it came to be used by historians, state officials, and architects during the 1960s and 1970s. I have argued that the 1960s in Ireland saw the development of what is now known as "historical revisionism," a narrative that sought to downplay the legacy of Ireland's colonial past and to critique the failures of Irish society since independence. The same years also saw the reorganization of the physical environment in Dublin: the creation of vast new suburbs, the building of modernist tower blocks, and the laying down of new highways and roads. I maintain that the critique of nationalist ideology embedded in the new historiography of revisionism found its material counterpart in the city's streets, public housing, and industrial infrastructure: over the face of the old city, a new industrial and corporate city was imposed.

The new history blamed previous nationalist narratives for being biased and one-sided. There was, the new historians insisted, a need for a more objective and rational approach to history, one that evaluated the facts of Irish history in a cool and calculated manner. In 1960s Ireland, revisionism manifested itself, too, in the production of space in Dublin: historical buildings were destroyed, and flat, concrete, and rational structures were erected in their place. As the new history assumed for itself the aura of objectivity, so too did the nation's architects and planners turn to a corporate international style of architecture, such as that developed by van der Rohe, Le Corbusier, and Gropius, in their search to create a city free from the weight of tradition and nationalism. Correspondingly, as architects and historians set about rewriting the past, the officials of the state, in order to solve Ireland's economic woes, turned to embrace international capital. In such an atmosphere, I have argued, nationalism needed to be reinterpreted and made safe for an emerging capitalist order. Architecture and urban planning, as always, reinforced and helped to create this new environment.

The connection between history and the urban environment takes a different turn in the 1990s. While writers, critics, architects, and planners in the 1960s had much at stake in repressing Ireland's recent nationalist history and all its attendant divisions, the globalization of the 1990s spurred a different kind of relationship between Irish culture and Irish nationalism. The historiography of the flourishing moment embraces an altered form of nationalism: its iconography, rhetoric, and even its controversial leaders. I have argued that the current shaky foundation of multinational capitalism cloaks it-self in the garb of tradition in order to lend itself a more permanent and loyal appearance. In chapter 4, I examined the spatial forms produced by the Celtic Tiger. The comparison of the Celtic Tiger to those economies of high growth in the Far East was meant to be laudatory, but, as I have argued, discourse always hides as much as it reveals. For every benefit associated with globalization (new indus-tries), one can find corresponding losses (the demise of older, indige-nous business). Again, my concern here has been with the relationship between history and globalization. The new pharmaceutical and financial companies that are coming to Dublin to avail themselves of attractive economic conditions require a new kind of urban space. Often situated on the fringes of the city, free from congested and po-tentially troublesome neighborhoods, the new assembly industries require the construction of new networks of roads, industrial parks, and tracts of housing. Financial services companies need high-tech buildings, providing the latest communications equipment. Mean-while, the growing Irish elite who work in the marketing, invest-ment, and advertising firms of Dublin's Tiger economy are not content with inhabiting the kind of city that they associate with a previous, less wealthy society. To satisfy the new economic situation, gentrified apartment blocks have sprung up in the heart of once undesirable neighborhoods. Young professionals seek the same quality of life that they would expect to find in other European cities. Entertainment districts and shopping centers have been built to cater to this con-temporary generation.

All these changes, I have suggested, are having an effect on how the nation remembers its own colonial and nationalist past. Increas-ingly, that history is less understood or debated than *used* in an at-tempt to market a generic sense of Irishness to tourists and locals alike. Rapidly transforming, globalizing cities lend themselves to reflection on what is being lost and how identities are being reshaped. In an Ireland that posits itself as a country finally coming of age, the unapologetically individualistic genre of memoir has attained a new level of popularity. In chapter 4 I gave a cultural reading of several new Dublin memoirs, each of which casts the city in a different light, drawing on personal memories to display the various ways in which collective and individual identities are being reshaped to meet the needs of a globalizing economy.

Dublin is more than the sum of its parts. Its streets, buildings, and suburbs reveal economic and political agendas, historical controversies, and genuine struggles over autonomy and national identity. Irish history has largely been determined by colonial conquest and postcolonial attempts to build the state. Dublin bears these imprints. Colonialism, nationalism, and their attendant conflicts and controversies have shaped the streets of Ireland's capital. Our understanding of physical space itself is lifeless without the animating forces of history, theory, and social debate. Much contemporary theory invokes spatial metaphors to empower its key concepts. Postcolonial theory employs the notion of center and periphery, metropole and colony, to understand the commercial and intellectual traffic between Europe and its holdings. Subaltern studies, in its theory of history, relies on the image of the visible and the invisible, what is representative and what is subterranean, to illuminate the ideas and populations that both typify and undermine the state. Foucault's panopticon and Habermas's public sphere are physical concepts of modern state control. Yeats famously prefigured these theories when he expressed the collapse of social order and the emergence of political extremes via his own spatial metaphor: "the centre cannot hold; / Mere anarchy is loosed upon the world." In this book I have attempted to theorize and explain how holding the city's center is more than a literary trope; controlling the representative, symbolic heart of the nation has been crucial to various movements, political, literary, and social, throughout the twentieth century. By combining critical and cultural theory with historical and architectural debate, I have attempted to demonstrate that Dublin's spatial history is not just the result of national and local energies, but that the currents and forces within Irish nationalism have always been part of wider, international cultural and intellectual trends. Dublin's urban planning and architecture stand at the crossroads between modernity and tradition, the local and the global, nationalism and colonialism. This approach, one that combines urbanism, modernism, and postcolonial theory, has, I hope, shed some light on our understanding of the built environment and on the way we define progress.

Notes

Introduction

1. See in particular King 1990.

2. See Robert K. Home, "The Grand Model of Colonial Settlement," in Home 1997, 8–35.

3. See Robert K. Home, "Port Cities of the British Empire: A Global Thalassocracy," in Home 1997, 62–84.

4. Edmund Spenser, *A View of the Present State of Ireland* (electronic text available at http://celt.ucc.ie/publishd.html).

5. The phrase itself has a history that predates Gramsci's examination of it, going back to debates within the Second International (1889–1914), where a dispute raged among European communist parties over what alliances the proletariat should form with other social classes and factions.

6. See Briggs 1959.

7. Society for the Improvement of Ireland, *Statement of the Proceedings of the Society for the Improvement of Ireland for the Year 1828 with an appendix, containing its rules and regulations, names of members, and other illustrative documents,* Dublin, A. Thom. Goldsmiths'–Kress Library of Economic Literature, no. 25471.

8. In rural areas, English settlers stamped their image on the landscape by building large houses, ranging in size from extensive farmhouses to Palladian and neoclassical mansions, separated from native settlements by vast gardens and parkland. These demesnes were laid out by leading landscape designers of the day according to the principles of the English natural garden:

expanses of smooth, open grass, loosely dotted with trees and other natural features, spread out in front of the house. Unlike the ornate and rigid French formal garden, the English garden and the Irish landed estate were intended to convey the comforting notion that the Anglo-Irish were part of the natural surroundings and that the social order was somehow inevitable. The "big house" itself, however, proudly proclaimed its foreign, romanesque lineage and featured pedimented windows, tight symmetry, Doric-columned porticos, and use of granite materials. The difference between the attempt to appear organic and the effort to stand out architecturally is symptomatic of the inherent contradiction of a foreign ruling class that wants to both belong and stand apart. In literature, these aristocratic homes came to serve as a metaphor for the fortunes of colonialism in Ireland. From the comic stories of Sommerville and Ross that portrayed respectable landlords engaging the uncooperative but lovable locals, through the Gothic novels of Bram Stoker and Le Fanu that represent the melancholy mood of a dying ascendancy, to the writings of Yeats, Lady Gregory, and others for whom the big house symbolized the ruined possibilities of a great and unpoliticized civilization, the architecture and culture of the big house have stood as an allegory for the shifting interpretations of colonialism in Ireland.

9. Wide Streets Commission 1802.

10. Ibid.

11. "An Act For Making a Wide and Convenient Way, Street, and Passage, From Essex-Bridge to the Castle of Dublin, And for Other Purposes Therein Mentioned" (Dublin, Printed by the Executor of George Abraham Grierson, 1758). George Semple was commissioned to widen Essex Bridge in 1756. In his preparation, he traveled to London to study the recently completed Westminster Bridge. The result was a new fifty-one-foot bridge over the Liffey that facilitated movement between Dublin Castle and the military barracks in the Phoenix Park (Fraser 1985, 103).

12. Wide Streets Commission 1802.

13. When the commissioners turned their attention in 1800 to removing any structural protrusions onto the quays, thereby increasing speed and mobility, they argued that the "opening of the quays on either side of the river" constituted "measures highly necessary for the accommodation of trade" (ibid.).

14. Fraser 1985, 113.

15. Ibid.

16. Wide Streets Commission 1802.

17. For example, the British Parliament in 1877 passed the Dublin Science and Art Museum Act. Its aim was "to authorize the Commissioners of Public Works in Ireland to acquire from the Royal Dublin Society and others

Lands for the Erection of a Science and Art Museum in Dublin, and to establish a National Library in Dublin" (1877 Local Act [40 and 41 Victoria], chap. ccxxxiv).

18. National Library of Ireland 1979.

19. The more powerful railway companies controlled the cross-channel boats. The terminus of the Great Northern Line, Dublin to Drogheda, was contracted between 1844 and 1846 at Amiens Street. Kingsbridge Station, terminus of the Great Western & Southern Lines, was built in 1845–46. Broadstone Street Station, home of the Dublin-Galway route, was completed in 1850. Each of these architecturally grand structures had connecting lines to Dublin's ports, whence Ireland's agricultural commerce was exported to industrial cities in England.

20. See Fremantle 1926, 84–86.

1. *Dublin of the Future* and the Emergence of Town Planning in Ireland

1. The American Revolution provoked a powerful and articulate campaign by Irish Protestants calling for the reconstruction of commercial legislation to give Ireland unrestricted access to world trade.

2. From 1782 the Irish Parliament in Dublin, until its abandonment under the terms of the Union in 1800, was the most autonomous of all Irish Parliaments under the Crown. By far the greatest development under Grattan's Parliament (named after the principal political leader in the Irish House of Commons) was the Renunciation Act, in which the British Parliament renounced its right to legislate for Ireland.

3. The United Irishmen's rebellion in 1798 was the most widespread and violent uprising yet against British rule in Ireland. Its radical political reform, to unite Catholic, Protestant, and Dissenter under the common name of Irishman, was inspired by the American and French Revolutions.

4. For a more complete understanding of the term *ascendancy,* see Terry Eagleton's "Ascendancy and Hegemony," in Eagleton 1995, 27–103.

5. See Oliver MacDonagh, "Ideas and Institutions," in Vaughan 1989, 193–216; also Deane 1985.

6. By 1830, for example, according to S. J. Connolly, "25,000 of the total 30,000 infantry in the United Kingdom were either in Ireland or at stations along the west coast of Great Britain from which they could be quickly dispatched across the Irish Sea" (1989). The country also maintained a paramilitary police force of 14,000. In addition, there were about 31,000 yeomen, mostly Protestant Orangemen (Comerford 1989).

7. See MacLaughlin 1994, 8–16.

8. *Irish Times,* 4 September 1913, 6.

9. *Irish Independent,* 15 September 1916, 2.

10. *Irish Worker,* 3 January 1914, 1.

11. *Freeman's Journal,* 30 September 1913, 5.

12. O'Beirne and Travers 1911, 568–69.

13. *Irish Architect and Craftsman* 6 (1914): 800.

14. See, for example, Geddes 1918, 1: 160: "For every reason then I essentially leave this old Bazar City as it stands, and without cutting any large new thoroughfares. Yet this is no mere policy of dull conservatism, of letting things alone as they are. There is a further alternative:—that of antisepsis and conservative surgery—in plainer terms, cleaning up, and clearing up.... By our small removals, straightenings, openings and replannings in detail, a network of clean and decent lanes, of small streets, and open places, and even gardens, is thus formed."

15. *Irish Architect and Craftsman* 6 (1914): 800. Other references to Unwin's 1914 Dublin stay can be found on pages 666, 707, 747, 743, 799.

16. See minute 607 (1914) of the *Minutes of the Municipal Council of the City of Dublin* (Dublin, Dublin Corporation): "That the Housing Committee be directed to acquire immediately, whether by private or compulsory purchase, Mr. Walker's interest in the 51 acres of land known as Marino, for the purpose of erecting housing thereon for the working classes." Geddes and Unwin's consultancy town planning report is included in the *Reports and Printed Documents of Dublin Corporation* (1915, document 78). It includes the following statement of support for the construction of garden suburbs in Dublin: "The least expensive and most useful method by which open space can be provided is by giving land in the form of gardens to each house. In this form the land will always yield on the average more than enough to pay the extra rent of the larger area.... The high price of land in Dublin is one difficulty.... To buy at the present high prices small plots in the centre, and build thereon the maximum number of houses, will therefore tend to keep up the value of land, and will do nothing to reduce the density of population, or to add to the number of good homes.... On the other hand, there is plenty of cheap land outside the central areas.... The tenants can have land at a cheap price per yard, and can afford to have a garden which will help them pay the rent. They will be healthier and more efficient workmen." Their memorandum no. 3 states that in terms of new locations for suburbs, "Marino is second to none in Dublin for accessibility, economy, and beauty." For discussion of the Marino layout, see Mervyn Miller, "Raymond Unwin and the Planning of Dublin," in Bannon 1985, 263–305; "Housing and Town-Planning Tour No. 8: Official Visit to Ireland," *Garden Cities and Town Planning,* October 1928, 210–22.

17. Georg Simmel, "Metropolis and Mental Life," in Sennett 1969, 47–61.

18. See Deane 1985.

19. These depictions of nationalism as essentially reactionary and violent will be elaborated on in chapters 3 and 4.

20. For a typical and foundational statement on the goals and methods of early town planning, see Abercrombie 1916.

21. Ralph Neville, "The Basis of British Efficiency," *Garden City* 1 (1904): 1–2.

22. Ibid., 1.

23. See, for example, the journal *Garden Cities and Town Planning*, whose early volumes include the following articles: "Alexandria, Old and New" (January 1923, 8–10); "Town Planning in Palestine" (November 1925, 267–69); Davis Trietsch, "Garden Cities for Palestine" (January 1923, 11–13); and "Town Planning in India" (August–September 1926, 167–70).

24. See, for example, the representative articles in *Garden City*: "Addresses by Sir Walter Foster, Mr. G. K. Chesterton, and Mr. Montagu Harris" (February 1905, 1–5), which included speeches on the topics of the "Advantages of Industrial De-Centralisation," "The Nightmare of Our Towns," and "The Existing City a Joke"; Evacustes Phibson, "Why Not Associated Homes?" (July 1905, 64).

25. *Irish Architect and Craftsman* 6 (1914): 800.

26. *Freeman's Journal,* 25 May 1911.

27. J. V. Brady, "Town Planning in Ireland," *Garden Cities and Town Planning* 1 (1911): 237–40.

28. The Housing of the Working Classes (Ireland) Act, commonly referred to as the Clancy Act, after its parliamentary sponsor. See Fraser 1996, 88–95.

29. Dublin City Council Reports (1915, report no. 78), 1: 736.

30. See, for example, minute 796 (1910) of the *Minutes of the Municipal Council of the City of Dublin*: "The motion was put by Alderman Kelly and seconded by Councillor O'Toole '[T]hat all references in the motion to a "Garden City" be eliminated, and the word "Houses" substituted therefore'" (513).

31. *Freeman's Journal,* 11 November 1913.

32. The Marino decision is also noted in minute 796 (1910) of the *Minutes of the Municipal Council of the City of Dublin*: "This Council hereby requests the Estates and Finance Committee to take into consideration at its next meeting this important matter [the creation of a garden suburb at Marino], and, in view, of giving much needed employment, that the said committee do report to the next monthly meeting of this Council as to the feasibility of the project" (513).

33. *Irish Builder and Engineer,* 26 November 1910, 728.

34. Horace Plunkett wrote on developments in the agricultural cooperative movement in Ireland in *Sociological Review,* a journal Geddes played a
large role in founding. See, for example, "The Sociological Aspects of the
Agricultural Revolution in Ireland" (1910, 185–96).

35. *Irish Architect and Craftsman* 6 (1914): 747.

36. Ibid., 799–800.

37. *Irish Builder and Engineer,* 19 May 1916, 215.

38. "The Results of Revolution," *Irish Builder and Engineer,* 13 May
1916, 202.

39. "Some Impressions of the Rebellion," *Irish Builder and Engineer,* 19
May 1916, 215.

40. "The Results of Revolution," *Irish Builder and Engineer,* 13 May
1916, 202.

41. Abercrombie and his Liverpool Department of Civic Design were
influenced by the École des Beaux Arts; he was an admirer of Hénard, the
French architect who was a disciple of Haussmann and an early student of
traffic flow systems.

2. Postindependence Ireland

1. See Frantz Fanon, "The Pitfalls of National Consciousness," in Fanon
1963, 148–205. Also see Benedict Anderson, "The Angel of History," in
Anderson 1991, 155–62.

2. See Sheehan 2002, 23–45.

3. The various projects undertaken by Dublin Corporation are included
in the Reconstruction Committee's minutes, which are collected in the *Reports and Printed Documents of Dublin Corporation* (1924 and 1925).

4. For a more detailed list of government remodeling, see Office of
Public Works 1999.

5. Dublin City Council Reports (1925), report no. 224, 401.

6. For a political and social history of the early years of the Irish Free
State, see Garvin 1996; Joseph Lee, "Consolidation, 1922–1932," in Lee
1989, 56–174; and Dermot Keogh, "A War without Victors: Cumann na
nGaedheal and the Conservative Revolution" and "De Valera and Fianna
Fáil in Power, 1932–1939," in Keogh 1995, 3–63, 64–107.

7. *Freeman's Journal,* 12 December 1922.

8. Mount Shannon Lodge, the estate of the Honorable Kathleen Lawless (Dublin Corporation Archives, box 18, Abbey Ref. 230645, Crumlin
North, Dublin City Library and Archive).

9. Chester Arthur, "Jazz and Skyscrapers," *Irish Statesman,* 25 June
and 2 July 1927, 374–75, 396–97.

10. "The Spoiling of Dublin Suburbs," *Irish Builder and Engineer,* 14 November 1925, 929, 933.

11. Acts of the Oireachtas, *Town and Regional Planning Act, 1934.* Available online at http://www.oireachtas.ie.

12. "Further figures supplied by the Corporation denote that of the 20,108 families living in one room in tenement houses..." (*Report of the Departmental Committee Appointed by the Local Government Board of Ireland to Inquire into the Housing Conditions of the Working Classes in the City of Dublin, Local Government Board* [London: H. M. Stationery office, 1914], 4).

13. *Irish Builder and Engineer,* 8 March 1923, 169.

14. See Bannon 1989, 32; Fraser 1996, 290; Roche 1982, 222–26.

15. *Manchester Guardian Commercial,* 10 May 1923, 42–43.

16. Ibid., 41.

17. The "million pound scheme" was a grant made available by the government of the Irish Free State for urban housing schemes. The sum was to be divided among the municipal authorities in the ratio of two pounds for every one provided by the local authority.

18. Modeled on British post–World War I labor guilds, which sought to cut out the capitalist in the provision of new housing. An Irish labor activist told Sinn Féin that the aim was to "show that workers were capable of building houses cheaper and better than they could be built by the capitalists of Dublin or any other city" (*Irish Times,* 2 August 1921).

19. See "The Present Position of Housing: As Viewed from the Government Standpoint," *Irish Builder and Engineer,* 19 February 1927, 106, 109–10, 113.

20. *Irish Times,* 8 June 1925.

21. "The Present Position of Housing: As Viewed from the Government Standpoint," *Irish Builder and Engineer,* 19 February 1927, 109.

22. Dublin Corporation archives, Cabra box 6, Abbey Ref. 230646. This is the source for the discussion of Cabra in the following paragraphs.

23. Dublin Corporation archives, Crumlin box 18, Abbey Ref. 230645.

24. Dublin Corporation archives, Cabra box 6, Abbey Ref. 230646.

25. These measures included changing the Irish Constitution in 1937 to remove remaining traces of the British Crown, refusing to pay the land annuities promised to the British government as compensation for land redistribution, and moving toward economic policies of increased protectionism and tariffs.

26. Dublin Corporation archives, Newfoundland Street box 76, Abbey Ref. 230654. This is the source for the discussion of the Newfoundland Street development in the following paragraphs.

27. Ken Lambla, "Abstraction and Theosophy: Social Housing in Rotterdam, the Netherlands," *Architronic* 8, no. 1 (January 1999), available online at http://architronic.saed.kent.edu/.

28. "The New Architecture Explained: The MARS Group Exhibition in London," *Irish Builder and Engineer,* 22 January 1938, 50.

29. "Architecture and Insularity," *Irish Builder and Engineer,* 14 June 1924, 513.

30. "Traditional and New Architecture," *Irish Builder and Engineer,* 26 June 1937, 574.

31. "Michael Scott: Man and Architect," *Build,* February 1975, 3.

32. Available online at http://www.irish-architecture.com/busaras/chapter_1e.html.

33. "Michael Scott: Man and Architect," *Build,* February 1975, 3.

3. Revisionism in Ireland

1. See Fintan O'Toole, "Faulty Towers," *Irish Times,* 14 January 1997; and "From High-Rise Hell to Hi-Tech Heaven?" *Irish Times,* 15 January 1997.

2. The most current technology was the French Balency system of poured concrete and rapid drying.

3. Some of the primary texts that address the revisionist controversy in Irish historiography are Brady 1994; Boyce and O'Day 1996; O'Ceallaigh 1994; and "Challenging the Canon: Revisionism and Cultural Criticism," in Deane 1992, 561–676.

4. Consider Marx's famous line in the *Communist Manifesto* about the "idiocy of rural life," which implies a link, at least in his schema, between urbanization and modernization. Weber, too, writes about how rationalization, bureaucratization, and a capitalist and modern work ethic develop alongside a mercantile "burgher" class in the early modern towns of Europe (see "The Spirit of Capitalism," in Weber 1985, 79–95).

5. See Kiberd 1994, 94–112.

6. "Editorial," *Forgnán,* January 1962.

7. "The Construction Industry and the Irish Economy," *Forgnán,* January 1962.

8. Michael Quinn, "1916: Progress Backwards," *Build,* January 1966.

9. The contradiction in Marx's *Communist Manifesto* between the power unleashed by capitalism and the enslaving uses to which that power is put demonstrates this point. For example, Marx writes of the advances made by modern industrialization: "Subjection of nature's forces to man, machinery, application of chemistry to industry and agriculture, steam navigation, rail-

ways, electric telegraphs, clearing of whole continents for cultivation, canalization of rivers, whole populations conjured out of the ground—what earlier century had even a presentiment that such productive forces slumbered in the lap of social labour" (1998, 56). In contrast, "the unceasing improvement of machinery...makes livelihood more and more precarious" (61).

10. Freud's metaphor in *Civilization and Its Discontents* depicts the unconscious in terms of a city: the old lies just below the surface of the new. In other words, there is but a thin layer between the present and the past. In Rome, for example, despite the modern lives being lived on the surface city, the contours of ancient streets and buildings still determine many aspects of everyday life: how and where people move in the city. Around the corner from the modern, or underneath the modern, there is always the old: powerful, influential, and often hidden.

11. In *The Birth of the Clinic* and *Discipline and Punish,* Foucault lays out, in immaculate detail, how modern institutions, such as the prison and the asylum, relied on objective and rational methods of science to analyze patients and punish prisoners. Scientific classifications and objective treatments that were intended to cure or help individuals were, he suggests, merely other ways of controlling and disciplining them. While modern welfare and medical practices make liberal claims, Foucault suggests they merely perpetuate the age-old concern with power, repression, control, and brutality.

12. See Frampton 1980, 262–69.

13. Dáil Éireann, Parliamentary Debates, 3 June 1959. Available online at http://www.oireachtas-debates.gov.ie.

14. "A striking fact," writes Loraine Donaldson, "is that 70 per cent of the new firms set up between 1959 and 1964 had foreign participation. These foreign firms accounted for 85 per cent of new investment....The pace [of growth] was set in the industrial sector by industrial exports which increased from an annual value of 32.8 million pounds in 1958 to 62.2 million pounds in 1963, i.e., by over 90 per cent....The foreign capital inflow increased from .8 million in 1960 to 22 million in 1963" (1966, 18, 44, 54).

15. "Comment," *Irish Builder and Engineer,* 12 March 1966.

16. Michael Quinn, "1916: Progress Backwards," *Build,* January 1966.

17. The biographies of these architects are briefly covered in Becker, Olley, and Lang 1997, 190–98.

18. St. Andrew's, a Protestant secondary school, had long been located in central Dublin (its football fields were in Montrose), where, for over a century, it had served the declining needs of the city's Presbyterian population. The school, after its sale to RTE, moved even farther out, to Blackrock, Co. Dublin, a traditionally Protestant village hugging the city's southern coastline. From there, the school could act as a magnet for Protestant families

living in Dublin's affluent, south-side suburbs. The city's Protestant population had, in effect, been moving southward ever since the Act of Union in 1800, but the migration intensified when Dublin Corporation became a predominantly Catholic body at the beginning of the century. Several of the south-side municipalities, such as Dun Laoghaire, Rathmines, and Rathgar, maintained a measure of legislative independence, however, and were, therefore, appealing places to live for many Protestants.

19. The National University Act of 1908 was part of the series of efforts made by the Conservative Party at the start of the twentieth century aimed at killing off home rule "with kindness." While it neglected to dismantle the Protestant-dominated Trinity College, it gave university status to Queen's College, Belfast, and established the Catholic-dominated National University of Ireland, which consisted of new universities in Dublin (later UCD), Galway, and Cork. This aroused the hostility of Ulster Unionists against what they called a scheme for "satisfying the monstrous demands of the Roman Hierarchy" (Boyce 1990, 229). In 1944, as Catholic archbishop of Dublin, McQuaid ordered, with reference to Trinity College, that no Catholic could attend: "Any Catholic who disobeys this law is guilty of mortal sin and while he persists in disobedience is unworthy to receive the Sacraments" (Keogh 1995, 146). McQuaid regarded the National University of Ireland, with its three constituent colleges, as a neutral educational establishment, which had to be regarded by Catholics as failing "to give true acknowledgement to the One True Faith" (ibid.). He considered UCD as being "sufficiently safe for Catholic students" (ibid.).

20. Acts of the Oireachtas, Local Government (Planning and Development) Act (1963). Available online at http://www.oireachtas.ie.

21. The stated "aims and achievements" of the first of Lemass's five-year plans (initiated in November 1958) were to "promot[e] economic development, both directly through State investment and indirectly through the encouragement of private enterprise by grants, loans, tax incentives and other means" (Government of Ireland 1963, 7). The Second Programme for Economic Expansion sought to "secure the widest and most effective use of the inducements offered by the State to firms to increase their efficiency. Generous grants and special loan facilities are available towards the cost of re-equipment and adaptation.... There must also be greater emphasis on research and development, and this may require co-operative effort because of the relatively small size of most Irish firms.... A 10% cut in protective tariffs was made on 1st January, 1963. A further cut will be made on 1st January, 1964" (35–36).

22. Dáil Éireann, Parliamentary Debates, 11 March 1970. Available online at http://www.oireachtas-debates.gov.ie.

23. *Building,* 25 February 1975.

24. Available online at http://www.irish-architecture.com/aai/journal/nine/esb.html.

25. Ibid.

26. "Stillorgan Shopping Centre: A New Concept in Ireland," *Build,* December 1966.

27. Ibid.

28. With this exercise in neocorporatism, Lemass was better able to introduce the Irish economy to international competition. Tariffs were reduced in 1963 and 1964 by 10 percent each year, and in 1965 the Anglo-Irish Free Trade Area Agreement was created.

29. *Ireland: The New Convention Country* (1966), directed by Robert Monks.

30. "Bank of Ireland Headquarters, Dublin: Architect's Account," *Build,* December 1972.

31. Office Premises Act (1958). Available online at http://www.acts.ie.

32. "Bank of Ireland Headquarters, Dublin: Architect's Account," *Build,* December 1972.

33. Ibid.

34. Lemass, according to several historians (Keogh 1995; Lee 1989), was the first Taoiseach to approach Northern Ireland not so much as a problem, but as a neighboring state, which required the development of friendly relations. In January 1965 he traveled to Belfast to meet the prime minister of Northern Ireland, Terence O'Neill. Lemass believed that the southern economy and culture required major changes before it would become attractive to Protestant northerners. He recognized that the Constitution would have to be changed and references to Catholicism removed, along with Dublin's territorial claim on the North. Idealistically, he hoped that an improved economy and goodwill gestures toward unionists might convince them to unify with the republic. Thirty years later, all these objectives have been achieved, and Protestants are more reluctant than ever to consider reunification.

35. Wright's report held advisory status only and, particularly at the regional level, was never formally adopted as a planning blueprint. Major elements of his proposal did, however, find expression in the Dublin County Development Plan of 1971.

36. The four proposed new towns are widely spread over the seven miles from Blanchardstown to Tallaght. It was proposed that each should be built to grow westward to a population of 60,000 to 100,000, or about 350,000 people in all, and that they should incorporate within them existing small towns. "It is essential," wrote Wright, "that each new town should be

planned to provide employment for most of its working population, and a shopping centre and other facilities that would meet all the ordinary weekly needs" (1967, 22).

37. Statistics are gathered from a series of newspaper articles, including the following: Nuala O'Faolain, "What the Planners Left Out of Tallaght," *Irish Times,* 19 February 1990; Frank McDonald, "Planners See New Vision of Tallaght," *Irish Times,* 29 June 1995; Paul White, "Suburban Sprawl without a Soul," *Irish Times,* 5 September 1989; Frank McDonald, "Happy Shiny Days Ahead for Tallaght as Planners Promise Radical Reform," *Irish Times,* 5 March 1998.

38. See Kristoff 1991; and Reps 1965.

39. For a polemic against the corporation's road-widening schemes, see Kelly 1976.

40. See note 3 above.

41. A long tradition of Marxist writing sees the colonial context as an aberration when set against the industrial European model of class development. Engels, in *The Condition of the Working-Class in England,* depicts the Irish as inherently unable to assimilate into the British proletariat mainstream. Bew and Patterson, in their contemporary attempt to produce a modern class history of Ireland, portray nationalism as intrinsically bourgeois (1982). Such writers privilege a complex and multilayered class analysis over their simplistic version of national identity.

42. David Lloyd, "Irish Studies in the Post-Colonial Frame," lecture delivered at the Ninth Annual Graduate Irish Studies Conference, University of Notre Dame, 10 March 1995.

43. Subaltern politics and struggles resist the theoretical and territorial paradigm of the nation, preferring to construct a history from below, a geography of resistance (the region, the village, and family and kinship networks, as opposed to national communities) that undermines and decenters the unity and coherence of both "official" nationalism and colonialism.

4. Memory and the City

1. "Survey Shows Dublin Is Fourth Most Expensive City in the EU," *Irish Times,* 15 June 2004.

2. Rob Norton, "The Luck of the Irish: If You Want to Visit Old Ireland You'd Better Get There Soon." *Fortune,* 25 October 1999, 194.

3. Many articles celebrate the new equation between economic prosperity and cultural growth. See, for example, "Dublin Leads the Way in Ireland's Cultural and Economic Resurgence" (*Architecture,* October 1998); "Goodbye Shamrock. Hello Kentia Palm" (*New Statesman,* 27 September

1996, 70); "In the Land of the Emerald Tiger" (*Irish Times,* 28 December 1996); "Ireland: Peaceful and Prosperous the Republic Confidently Faces the 21st Century" (*Europe,* July–August 1995, 7); "Europe's Back Office: In a World Increasingly Ruled by Giant Financial Centers, Dublin Is More Than Holding Its Own" (*Economist,* 16 November 1996, 83); and "Ireland's New Face" (*Newsweek,* 15 December 2003).

4. For an important essay on the use of ancient history by the current forces of neoliberalism in Ireland, see Luke Gibbons, "The Myth of Modernization in Irish Culture," in Gibbons 1996, 82–93.

5. Taxation statistics taken from "The Irish Financial Industry: Europe's Back Office," *Economist,* 16 November 1996, 83–84. Ireland, according to the conservative Heritage Foundation, has one of the world's most pro-business environments, especially for foreign businesses and foreign investment. Beginning in the early 1990s, successive Irish governments, writes the Heritage Foundation, lowered the Irish corporate tax rate to "far below the EU average of 30 percent. Not surprisingly, Ireland has become a major center for U.S. investment in Europe, especially for the computer, software, and engineering industries. Although accounting for 1 percent of the euro-zone market, it receives nearly one-third of U.S. investment in the EU. GDP growth totaled 6.3 percent in 2002.... U.S. employers find that the marginal cost of employing workers... [is] less expensive than in the major Western European states" (available online at http://www.heritage.org/research/features/index/country.cfm?id=Ireland).

6. Available online at http://www.intel.com.

7. Gibbons, "The Myth of Modernization in Irish Culture," in Gibbons 1996, 89–90.

8. Christina Barron, "Calling Ireland: Call Centers Are the New Booming Business," *Europe,* July–August 1995, 16.

9. U.S. Bureau of Labor Statistics, "International Comparisons of Hourly Compensation Costs for Production Workers in Manufacturing, Revised Data for 2002." Available online at http://www.bls.gov/news.release/ichcc.t02.htm.

10. Tourism became the country's largest industry in 1988, when it employed more than 124,000 people and brought in over 2.3 billion pounds in foreign revenue (Fintan O'Toole, "In the Land of the Emerald Tiger," *Irish Times,* 28 December 1996).

11. Interview in *Newsweek,* 13 October 1987.

12. "Emigration Now Often to Be Welcomed, Speakers Say," *Irish Times,* 15 August 1996.

13. Ibid.

14. Interview in *Newsweek,* 13 October 1987.

15. The consent clause, which introduces the Belfast Agreement, states that any change in the status of Northern Ireland will only come about with the consent of a majority of its people. It accepts that while a substantial minority in the North, and a majority on the island as a whole, want a united Ireland, the majority in the North currently has the final say over Northern Ireland's status within the Union. Both governments are obliged to give effect to the wishes of the majority of the people of the North, if that wish changes. The agreement also recognizes "the birthright of all the people of Northern Ireland" to identify themselves and be accepted as Irish, British, or both.

16. *Constitution of Ireland* (Dublin: Government of Ireland Publications, 1937), Article Two.

17. Ibid.

18. Ibid., Article Three.

19. "This Is No 'Deal' for Nationalist Ireland," *Sunday Business Post,* 12 April 1998.

20. "New Confidence, New Thinking Hastens Change," in "The Path to Peace," supplement to *Irish Times,* 11 April 1998.

21. "Economic Prosperity Puts Dublin in Gridlock," *USA Today,* 12 April 2000.

22. See Ruth McManus, "Dublin's Changing Tourism," *Irish Geography* 34 (2001): 108.

23. As David Harvey writes about the contemporary Western city: "The frenetic pursuit of the consumption dollars of the affluent has led to a much stronger emphasis on product differentiation.... Producers have, as a consequence, begun to explore the realms of aesthetic preferences in ways that were not so necessary under a Fordist regime of standardized accumulation through mass production" (1989b, 269).

24. The Carton estate, for example, has almost a thousand years behind it and has just been converted into an approximately $65 million golf course. The original house was built by the Fitzgerald family in 1176, after the Norman invasion of Ireland. Membership in the new golf course currently stands at $15,000 a year.

25. House prices have risen at well over 10 percent per year in Dublin during the last ten years. Average three-bedroom homes may now sell for half a million dollars. With such profits to be had in real estate, it is hardly surprising that these same years have witnessed a series of political scandals in which property developers, speculators, and builders were discovered to be bribing politicians for information about the next piece of agricultural land scheduled to be rezoned for housing. (This land could then be bought cheaply before its value exploded.) In such a climate, the property market has been flooded with surplus capital as citizens, banks, and investors are

eager to buy, hold, and resell whatever is available. Whether the bubble will burst and prices fall back to a more realistic level is a subject of great debate. One of the results of the exaggeration in Dublin's property market is that many younger couples (who did not already have a foot on the property ladder before the Celtic Tiger) cannot afford to buy a home or are working excessively to pay for their mortgage. Signs of discontent are beginning to emerge as an overburdened public begins to demand some form of debt relief, increased rates of subsidized housing, and the creation of an improved infrastructure to meet the demands of the growing, expensive city.

26. "Europe's Back Office: In a World Increasingly Ruled by Giant Financial Centers, Dublin Is More Than Holding Its Own," *Economist,* 16 November 1996.

27. "Urban and Rural Renewal Tax Incentive Schemes," Department of Finance, document no. TSG99/32. Available online at http://www.finance .gov.ie/viewdoc.asp?DocID=1165.

28. The HARP framework covered 260 acres of central Dublin, from O'Connell Street to Smithfield, and included many historical markers, such as Collins Barracks. One goal of the plan was to create a pedestrian route through part of the northern inner city. Ten million euros was provided by the European Union's Urban and Village Renewal Programme, which was a significantly lower amount than the forty million put into Temple Bar's twenty-eight acres.

29. *Modern Dublin,* pamphlet no. BE (Built Environment) 20, published by Enfo (the Department of the Environment and Local Government's educational unit). Available online at http://www.enfo.ie/leaflets/bs20.htm.

30. Ibid.

31. The consultancy firm KMPG, along with the architectural firm of Murray O'Laoire and the Northern Ireland Economic Research Center, was commissioned by the government to produce a review of the workings of renewal schemes since 1986. The report they issued revealed that residential units were "small and spatially repetitive," with "a prevalence of small bathrooms and kitchenettes, many of them internalized with little natural light or ventilation," and a lack of semipublic and private external space. The report's most general finding was the lack of integration between the local communities and the new residents (KPMG et al. 1996).

32. Speech by the Taoiseach at the launch of a development for Smithfield Market, 15 April 2002, government press release.

33. Ester Laushway, "Temple Bar: Dublin's Young Heart," *Europe,* 1 July 1996.

34. In the United States, HUD (Department of Housing and Urban Development), under the HOPE VI project, has demolished 135,000 units of

older public housing but has created only 60,000 units in the style of new urbanism (Sabrina Williams, "From Hope VI to Hope Sick," *Dollars and Sense,* July–August 2003).

35. "The share of [Local Authority] housing stock...had fallen to less than 9 per cent by 1996," writes Tony Fahey, "half its relative size of 30 years previously.... The present relative smallness of social housing construction arises par" (1999, 37, 39). In other words, housing is increasingly being left to the free market. For statistics on social housing, see also the Web site of the Irish Council for Social Housing (http://www.icsh.ie). The official housing strategy of Dublin City Council, the heir to Dublin Corporation, announced in 2001 as part of the Dublin city development plan that "the demand for social housing in Dublin City and Counties is projected to grow significantly over the period 2001–2005 inclusive (over 7,000 extra applicants are expected in the city)." Available online at http://www .dublincity.ie.

36. A 1994 study revealed that over 90 percent of tenants who lived in new inner-city apartments intended to move in the next two years, and that 75 percent of these planned on relocating to the suburbs (Jacinta Prunty, "Residential Urban Renewal Schemes, Dublin 1986–1994," *Irish Geography* 28 [1995]: 143).

37. I am working here from Saskia Sassen's definition of a global city: not a place that is home to the headquarters of major corporations, but a site that contains the features—telecommunications, fiscal incentives, labor supply—that allow that city to perform the functions of business that large international firms increasingly outsource to profitable and peripheral locations. These functions might include, for example, data processing, telemarketing, software design, and banking services. Along with these financial services, global cities also need to be able to sell "world-class" entertainment and culture to their transnational underwriters ("Whose City Is It? Globalization and the Formation of New Claims" [available online at http://www .ifs.tu-darmstadt.de/fileadmin/lopofo/]).

38. "'Fortune' Magazine Says Dublin Is the Business," *Irish Times,* 4 November 1997.

39. Linda Higgins, "The Quay to Happiness," *Irish Independent,* 14 January 1997.

40. Copper Alley received its name from the copper money coined and distributed there by Lady Alice Fenton, widow of Geoffrey Fenton, secretary of state in Ireland, 1581–1608. Crow Street was named after William Crow, chief chirographer to the House of Commons in 1597.

41. Group 91 came together in 1991 to design a new housing scheme in the Liberties section of Dublin. In the spirit of new urbanism, the project

(presented in the form of an exhibition, "The Making of a Modern Street") promoted mixed residential and commercial development, with internal court-yards, recessed balconies, interior terraces (even a pergola), corner columns, and entrance archways, for seven infill sites at the corner of Meath Street and South Earl Street.

42. Catherine Slessor, "Irish Reels," *Architectural Review* 1151 (January 1993).

43. "Clouds in My Cappuccino," interview in *Irish Times,* 18 April 2000.

44. Fintan O'Toole, "In the Land of the Emerald Tiger," *Irish Times,* 28 December 1996.

45. For a detailed discussion of this history see the chapters, "The Ring-strasse, Its Critics, and the Birth of Urban Modernism" and "Politics and Patricide in Freud's *Interpretation of Dreams,*" in Schorske 1981.

46. Reviewer reaction to these memoirs has been varied and diverse. O'Faolain and Sheridan are both minor celebrities in Ireland, and their books were widely received. Sheridan went on to write a follow-up memoir to *44 Dublin Made Me,* and O'Faolain's next work was a much publicized novel. One reviewer dismissed Sheridan's story as a "series of set-pieces that never deliver the emotional climax they strive for" (Toibin Harshaw, "My Heart Belongs to Da," *Book Review Desk,* 13 June 1999). The British paper *Guardian* locates Sheridan in a long line of Dublin writers who have told the same story and told it better (Joe Ambrose, "Da-da-Dublin," *Guardian,* 8 May 1999). Most reviews of O'Faolain's work focus on the emotional under-pinnings of her life. They highlight the hard choices forced on a liberal, feminist woman in a traditionally patriarchal society. "Her real strength," writes a *Time* Magazine reviewer, "is in her close-to-the-bone rendering of the sadness lurking at the edges of every adult life" (Margaret Carlson, "Now Isn't That the Truth?" *Time,* 8 June 1998). Crowley's book did not receive the same kind of attention that Sheridan's and O'Faolain's did, pos-sibly because she is a relatively unknown writer. The press that she did re-ceive, however, generally recognizes her literary merit and subtlety: she "shun[s] the idea of telling the reader precisely what Ireland is all about, and why exactly the Irish are the way they are . . . [her work] is that of in-vestigation, not dogma . . . she has a need to evoke an Ireland that has passed" (Clancy Ambrose, "Irish Elsewheres," *Nation,* 23 March 1998). None of these reviews, however, addresses the form of memoir writing itself and the cultural context of its current Irish incarnation.

Bibliography

Aalen, F. H. A. 1990. *The Iveagh Trust: The First Hundred Years, 1890–1990*. Dublin: Iveagh Trust.

Aalen, F. H. A., Kevin Whelan, and Matthew Stout, eds. 1997. *Atlas of the Irish Rural Landscape: Ireland*. Cork, Ireland: Cork University Press.

Abercrombie, Patrick. 1916. "Study before Town Planning." *Town Planning Review* 6: 171–90.

———. 1922. *Dublin of the Future*. London: Hodder & Stoughton.

Abercrombie, Patrick, and J. H. Forshaw. 1943. *County of London Plan: Prepared from the London County Council*. London: Macmillan.

Aberdeen, Marquess of (John Campbell Gordon), and Ishbel Gordon. 1925. *We Twa'*. London: W. Collins.

Abrams, Charles. 1961. *Urban Renewal Project in Ireland (Dublin)*. New York: United Nations.

Adshead, A. D. 1908. "An Introduction to Civic Design." *Town Planning Review* 1: 3–17.

Anderson, Benedict. 1991. *Imagined Communities*. London: Verso.

Archer, John. 2002. "Landscape and Identity: Baby Talk at the Leasowes." *Cultural Critique* 51: 148–85.

Arnold, Matthew. 1900. *The Study of Celtic Literature*. London: Smith, Elder.

Artifex. 1930. "Greater Dublin—Complexities and Possibilities." *Dublin Magazine* 1: 37–43.

Bannon, Michael. 1985. *The Emergence of Irish Planning, 1880–1920.* Dublin: Turoe Press.

———. 1988. "The Capital of the New State." In *Dublin through the Ages.* Dublin: College Press, 133–50.

———. 1989. *Planning: The Irish Experience, 1920 to 1988.* Dublin: Turoe Press.

Becker, Annette, John Olley, and Wilfried Wang, eds. 1997. *Ireland: Twentieth-Century Architecture.* Munich: Prestel.

Behan, Dominic. 1965. *My Brother Brendan.* New York: Simon & Schuster.

Benjamin, Walter. 1968. *Illuminations.* Ed. Hannah Arendt. New York: Schocken Books.

Bennett, Douglas. 1991. *Encyclopedia of Dublin.* Dublin: Gill & Macmillan.

Bew, Paul, Ellen Hazelkorn, and Henry Patterson. 1989. *Dynamics of Irish Politics.* London: Lawrence & Wishart.

Bew, Paul, and Henry Patterson. 1982. *Seán Lemass and the Making of Modern Ireland, 1945–66.* Dublin: Gill & Macmillan.

Blomfield, Reginald. 1934. *Modernismus.* London: Macmillan.

Boland, Kevin. 1968. "Ireland: The Planning Scene." *Christus Rex* 22: 173–205.

Boyce, George D. 1990. *Nineteenth-Century Ireland: The Search for Stability.* Dublin: Gill & Macmillan.

———. 1995. *Nationalism in Ireland.* London: Routledge.

Boyce, George D., and Alan O'Day. 1996. *The Making of Modern Irish History: Revisionism and the Revisionist Controversy.* London: Routledge.

Boyer, Christine. 1983. *Dreaming the Rational City: The Myth of American City Planning.* Cambridge, Mass.: MIT Press.

Brady, Ciaran, ed. 1994. *Interpreting Irish History: The Debate on Historical Revisionism.* Dublin: Irish Academic Press.

Briggs, Asa. 1959. *The Age of Improvement.* London: Longman's.

Brown, Terence. 1985. *Ireland: A Social and Cultural History, 1922 to the Present.* Ithaca, N.Y.: Cornell University Press.

———. 2000. "Architecture in Independent Ireland." In *Building for Government: The Architecture of State Buildings, 1900–2000,* 21–23. Dublin: Government Publications.

Buck-Morss, Susan. 1989. *The Dialectics of Seeing: Walter Benjamin and the Arcades Project.* Cambridge, Mass.: MIT Press.

Butler, R. M. 1916. "The Reconstruction of O'Connell Street." *Studies* 5: 570–76.

Cairns, David, and Shawn Richards. 1988. *Writing Ireland: Colonialism, Nationalism, and Culture.*

Campbell, Hugh. 1994. "Interpreting the City." Diss., Trinity College, Dublin.

Chambers, William. 1968. *A Treatise on the Decorative Part of Civil Architecture.* New York: Benjamin Blom.

Chatterjee, Partha. 1986. *Nationalist Thought and the Colonial World.* Minneapolis: University of Minnesota Press.

Cherry, Gordon, ed. 1981. *Pioneers in British Planning.* London: Architectural Press.

Civics Institute of Ireland. 1925. *The Dublin Civic Survey.* London: University of Liverpool Press.

Comerford, R. V. 1989. "Ireland, 1850–70: Post-Famine and Mid-Nineteenth Century Ireland." In Vaughan 1989, 372–94.

Connolly, James. 1987. *The Collected Works.* 2 vols. Dublin: New Books Publications.

Connolly, S. J. 1989. "Mass Politics and Sectarian Conflict, 1823–30." In Vaughan 1989, 74–107.

Conroy, Eddie. 1997. "Centre and Periphery: Housing in Ireland." In Becker, Olley, and Wang 1997, 54–60.

Cooney, John. 2000. *John Charles McQuaid: Ruler of Catholic Ireland.* Dublin: O'Brien Press.

Copcutt, Geoffrey. 1967. "Physical Planning in Ireland." *Build* 3 (February): 17–21.

Corcoran, Mary. 1998. "The Re-Enchantment of Temple Bar." In *Encounters with Modern Ireland,* ed. Michael Peillon, 9–24. Dublin: IPA.

Cowan, P. C. 1918. *Report on Dublin Housing.* Dublin: Cahill.

Craft, Maurice. 1970. "The Development of Dublin: Background to the Housing Problem." *Studies* 59: 301–13.

———. 1971. "The Development of Dublin: The Southern Suburbs." *Studies* 60: 68–80.

Cronin, Mike. 2000. "Golden Dreams, Harsh Realities: Economics and Informal Empire in the Irish Free State." In *The Politics of Independence,* ed. Mike Cronin and John Regan. New York: St. Martin's Press, 144–64.

Crowley, Elaine. 1996. *A Dublin Girl: Growing Up in the 1930s.* New York: Soho.

Cubitts Haden Sisk. 1966. *Ballymun Housing Project.* Dublin: Cubitts Haden Sisk.

Curl, James Stevens. 1986. *The Londonderry Plantation: 1609–1914.* Southampton, U.K.: Camelot Press.

Curtis, Liz. 1995. *The Cause of Ireland.* Dublin: Beyond the Pale Publications.

Curtis, William. 1982. *Modern Architecture since 1900.* Oxford: Phaidon.

Daly, Mary. 1984. *Dublin, the Deposed Capital: A Social and Economic History, 1860–1914.* Cork, Ireland: Cork University Press.

———. 1992. *Industrial Development and Irish National Identity.* Dublin: Gill & Macmillan.

Deane, Seamus. 1985. "Civilians and Barbarians." In Field Day Theatre Company 1985, 33–42.

———, ed. 1992. *The Field Day Anthology of Irish Writing.* Vol. 3. Derry: Field Day Publications.

———. 1997. *Strange Country: Modernity and Nationhood in Irish Writing since 1790.* Oxford: Oxford University Press.

Defries, Amelia. 1928. *Interpreter Geddes: The Man and His Gospel.* New York: Boni & Liveright.

Dillon, T. 1945. "Slum Clearance." *Studies* 34: 13–20.

Donaldson, Loraine. 1966. *Development Planning in Ireland.* New York: Frederick A. Praeger.

Eagleton, Terry. 1995. *Heathcliff and the Great Hunger: Studies in Irish Culture.* New York: Verso.

Edwards, Trystan A. 1914. "A World Centre of Communication." *Town Planning Review* 5: 4–30.

Fahey, Tony. 1999. *Social Housing in Ireland.* Dublin: Oak Tree Press.

Fallon, Brian. 1988. *An Age of Innocence.* Dublin: Gill & Macmillan.

Fallon, Gabriel. 1938. "The Celluloid Menace." *Capuchin Annual,* 248–60.

Fanon, Frantz. *The Wretched of the Earth.* New York: Grove Press.

Field Day Theatre Company. 1985. *Ireland's Field Day.* Notre Dame, Ind.: Notre Dame University Press.

Figgis, Darrell. 1922. "Planning for the Future: An Address before the Architectural Association of Ireland on Tuesday, March 28, 1922." Dublin: Talbot Press.

Finegan, John. 1978. *The Story of the Monto: An Account of Dublin's Notorious Red Light District.* Cork, Ireland: Mercier Press.

Fitzgerald, Garret. 1968. *Planning in Ireland.* Dublin: Institute of Public Administration.

Fitzpatrick, David. 1989. "Ireland since 1870." In Foster 1989, 213–75.

Foras Forbartha. 1973. *Office Location and Regional Development.* Dublin: Foras Forbartha.

Foster, Roy, ed. 1989. *Oxford Illustrated History of Ireland.* Oxford: Oxford University Press.

Frampton, Kenneth. 1980. "New Brutalism and the Architecture of the Welfare State: England 1949–59." In *Modern Architecture,* 262–69. London: Thames & Hudson.

Fraser, Murray. 1985. "Public Building and Colonial Policy in Dublin, 1760–1800." *Architectural History: Journal of Architectural Historians of Great Britain* 28: 102–23.

———. 1996. *John Bull's Other Homes: State Housing and British Policy in Ireland, 1883–1922.* Liverpool: Liverpool University Press.

Fremantle, Sir Selwyn. 1926. "Town Planning in the East." *Garden Cities and Town Planning,* February, 84–86.

Freud, Sigmund. 2001. *The Standard Edition of the Complete Psychological Works of Sigmund Freud.* Vol. 21, 1927–1931. London: Hogarth Press.

Frisby, David. 1985. *Fragments of Modernity.* Cambridge: Polity Press.

Ganguly, Keya. 2001. *States of Exception.* Minneapolis: University of Minnesota Press.

Garvin, Tom. 1987. *Nationalist Revolutionaries in Ireland, 1858–1928.* Oxford: Clarendon Press.

———. 1996. "State Building after the Treaty." In *1922: The Birth of Irish Democracy.* Dublin: Gill & Macmillan, 156–89.

Geddes, Patrick. 1908. "The Survey of Cities." *Sociological Review* 1: 72–79.

———. 1918. *Town Planning towards City Development: A Report to the Durbar of Indore.* 2 vols. Indore, India: Holkar State Printing Press.

Gellner, Ernst. 1983. *Nations and Nationalism.* Ithaca, N.Y.: Cornell University Press.

Gibbons, Luke. 1992. "Introduction. Challenging the Canon: Revisionism and Cultural Criticism." In Deane 1992, 561–69.

———. 1996. *Transformations in Irish Culture.* Cork, Ireland: Cork University Press.

Glendenning, Miles, and Stefan Muthesius. 1994. *Tower Block: Modern Public Housing in England, Scotland, Wales, and Northern Ireland.* New Haven, Conn.: Yale University Press.

Government of Ireland. 1963. *Second Programme for Economic Expansion.* Dublin: Government Publications.

Guha, Ranajit. 1982. "On Some Aspects of the Historiography of Colonial India." In *Subaltern Studies I: Writings on South Asian History and Society,* ed. Ranjit Guha. Delhi: Oxford University Press, 1–7.

———. 1997. *Dominance without Hegemony.* Cambridge, Mass.: Harvard University Press.

Habermas, Jürgen. 1990. *The Philosophical Discourse of Modernity.* Cambridge, Mass.: MIT Press.

Hadfield, Andrew, and John McVeagh, eds. 1994. *Strangers to That Land: British Perceptions of Ireland from the Reformation to the Famine.* Gerrards Cross, Cornwall, England: Colin Smythe.

Hall, Peter. 1996. *Cities of Tomorrow: An Intellectual History of Urban Planning and Design in the Twentieth Century.* Oxford: Blackwell.

Hampl, Patricia. 1999. *I Could Tell You Stories.* New York: W. W. Norton.

Harvey, David. 1989a. *Condition of Postmodernity.* Oxford: Blackwell.

———. 1989b. *The Urban Experience.* Baltimore, Md.: Johns Hopkins University Press.

Home, Robert. 1997. *Of Planting and Planning: The Making of British Colonial Cities.* London: E & F. N. Spon.

Horner, Arnold. 1992. "From City to City-Region: Dublin from the 1930s to the 1990s." In *Dublin City and County: From Prehistory to Present,* ed. F. H. A. Aalen and Kevin Whelan, 327–58. Dublin: Geography Publications.

Housing and Town Planning Association of Ireland. 1911. *Housing and Town Improvement.* Dublin: Housing and Town Planning Association of Ireland.

Howard, Ebenezer. 1951. *Garden Cities of Tomorrow.* London: Faber & Faber.

Hutchinson, John. 1987. *The Dynamics of Cultural Nationalism.* London: Allen & Unwin.

Hutton, A. W., and H. J. Cohen. 1902. *The Speeches of W. E. Gladstone on Home Rule, Criminal Law, Welsh and Irish Nationality, National Debt, and the Queen's Reign.* London: Methuen.

Jacobs, Jane. 1961. *The Death and Life of Great American Cities.* New York: Random House.

Jeffrey, Keith. 2000. *Ireland and the Great War.* Cambridge: Cambridge University Press.

Joyce, James. 1986. *Ulysses.* New York: Random House.

Kearns, Kevin. 1983. *Georgian Dublin: Ireland's Imperilled Architectural Heritage.* London: David & Charles.

Kelly, Deirdre. 1976. *Hands Off Dublin.* Dublin: O'Brien Press.

Keogh, Dermot. 1995. *Twentieth-Century Ireland: Nation and State.* New York: St. Martin's Press.

Keynes, John Maynard. 1933. "National Self-Sufficiency." *Studies* 22: 177–93.

Kiberd, Declan. 1979. "Story-Telling: The Gaelic Tradition." In *The Irish Short Story,* ed. P. Rafroidi and T. Brown, 13–27. Lille, France: Publications de l'Université de Lille III.

———. 1994. "Postcolonial Ireland: Being Different." In Ó'Ceallaigh 1994, 94–113.

———. 1996. *Inventing Ireland: The Literature of the Modern Nation.* Cambridge, Mass.: Harvard University Press.

———. 2000. "The View from Enniskillen." *New Left Review,* May–June, 153–58.

King, Anthony D. 1990. *Urbanism, Colonialism, and the World Economy: Cultural and Spatial Foundations of the World Urban System.* London: Routledge.

Kitchen, Paddy. 1975. *A Most Unsettling Person.* London: Gollancz.

KPMG, Murray O'Laoire Associates, Northern Ireland Economic Research Centre, and Dept. of the Environment. 1996. *Submission on the Study of Urban and Renewal Schemes.* Dublin: Government Stationary Office.

Krier, R. 1987. "Tradition—Modernity—Modernism: Some Necessary Explanations." *Architectural Design* 57: 1–2.

Kristoff, Spiro. 1991. "The Grid." In *The City Shaped: Urban Patterns and Meanings through History,* 95–157. New York: Little, Brown.

Le Corbusier. 1946. *Towards a New Architecture.* London: Architectural Press.

Lee, J. J. 1983. *The Modernization of Irish Society, 1848–1918.* Dublin: Gill & Macmillan.

———. 1984. "The Social and Economic Ideas of O'Connell." In *Daniel O'Connell: Portrait of a Radical,* ed. Kevin B. Nowlan and Maurice R. O'Connell, 70–87. Dublin: Apple Tree Press.

———. 1989. *Ireland, 1912–1985.* Cambridge: Cambridge University Press.

Legates, Richard, T. and Frederick Stout, eds. 1999. *The City Reader.* London: Routledge.

Lloyd, David. 1999. *Ireland after History.* Cork, Ireland: Cork University Press.

Local Government Board. 1914a. *Report of the Departmental Committee Appointed by the Local Government Board for Ireland to Inquire into the Housing Conditions of the Working Classes in the City of Dublin.* London: H. M. Stationery Office.

———. 1914b. *Appendix to the Report of the Departmental Committee Appointed by the Local Government Board for Ireland to Inquire into the Housing Conditions of the Working Classes in the City of Dublin.* London: H. M. Stationery Office.

MacCannell, Dean. 1989. *The Tourist.* New York: Shocken Books.

MacDonagh, Oliver. 1989. "Ideas and Institutions." In Vaughan 1989, 193–216.

MacLaran, Andrew. 1993. *Dublin: The Shaping of a Capital.* London: Belhaven Press.

MacLaughlin, Jim. 1994. *Ireland: The Emigrant Nursery and the World Economy.* Cork, Ireland: Cork University Press.

Malton, James. 1978. *Malton's Dublin.* Dublin: Dolmen Press.

Marx, Karl. 1998. *Communist Manifesto*. London: Signet Classics.

Matthew, Colin. 2000. *Short History of the British Isles: The Nineteenth Century*. Oxford: Oxford University Press.

Maume, Patrick. 1999. *Long Gestation: Irish Nationalist Life, 1891–1918*. Dublin: Gill & Macmillan.

McCabe, J. F. 1925. "Town and Country." *Dublin Magazine* 2–3: 675–79.

McCarthy, Conor. 2000. *Modernisation: Crisis and Culture in Ireland, 1969–1992*. Dublin: Four Courts.

McCartney, Donal. 1999. *UCD: A National Idea: The History of University College, Dublin*. Dublin: Gill & Macmillan.

McDonald, Frank. 1985. *The Destruction of Dublin*. Dublin: Gill & Macmillan.

———. 2000. *The Construction of Dublin*. Kinsale, Co. Cork, Ireland: Gandon Editions.

McDowell, R. B., ed. 1991. *The Writing and Speeches of Edmund Burke*. Vol. 9. Oxford: Clarendon Press.

McGrath, Brendan. 1992. "Suburban Development in Ireland." *Planning Perspectives* 7: 27–46.

McGrath, Fergal. 1931. "The Sweep and the Slums." *Studies* 20: 529–54.

———. 1932. "Homes for the People." *Studies* 21: 269–82.

McGregor, John James. 1821. *New Picture of Dublin*. Dublin: Johnson & Deas.

McKenna, Lambet. 1919. "The Housing Problem in Dublin." *Studies* 5: 279–95.

McManus, Ruth. 2002. *Dublin, 1910–1940: Shaping the City and Suburbs*. Dublin: Four Courts.

McSheffrey, Gerald. 2000. *Planning Derry: Planning and Politics in Northern Ireland*. Liverpool: Liverpool University Press.

Meller, Helen. 1990. *Patrick Geddes: Social Evolutionist and City Planner*. London: Routledge.

Miller, Mervyn. 1992. *Raymond Unwin: Garden Cities and Town Planning*. Leicester: Leicester University Press.

Miller, Nancy K. 2000. "But Enough about Me, What Do You Think of My Memoir?" *Yale Journal of Criticism* 2: 421–36.

Moody, T. W. 1994a. "Irish History and Irish Mythology." In Brady 1994, 71–86.

———. 1994b. "A New History of Ireland." In Brady 1994, 38–53.

Moody, T. W., and R. D. Edwards. 1994. "Preface to *Irish Historical Studies*." In Brady 1994, 35–37.

Mooney, Miss. 1907. "Some Remedies for Overcrowded Districts." *Journal of the Statistical and Social Inquiry Society of Ireland* 12: 50–60.

Moran, Austen, and Bob Purdie, eds. 1980. *Ireland: Divided Nation, Divided Class.* London: Ink Links.

Moran, James. 1923. "The Reconstruction of Greater Dublin." *Manchester Guardian Commercial,* 10 May, 42–43.

Mulhern, Francis. 1998. *The Present Lasts a Long Time.* Cork, Ireland: Cork University Press.

Mumford, Lewis. 1961. *The City in History: Its Origins, Its Transformations, and Its Prospects.* New York: Harbinger.

National Library of Ireland. 1979. *Illustrations to the History of the National Library of Ireland, 1877–1977.* Dublin: National Stationery Office.

O'Beirne, Thomas, and Charles Travers. 1911. *Report of the Health Committee.* Dublin City Council Reports, No. 54.

O'Brien, Keith. 1993. "Dublin as a Location for International Financial Services: The Dublin International Financial Services Centre." Master's thesis, Trinity College, Dublin.

Ó'Cathasaigh, Aindrais, ed. 1997. *James Connolly: Lost Writings.* London: Pluto.

Ó'Ceallaigh, Daltun. 1994. *Reconsiderations of Irish History and Culture.* Dublin: Leirmheas.

O'Faolain, Nuala. 1996. *Are You Somebody? The Accidental Memoir of a Dublin Woman.* New York: Owl Books.

O'Faolain, Sean. 1980. *King of Beggars.* Dublin: Poolbeg Press.

———. 1992. "The Gaelic Cult." In Deane 1992, 573–76.

Office of Public Works. 1999. *Building for Government: The Architecture of State Buildings, 1900–2000.* Dublin: Government Publications.

O'Flaherty, Liam. 1925. *The Informer.* New York: Signet Classics.

O'Gorman, John. 1936. "Building and Order." *Capuchin Annual,* 118–32.

O'Hearn, Denis. 2000. "Globalization, 'New Tigers,' and the End of the Developmental State." *Politics and Society* 28: 67–92.

O'Leary, Liam. 1990. *Cinema Ireland, 1896–1950: From the Liam O'Leary Archives.* Dublin: National Library of Ireland.

Olley, John. 1997. "Geragh." In Becker, Olley, and Wang 1997, 114–15.

O'Neill, Helen. 1971. *Spatial Planning in the Small Economy: A Case Study of Ireland.* New York: Praeger Publishers.

O'Sheehan, J., and E. de Barra, eds. 1940. *Ireland's Hospitals, 1930–1955.* Dublin: Hospitals' Trust.

Prunty, Jacinta. 1995. "Residential Urban Renewal Schemes, Dublin, 1986–1994." *Irish Geography* 28: 131–49.

Pyle, Fergus, ed. 1968. *1916: The Easter Rising.* London: McGibbon & Kee.

Reps, John. 1965. "Checkerboard Plans and Gridiron Cities." In *The Making of Urban America,* 294–325. Princeton, N.J.: Princeton University Press.

Robertson, Manning. 1925. *Laymen and the New Architecture.* London: John Murray.

Roche, Desmond. 1982. *Local Government in Ireland.* Dublin: Institute of Public Administration.

Rossi, Aldo. 1982. *The Architecture of the City.* Cambridge, Mass.: MIT Press.

Rothery, Sean. 1991. *Ireland and the New Architecture, 1900–1940.* Dublin: Lilliput Press.

Rowe, Colin. 1994. *The Architecture of Good Intentions.* London: Academy Editions.

Ruckenstein, Lelia. 2003. *Everything Irish: The History, Literature, Art, Music, People, and Place of Ireland from A to Z.* New York: Ballantine Books.

Saorstat Eireann. 1932. *Irish Free State: Official Handbook.* Dublin: Talbot Press.

Schaechterle, Karl-Heinz. 1976. *Dublin Traffic Planning: General Traffic Plan, Part 1: Traffic Investigation concerning the Future Main Road Network, Carried Out in Accordance with the Instructions of the Corporation of Dublin.* Ulm, Ireland: Dublin Corporation.

Schorske, Carl. 1981. *Fin-de-Siècle Vienna.* New York: Vintage.

Scott, Michael. 1995. *Michael Scott, Architect: In Casual Conversation with Dorothy Walker.* Kinsale, Co. Cork, Ireland: Gandon Editions.

Sennett, Richard, ed. 1969. *Classic Essays on the Culture of Cities.* Englewood Cliffs, N.J.: Prentice Hall.

Shaw, Father Francis. 1972. "The Canon of Irish History—A Challenge." *Studies* 61: 153–90.

Sheehan, Patrick. 2002. *Ireland into Film: The Informer.* Cork, Ireland: Cork University Press.

Sheerin, Emer. 1998. "Heritage Centres." *Encounters with Modern Ireland,* ed. Michael Peillon, 39–48. Dublin: IPA.

Sheridan, Peter. 1999. *44 Dublin Made Me.* New York: Penguin.

Stieber, Nancy. 1998. *Housing Design and Society in Amsterdam: Reconfiguring Urban Order and Identity, 1900–1920.* Chicago: University of Chicago Press.

Sutcliffe, Anthony. 1981. *Towards the Planned City: Germany, Britain, the United States, and France, 1780–1914.* Oxford: Basil Blackwell.

Sweeney, Paul. 1999. *The Celtic Tiger: Ireland's Continuing Economic Miracle.* Dublin: Oak Tree Press.

Temple Bar Properties. 1996. *Temple Bar: The Power of an Idea.* Kinsale, Co. Cork, Ireland: Gandon Editions.

Thompson, Spurgeon. 1997. "James Joyce and Tourism in Dublin." *New Hibernia Review* 1: 136–55.

Thornley, David. 1964. "Ireland: The End of an Era?" *Studies* 53: 1–17.

Townsend, Charles. 1983. *Political Violence in Ireland.* Oxford: Clarendon Press.

Ui Breasail. 1911. *"Ui Breasail": Catalogue of the Great Health, Industrial, and Agricultural Show, Ballsbridge, Dublin, May 24th to June 7th.* Dublin.

Vaughan, W. E., ed. 1989. *A New History of Ireland.* Vol. 5, *Ireland under the Union, 1800–1870.* Oxford: Clarendon Press, 193–216.

Walsh, Brendan. 1979. "Economic Growth and Development, 1945–1970." In *Ireland, 1945–70,* ed. J. J. Lee, 27–37. Dublin: Gill & Macmillan.

Waters, John. 1998. *An Intelligent Person's Guide to Modern Ireland.* London: Duckworth.

Weber, Max. 1985. *The Protestant Ethic and the Spirit of Capitalism.* London: Unwin Paperbacks.

Whyte, Iain Boyd, ed. 2003. *Modernism and the Spirit of the City.* New York: Routledge.

Wickham, Mary. 1998. "An Intelligent Island." In *Encounters with Modern Ireland,* ed. Michael Peillon, 81–91. Dublin: IPA.

Wide Streets Commission. 1802. *City of Dublin: Wide and Convenient Ways, Streets, and Passages.* Dublin: Wide Streets Commission.

Williams, Raymond. 1983. *Keywords.* London: Fontana.

Wilson, William H. 1964. *The City Beautiful Movement.* Baltimore, Md.: Johns Hopkins University Press.

Wright, Myles. 1967. *The Dublin Region: Advisory Plan and Final Report.* Dublin: Government Publications Office.

Yeates, Pádraig. 2000. *Lockout: Dublin 1913.* Dublin: Gill & Macmillan.

Index

Andrew Kincaid is assistant professor of English at the University of Wisconsin–Milwaukee.

www.ingramcontent.com/pod-product-compliance
Lightning Source LLC
Chambersburg PA
CBHW061718270326
41928CB00011B/2022